"God's servant Calvin McBride, a deacon at the Pentecostal Assembly Church of God in Christ, is a self-motivated, self-taught historian, who has thoroughly researched the history of one of the most prominent and influential African-American preachers in this country. I encourage all pastors, preachers, teachers, and laypersons to read this rich and exciting piece of history concerning the contributions of this man to the Christian Methodist Episcopal Church and the Church of God in Christ."
—**Rev. Kip T. Cole, B.S., M.Div.**
B.S., Union University; M.Div., Samford University, Beeson School of Divinity.

"This inspiring and well-documented book of an incredibly gifted and anointed servant leader of the late nineteenth and early twentieth centuries is a must read for the body of Christ. This book chronicles a spiritual leader's deep desire to preach the Gospel and passionate desire to win souls for Christ, which leads to more pastoral and ministerial challenges in the Christian Methodist Episcopal Church. Eventually, this servant leader's spiritual cross-over became very instrumental to Bishop Charles Harrison Mason in pioneering a new spirituality—the Church of God in Christ."
—**Elder Christopher A. Reed, B.S., M.P.A.**
B.S., Austin Peay State University; M.P.A., University of Tennessee, Knoxville; Asst. Vice President for Auxiliary Enterprises, Jackson State University.

"I found this book to be inspiring, motivational and enthusiastic. I've read many excerpts of the life of Elder Robert Eber Hart but never felt so connected to a person until I read "Walking Into A New Spirituality." It was as if the pages came to life and I was taking the journey with him. Anyone interested in traveling through the history of COGIC or always wanted a glimpse of our forefathers should read this book. I recommend this book to all who have a desire to be enlightened on a daily basis walking into a new spirituality, chronicling the life, ministry, and contributions of Elder Robert Eber Hart."
—**Elder Eddie Whitelaw, B.S.**
B.S., Lane College; Pastor, Unity Temple COGIC, Jackson, Tennessee.

"Calvin McBride has shown us his unique literary ability in the life journey of Robert E. Hart's transition from one denomination (Christian Methodist Episcopal Church) to another (Church of God in Christ). He has plunged us into the history of not only an individual but has transported us as well into the history of African-Americans as it relates to the church as an institution. The book has been well written and will service well those who embrace history."

—Stevey M. Wilburn, Sr., B.A., M.Div., D.Min. B.S., Lane College; M.Div., Phillips School of Theology (ITC); D.Min., Memphis Theological Seminary; Pastor, Mt. Olive Cathedral CME Church, Memphis, Tennessee.

GRACIOUS LORD

When, gracious Lord, when shall it be
That I shall find my all in thee?
The fullness of thy promise prove,
The seal of thy eternal love.

A poor blind child I wander here,
If haply I may feel thee near;
O dark! dark! dark! I still must say,
Amidst the blaze of gospel day.

Thee, only thee, I fain would find,
And cast the world and flesh behind;
Thou, only thou, to me be giv'n,
Of all thou hast in earth or heav'n.

When from the arm of flesh set free,
Jesus, my soul shall fly to thee;
Jesus, when I have lost my all,
I shall upon thy bosom fall.

—Charles Wesley Lane, October 1900

Walking Into A New Spirituality

Walking Into A New Spirituality

✦

Chronicling the Life, Ministry, and Contributions of Elder Robert E. Hart, B.D., LL.B., D.D., to the CME Church and COGIC: With Some Additional COGIC History

Convocation Centennial Edition

Deacon Calvin S. McBride

Walking Into A New Spirituality
Chronicling the Life, Ministry, and Contributions of Elder
Robert E. Hart, B.D., LL.B., D.D., to the CME Church and
COGIC: With Some Additional COGIC History

iUniverse books may be ordered through booksellers or by contacting:

iUniverse
1663 Liberty Drive
Bloomington, IN 47403
www.iuniverse.com
844-349-9409

ISBN: 978-0-5954-6257-5 (sc)

Print information available on the last page.

iUniverse rev. date: 09/09/2020

For my beautiful wife, and precious children

Sharon Annette McBride

Calvin de'Von McBride

Calah Chanel McBride

Thank God for a loving family

IN MEMORIAM OF ALFRED Z. HALL, JR.
GENERAL SECRETARY OF THE
CHURCH OF GOD IN CHRIST
2000-2007

I commemorate this book to the legacy of the late A. Z. Hall, Jr., (1943-2007) who was pastor of the Pentecostal Assembly Church of God in Christ in Jackson, Tennessee. He was my pastor, and I was one of his deacons. I have been in COGIC a little over three years, and Elder Hall was the primary reason I joined COGIC. I was already saved; however, I needed seasoned leadership and a father in the ministry, which Elder Hall provided in abundance. I will always remember my pastor—the man that gave me so much in so little time, the man that I learned so much from, and the man that stood in Christ's stead, "Declaring the Works of the Lord!" Amen.

Contents

ACKNOWLEDGMENTS

Although I did all of my own research and writing for this book, there were many friends and history enthusiasts' who cheered me along the way. First of all, I give thanks to the Almighty God and his precious Holy Ghost, who planted his gifts of reasoning and thoughts in my mind so that all the words of wisdom and knowledge were channeled through to complete this book. It has taken two years to complete, but I was blessed with an abundance of time, which enabled me to pour myself into the research and writing of the book.

I am deeply thankful to all of my friends in the ministry who took the time to review this book and submit their opinion. I must also acknowledge the significance of the foreword by Evangelist Barachias T. Irons, who in the stead of our late pastor, Elder A. Z. Hall Jr., graciously submitted to the task.

A special thanks goes to Eddie M. Mercer for her guiding and untiring efforts in editing this difficult manuscript.

I must express how much I enjoyed pursuing the hidden history as well as the obvious history of COGIC and learning for the first time myself of the rich history bequeathed to us through this great religious institution by the beloved saints. I am eternally grateful God has allowed me to do this work while it is yet still day.

FOREWORD

The moment of one's entrance into the world, the steps of one's life journey begins. We walk through childhood, adolescence, and adulthood. These numerical stages of life, however, are mere numbers. They cannot tell of the real journey one is on and what venues our daily steps take us into and out.

In this historical piece of extraordinary literature, Calvin McBride has walked us through the life journey of an incredible clergyman, Elder Robert Eber Hart. Elder Hart began his journey just after freedom had come to his ancestors from slavery. His quest for the knowledge and understanding of God led him to follow after truth in scripture.

His journey led him through educational pursuits, both secular and seminarian, but it was his desire for an even more personal experience with the Lord that carried him to a bridge of change.

As you read this chronicle of events in the life of Elder Hart, may you find yourself examining your ways and looking to the Lord for his assurance that your life steps are following the path that He ordered for you.

Evangelist Barachias T. Irons
Pentecostal Assembly COGIC, Jackson, Tennessee
Assistant General Secretary of Publications, COGIC

INTRODUCTION:
ANOINTED TO SERVE
IN BOTH DENOMINATIONS

In order to grasp the full impact and contributions made to the Church of God in Christ (COGIC) by Dr. Robert Eber Hart, we must first take an overview of his early life and labor in the ministry before he matriculated into the Church of God in Christ. Dr. Hart spent all of his early Christian life in the Colored Methodist Episcopal Church (CME). This is where he received the foundation and classical training that prepared him for his pioneering role in COGIC. The CME denomination changed its name from Colored Methodist Episcopal in 1956, to Christian Methodist Episcopal. Dr. Hart's affiliation in the CME Church and the University of West Tennessee Medical College (both institutions where I had relatives serving) was the reason I kept a file on him for years. When I saw his name mentioned in 2005 associated with the history of COGIC, I knew then a book would be appropriate and forthcoming.

The Colored Methodist Episcopal Church was formed out of the white Methodist Episcopal Church, South, after the Civil War and the freeing of the slaves. While they were slaves, Dr. Hart's parents were likely members of the Methodist Episcopal Church, South. The Colored Methodist Episcopal Church was organized in Jackson, Tennessee, December 15, 1870, when the white and black brethren of the Methodist Episcopal Church, South, met for their yearly conference. There were about 206,000 former slaves that were members of the denomination. The blacks attending the conference felt that it was time to organize their own denomination and conference. The white brethren were very receptive to their idea, and it was overwhelmingly agreed to allow the black brethren to move forward with their own organization. They gave the black brethren their blessings, and a new Black Methodist denomination was birthed with great excitement and expectations.

One generation later, the Colored Methodist Episcopal Church had made tremendous progress saving souls, establishing churches, schools, missions, and educational programs. By 1900, the denomination had grown from about 25,000 members in 1870 to 150,000. These challenging efforts were successful largely because of the excellent leaders appointed to the ecclesial positions. The ecclesial leaders chosen to take the church from its inception and into the early twentieth century were highly qualified. They were men of vision: humble servants of God, full of wisdom, and pious men. They were competent leaders such as Bishops William H. Miles, Richard H. Vanderhorst, Joseph A. Beebe, Lucius H. Holsey, Isaac Lane, Robert S. Williams, and Elias Cottrell.

Bishop Joseph A. Beebe took Dr. Hart under his "wings" and became his mentor, investing a great deal of time in Dr. Hart's training and preparation. Dr. Hart, at a relatively young age, was given a lot of responsibility in the ministry; and he succeeded at every level. He was appointed to some of the largest and most prestigious churches in the Colored Methodist Episcopal Church. He was one of a few within the denomination and country that received a college education before the twentieth century; thereby, earning a place in history only a few obtained. He possessed certain God-given talents, gifts, and abilities that enabled him to become a powerful preacher, teacher, evangelist, and financier in the body of Christ. All of these attributes were going to be very beneficial to COGIC as he moved closer to *"Walking Into A New Spirituality"* at the beginning of the twentieth century.

Dr. Hart withdrew from the CME denomination in 1905; however, he didn't leave the body of Christ. He was already fellowshipping with the Sanctified Church and attending holiness meetings in Jackson, Mississippi, and other places organized by Charles P. Jones, Charles H. Mason, William S. Pleasant, and John A. Jeter, all originally Baptist preachers. In 1907, after the right hand of fellowship was withdrawn from Charles H. Mason by Charles P. Jones and the Ministerial Council of the Church of God in Christ (the name adopted by the convention in 1906), Dr. Hart became one of Mason's strongest supporters. He was present at the meeting in Memphis called by Mason in 1907, which was the founding and reorganizing of COGIC and its first General Assembly and Holy Convocation held in November of the same year. Dr. Hart's contributions to COGIC were phenomenal in a variety of ways and they proved to be very helpful during the formative years in organizing and building this new Black Pentecostal-Holiness denomination that had its beginning in the latter part of the nineteenth century. The denomination was birthed out of what is considered by many as the most significant God initiated religious movement the modern world has ever seen—The Azusa Street Revival!

Bishop Mason welcomed and embraced Dr. Hart's experience, gifts, abilities, and used them in many areas of the church. Mason possessed an uncanny wisdom of where to place people so that they would be the most effective and productive. This wisdom can become one of the greatest assets of any leader when he or she understands how to effectively use their staff. During the formative years, Dr. Hart was a close confidant of Mason, advising him on many issues facing the church, particularly on legal matters. From 1901-09, Dr. Hart was a non-practicing attorney until May 1909, when Bishop Mason and the officers of his church decided to retain Dr. Hart as their attorney to represent them in the lawsuit filed in Memphis by the Charles P. Jones faction of the church that broke with the Mason faction of COGIC. Subsequently, Dr. Hart became the representing counselor for COGIC until his death in 1921. Dr. Hart frequently traveled with Bishop Mason and was a first-hand eyewitness to many miracles and the supernatural works God performed through Bishop Mason. Dr. Hart knew the law, and he was an incalculable companion to Bishop Mason when he was traveling, especially during the times Mason was jailed for preaching sanctification and holiness.

It might appear that Dr. Hart had an early or what some would call an untimely death compared to the number of years other early pioneers served the church. There aren't any untimely deaths in the eyes of God. All men live and work until their appointed time when their destiny is fulfilled in God. Dr. Hart accomplished in a few years through the CME Church and COGIC what would take most men a lifetime. He left an impeccable record upon the minds of many in both denominations.

Special attention has been given to Bishop Mason's siblings, the women of the church, and whom I call his "inner circle," because not enough information has been documented about their lives and contributions. It's important to know the socio-political and the socio-religious factors and what effect COGIC as a denomination had in these sectors. However, it is also equally important to know some of the various ways in particular that the saints lived as individuals and as families from day to day, such as how and when they died, survived, struggled, supported themselves, and worked together as families and church members.

These are some of the areas in which I tried to provide as much information as possible in order that the readers would have a slight sense of familiarity with the person or family.

It's extremely important as we approach the one hundredth anniversary celebration of the founding of the Holy Convocation of the Church of God in Christ that we pass on to the next generation the rich legacy the "old saints" extended to us through their prayers to overcome hard trials, challenges, persecutions, and doubts, all of which they overcame. With faith and endurance, they succeeded and witnessed the wonderful works God performed through Bishop Mason and the early pioneering saints that made up the Church of God in Christ.

Above all things, it's my passionate desire that this book will first inform and then serve as a stepping stone to theologians, historians, teachers, genealogists, researchers, and students toward their quest. I wish that I could have spent more time traveling and researching events for this book; however, mandates wouldn't allow it. God knows it has been very challenging for me because it is my first book, and all of it was typed with my right index or middle finger; however, I was determined to complete it myself. Nevertheless, I finished my course and the race is over. My greatest appreciation and thanks to my wife and daughter for their tolerance of me, especially during the times when I threatened them (smiling) to dismiss themselves from the computer so that I could be seated. I honor my ancestors for being such outstanding preservationists of the family's memorabilia, which is the main reason I can now reminisce over my memories of sitting on the floor as a young lad looking at family photographs well over a hundred years old. I also enjoyed flipping through the family Bible, looking at tintypes, and listening to the family's slave stories fascinated by every word I heard. I guess from all of this, my motivation and interest in history and this book evolved. It's my desire to see this book become the catalysis that ignites a reason for others to research and document the accomplishments and contributions of others in COGIC and make them available to a generation that needs to know.

Calvin Stanford McBride
Deacon, Pentecostal Assembly COGIC
Jackson, Tennessee

1

THE MAKING OF A PREACHER: ROBERT EBER HART

Although many black men were called by God to preach the gospel in the nineteenth century, only a few experienced such a rewarding and fascinating life in the ministry as Robert Eber Hart. He was born March 10, 1863, in Macon, Bibb County, Georgia, sixty-nine days after the Emancipation Proclamation was signed by Abraham Lincoln on January 1, 1863. He was the third child of five children born to Jubiter and Phillis Hart. His father was a carpenter and his mother stayed home and raised the children. Jubiter was born in Georgia in 1825, and Phillis was born May of 1847 in Georgia. Dorman was her maiden name.

By 1860, some 6,890 slaves lived in Macon. Slaves in middle Georgia were used for several tasks. Though many worked in cotton production, other slaves tended kitchen gardens, mended clothes and worked at weaving cloth. They built railroads, operated trains and worked on steamboats. The city of Macon used slaves to maintain the streets. Many businessmen preferred slaves over free men. The Macon Telegraph described slave labor in textile mills as "more docile, more constant and cheaper than freemen." When it came to living conditions, slaves were at the mercy of their owners, and many provided only the most basic needs. Several Georgia slaves reported that they lived in poorly constructed, one-room log cabins with few furnishings. They had to prepare all their meals, most of them cooked in fireplaces. Though many masters allowed their slaves to grow vegetables, the food allowance was meager. At rare times, such as Christmas, owners supplemented their slaves' normal diets of meat and meal with the addition of fruit. The types of food varied from plantation to plantation, and there was rarely enough of it. On some farms, a designated slave cook would prepare the meals. In these cases, food would be cooked in one pot and poured into a large container from which all slaves had to eat. The late William Randall's grandmother told him a story about "having all of their food put together in a trough and eating from it with wooden spoons." [1]

According to the U.S. Census in 1870, Phillis Hart moved her family from Macon to Monroe, Georgia, around 1869, a distance of about a hundred miles. The U. S. Census of 1870 was the first census taken after the slaves were freed when their names were first documented in this society as free American citizens. Phillis Hart was forty-five years old and keeping house; Arthur was seventeen years old and a farm laborer; Reynolds was twelve years old and a farm laborer; Robert was eight years old; Ella was four years old, and Nicy was two years old. [2] There was a very noticeable difference documented concerning the color of Ella, being a mulatto when all the other children were listed as black. Their father, Jubiter, wasn't living with them; therefore, he wasn't enumerated within this household but as head of another household. He and Phillis were divorced and Jubiter had remarried. Ella, being the only child listed as mulatto, may give us a hint into the reason why they divorced. They could have divorced because of problems surrounding the biological father of Ella. Their former white slave owner might have fathered the child with Phillis, causing deep resentment toward Phillis coming from Jubiter. Although Phillis and Jubiter had another child after Ella, the emotional scars from her unwanted relationship with their former white slave owner could have later proved too much for the couple to handle. Jubiter was the biological father of Robert, validated by Robert's death certificate. [3]

While growing up in Macon, Robert first attended school around the home fireplace and then Lewis Normal Institute, a school constructed in Macon by the American Missionary Association in 1868 as a gift to the colored people in honor of General John Lewis, an agent of the Freemen's Bureau in Georgia. Two years earlier the Association founded Fisk School, which later became Fisk University in Nashville, Tennessee.

Robert's conversion to the Christian faith occurred in his youth and was followed a few years later by a clear and impressive call to the ministry. He obeyed and gave himself to be the servant of servants. He and his family probably went to church with their white slave owners until the slaves were freed; and after the

Colored Methodist Episcopal Church was organized, they joined the new denomination.

His first theological academic training was at Selma University. The University was founded in 1878 as the Alabama Baptist Normal and Theological School to train blacks to become ministers and teachers. Around 1881, the school was incorporated but wasn't officially named Selma University until 1908.

There came an urgent call for a young man of his caliber, so his first labors in the ministry of Christ were given to the Colored Methodist Episcopal Church in the South Georgia Conference. After a short but successful tour in the South Georgia Conference, there came a second call; and he was transferred to the Alabama Conference of the CME Church and was placed in charge as pastor of the church at Selma. This was his first appointment as pastor of a church. His success in Selma was so gratifying and he was such a "powerhouse" in the pulpit that he was then sent to the church at Tuscaloosa to arouse it from its lethargic condition and inspire it with some of his burning enthusiasm. This he succeeded in doing.

Preparation for Ministry

While in Tuscaloosa, he took advantage of the proximity of his charge as pastor of the CME Church there to attend the Southern Presbyterian Theological Institute. The Seminary opened its doors and received the first students in 1877 for the training of colored male ministers, which was under the control of the General Assembly of the Southern Presbyterian Church. The course of study covered a period of four years and was centered on the Holy Bible. There was no charge for tuition to any properly qualified colored candidate for the ministry. The Southern Presbyterian Church paid the cost of the board, medical attention, and the textbooks. Near the end of the nineteenth century the school enlarged its academic program and changed its name to Stillman Institute in honor of Charles Allen Stillman, who petitioned the General Assembly to establish a training school for black male ministers. Known today as Stillman College, the school has seen considerable growth over the years.

Early as 1886, at the age of twenty-three, Rev. Hart was pastoring his first congregation. He was later transferred from the Alabama Conference back to the Georgia Conference, and like the apostles of old, the reformers and the founders of Methodism, he waited not for sinners to come and ask him the way, but he went to them, down into the vices and iniquity in the cities of Norcross and Atlanta, Georgia, to persuade them to escape the clutches of the devil. As many as 175 souls were gloriously converted at Atlanta under his ministry and many strangers went away, not being converted, but with the aurous of conviction in their hearts to yield at a later time in life.

Madison H. Flewellen, a presiding elder in the CME Church, probably placed the first article in reference to Rev. Hart in the *Christian Index*, the official newspaper of the Colored Methodist Episcopal Church. He told of Rev. Hart's location and activities:

*I am now at Norcross with **Brother R. E. Hart.** We are holding services in the new church; it is not finished but will be in a short time. **Brother R. E. Hart** is doing a great work in this little town. He is teaching, preaching, and building a church. I do not know which thinks the most of him, his pupils in school or the members in the church, or the young ladies in the town. But **Brother Hart** understands how to march upon the line.* [4]

In November of 1868, two years before the organization of the Colored Methodist Episcopal Church, the *Christian Index* newspaper was being published by the white Methodist Episcopal Church, South for its colored members. The paper was being published monthly in Memphis, Tennessee.

Bishop Joseph A. Beebe (1832-1902), the third man to be elected to the office of Bishop in the Colored Methodist Episcopal Church, saw greatness in this young minister and gave him the opportunity to further develop by transferring him in December of 1888 to his first major charge as pastor of the Butler Street CME Church in Atlanta, Georgia. While in Atlanta, his residence was a small cottage in the rear of a house at 65 Fort Street. Rev. Hart was encouraged by Bishop Beebe and he seized upon the opportunity and enrolled in Gammon Theological Seminary, located on the campus of Clark Atlanta University. His school life in the Seminary was characterized by his dedication to the mental and spiritual challenges before him that enabled him to exceed the hopes of all that knew him. He graduated in 1889 with a Bachelor of Divinity degree in one of the strongest classes that marched from Gammon. He left an enviable record as a student and scholar. Gammon Theological Seminary was founded first as Gammon School of Theology as a department of religion and philosophy at Clark University in 1869. In 1883, Gammon Theological Seminary was founded by the Methodist Episcopal Church and remained a part of Clark University. Gammon today is the United Methodist component of a consortium of six historical African-American Theological schools known as The Interdenominational Theological Center (ITC). As recent as 1970, the Charles H. Mason Theological Seminary was added to the Interdenominational Theological Center on the campus of Clark Atlanta University.

A Pastor and a Street Preacher

The second mention of Rev. Hart in the *Christian Index* was briefly in an editorial written by Rev. Fayette M. Hamilton, editor and manager of the *Christian Index*, when he noted some worthwhile comments made by Rev. Hart but condensed them to the following statement:

*"**Rev. R .E. Hart** replied in a few well-chosen remarks."* [5] Rev. Hamilton said to be the most prominent man exclusive of the bishops of the CME Church, was born near Washington, Arkansas, September 3, 1858. He attended the schools of his state, private and public. Afterwards, he spent sixteen months in the Southern Presbyterian Theological Institute at Tuscaloosa, Alabama, the same school that Rev. Hart attended. Rev. Hamilton made another comment about Rev. Hart in the same issue of this paper when he extolled the young preacher saying:

Rev. R.E. Hart *is a young man full of promise, and the C.M.E., Church has reasons to feel proud of him.* [6]

Another article in the *Index* a few days later complimented Rev. Hart on a sermon he preached from Psalms: 120 at Sidney Park CME Church for their week of church dedication at Columbia, South Carolina; and then he was teased by the writer of the article concerning his marital status:

Rev. R.E. Hart *was very much pleased with his visit. He wants to marry but is undecided where to cast his lot He was very much attracted by two of Columbia's fair belles, but could not decide which he like better, poor fellow, he had to leave before coming to a conclusion, but says he is determined to go back next summer.* [7]

Dr. Charles Henry Phillips, although it was a short comment, expressed his confidence in Rev. Hart through the pages of the *Christian Index:*

R. E. Hart has the bearing of an orator. He is a good talker and will surely make his way. **[8]**

Charles H. Phillips, B.A., B.D., M.A., M.D., D.D., LL.D., was born January 17, 1858, in Milledgeville, Georgia. He was the eighth man elected to the bishopric of the CME Church in 1902 and was probably the most educated man in the denomination. Inside and outside of the denomination, he was revered as the "prince" of Black Methodism. There was quite a "stir" surrounding the campaign of Dr. Phillips's running for bishop in 1902. The question in rumor was whether Dr. Phillips (dark-skinned) was going to be the next bishop or would a light-skinned man be elected to the office, replacing Bishop Joseph Beebe (dark-skinned) after his death in 1902. Rev. Hart and Bishop Phillips several years later had some very serious doctrinal differences and conflicts, which led to a split in their relationship and Rev. Hart leaving the denomination.

Rev. Hart's gifts, talents, and the confidence his peers had in him were frequently expressed through the pages of the *Christian Index*. He was a man of God that clearly had a burden for souls, and he boldly proclaimed the Word of God from the pulpit to the streets. This can better be understood from this description of a street scene in Atlanta, Georgia:

*Last Sunday was the scene of a large baptizing by **Rev. R. E. Hart**, pastor of the Butler St., C. M. E., church. A sermon was preached on Mitchell Street on the way to the baptizing pool. Then they proceeded on their line of march to Rev. S. E. Poe's church, corner of Hunter and Davis Streets, where about 23 or 25 applicants were baptized. **Rev. Hart** had about 63 to baptize in all besides taking in forty-two others in the church. These are the fruits of a series of open air meetings on the corner of Decatur and Ivy Streets and at **Rev. Hart's** church.* **[9]**

The Johnson-Hart Nuptial

Rev. Hart in a previous article had already expressed that he was interested in finding for himself a good wife. At the end of his third year as pastor of Butler Street CME Church, just before his transfer from Atlanta to Columbia, South Carolina, he met someone that surpassed all his hopes and expectations. On December 24, 1891, in the presence of a large congregation at Butler Street CME Church, Dr. W. P. Thirkield, President of Gammon Theological Seminary, united Rev. Robert E. Hart and Miss Cornelia Triplett Johnson in marriage.

Miss Johnson, a Christian woman and graduate of Clark Atlanta University and a teacher in the public schools of Atlanta; was a lady esteemed by all for the many excellent qualities she possessed. She was known to be an enthusiastic church and Sunday school worker with a humble spirit. Cornelia was born in March of 1868 in Atlanta, (Fulton County) Georgia, to Washington and Emma Johnson, and she was the younger of two children. Her father, a carpenter by trade, and her mother, a housekeeper, had both been slaves. He was born in Virginia in 1834, and she in Georgia in 1846. [10]

A Capable Orator and Pulpiteer

Rev. Hart was transferred by Bishop Beebe at the General Conference in 1891 to Sidney Park CME Church in Columbia, South Carolina, to pastor. He continued to preach a "burning gospel" and spoke well of the South Carolina Conference. A few weeks after taking over as pastor, he "shook" Sydney Park in a great revival who boasted in the Lord of over 1,000 members. On June 30, 1892, Rev. Hart had been at Sidney Park only six months when the church burned and they didn't have any insurance. Almost immediately they began plans to erect a new edifice. Rev. Hart assured everyone that the glory of the latter house would be greater than the first. He warned people not to think that they had plunged themselves in a "gulf of debt." Neither did they take out a mortgage from a building and loan association, but they setup rally after rally to raise money for the desired amount. In some rallies, they would raise over a thousand dollars, in others five hundred, three hundred, and less. Rev. Hart expected the new cornerstone to be placed by November of 1893; however, completion of the church wasn't until 1894. Isaac H. Anderson, managing editor of the *Christian Index,* placed the following tidbit in its personal mention section:

Rev. R. E. Hart *of Sidney Park raised the largest purse of any minister in the connection; over $7000.00 for 1893.* **The Rev. Hart** *made a grand fight and won a great victory; he is a credit to our Methodism.* [11]

Rev. Hart was chosen as a delegate to the General Conference of the CME Church in 1892 when the sixth and seventh bishops of the Colored Methodist Episcopal Church were elected. There were eighteen men on the ballot running for the office of bishop, and Rev. Hart was one of them. He received only one vote along with Rev. Daniel W. Featherston, my great-grandfather. Of course, they were both extremely short of the number necessary to be elected bishop. It appears this was the first and last time Dr. Hart's name was on a ballot for bishop.

Hart was an excellent speaker and debater and was often on his feet at conferences making a "point." When on his feet, he weighed in at about 225 pounds, making him one of the heaviest men at the conference. He distinguished himself not only as an outstanding preacher but also a help to his brethren in the time of need. When a fellow pastor received a new appointment to a church and didn't have enough money to reach his destination in South Carolina, Rev. Hart and his wife provided him with the money and some simple accommodations. Bishop Isaac Lane visited Rev. Hart and Sidney Park Church while on a tour of the South Carolina and Virginia Conference. He said, "I found Rev. Hart to be most accommodating and pleasant."

The Columbia District Conference began meetings on July 16, 1896; and services lasted all week with preaching day and night. On Sunday, the last day of the meeting at 11:00 am Rev. Hart preached the closing sermon; and the *Index* recorded the comments of an attendee:

Sunday at 11 a. m. **Dr. Hart** *of Sidney Park fired one of his biggest guns. He used as the subject of his discourse: "A New Heaven and a New Earth." I tell you what, Aunt Dilly hopped."* [12]

The eleventh session of the South Carolina Annual Conference of the CME Church met at Allendale, South Carolina, November 25, 1895. On Thursday, Thanksgiving Day the reports from the pastors were given; after which, the business was waived to hear a sermon by Rev. Robert E. Hart, pastor of Sidney Park Church. One attendee felt the need to pass these joyful comments to the *Index*:

He used as a text Matthews 24:12-13. The golden truths that fell from the lips of the master mind were afflatus. It seemed while he was preaching that every soul was carried into ecstasy. His exegesis was plain, yet intricate, metaphysical, and philosophic. It was the sermon of his life. [13]

In previous paragraphs, Rev. Hart has also been referred to as Dr. Hart. He was first called Dr. Hart in 1893 after pastoring Sidney Park Church for two years. Rev. Hart earned a Bachelor of Divinity, but not a Ph.D.; however, an honorary Doctor of Divinity degree was conferred upon him, but not until several years later. So why was this title given to him prematurely? First of all, it was rare for African-Americans to have a college degree at that time. In 1889, when Dr. Hart earned his Bachelor of Divinity degree, there were considerably fewer than two thousand blacks in the whole country that had college degrees. Therefore in 1893, it was very prestigious to have a college degree; secondly, it was more prestigious when African-American men that had degrees were appointed to pastor mega churches of their day. My analysis is that they were highly respected as educated men; and the "non-earned" titles helped boost the image of the person, the race, and denomination.

Dr. Robert E. Hart for Bishop

By 1897, the popularity of Dr. Hart in the CME Church had reached a new level. His success as a pastor and his pulpit skills had earned him respect and an excellent reputation among the bishops and his colleagues. The following statement came from Rev. J. W. Wills through the pages of the *Index:*

> *"If we must have another Bishop in our next General Conference, give us Rev. G. W. Stewart of Alabama, or **Rev. R. E. Hart** of South Carolina.]* [14]

A similar response came from Rev. T. J. Moppins of the Kentucky Conference of the CME Church, who was often an outspoken critic of the "color line" that existed in the church between the light-skinned bishops and the dark-skinned bishops. He wrote an article to the *Christian Index* where he pleaded to the bishops to appoint men of intellectual value who didn't dread small towns and the cities, men who did not dread education, and men that realized great things were expected of them. He asked, "As a bishop appoint men that are gentlemen and scholars." He suggested as editor of the *Christian Index*, elect Dr. R. E. Hart to this position. No doubt, opinions and comments like these only reinforced Dr. Hart's ambitions and aspirations while improving his circumstances and opportunities in the denomination. Two months after Rev. Moppins's article appeared in the *Index*, Dr. Hart was transferred to the Virginia Conference and appointed pastor of Israel Metropolitan CME Church in Washington, D.C., in December of 1896. This was probably the "most prominent" of all appointments in the CME Church at the time. However, I'm not suggesting that Rev. Moppins article had anything to do with the decision to relocate Rev. Hart to the Virginia Conference. It was only a letter of support. Dr. Hart was only thirty-three years old and well prepared to take over his new post. His new congregation was well pleased with him and he with them. One parishioner predicted, "They will most assuredly succeed because his administration has every indication of being crowned with success."

Dr. Hart was a powerful speaker and this was well characterized by a parishioner that was present at a church service and heard Dr. Hart's sermon and later made these comments:

Rev. R. E. Hart made a speech which was actually the speech of his life and after which the people from all over the house came and shook his hand. Well, I never realized such a time; it seemed that the very name C. M. E., stirred the people up. [15]

He was as powerful a preacher out of the pulpit as he was in the pulpit, and he never gave up street preaching. On one occasion when a presiding elder from the South came to visit him in Washington, the two of them spent two weeks on the street preaching the gospel. This clearly shows that Dr. Hart had a passion for saving souls and wasn't caught up in religiosity that could come from pastoring a very large church and congregation. Everywhere Dr. Hart went he made an impression on the people and was known as a humble servant of Christ. He was one of the favorite speakers at conferences and was considered a towering giant in the Colored Methodist Episcopal Church. He was often called upon to present the bishops to the Conference because he was such an outstanding orator.

Bishop Robert S. Williams, the sixth man to be ordained to the bishopric of the CME Church in 1892, was the representative for the Colored Methodist Episcopal Church to the Third Ecumenical Conference, which was to be held in London, England, in 1901. He called upon Dr. Hart to aid him in arranging and negotiating the trip. The two of them made plans for the trip to London at the meeting for the conference in the Missionary Room of the Publishing House of the Methodist Episcopal Church, South, in New York, on June 14, 1899. Although Dr. Hart wasn't chosen to make the trip, it was good close working relationships like this with the bishops that prompted some preachers to suggest that Dr. Hart would be a good choice for bishop.

Rev. G. I. Jackson, pastor of Capers Chapel CME Church in Nashville, Tennessee, didn't mind sharing his thoughts about Dr. Hart for bishop in the *Index*:

Rev. R. E. Hart of Washington, D. C., was with us on the 1ˢᵗ of June and preached us two very important sermons and made a great name for him in the city of Nashville. He is one that will make a future Bishop for our Church. [16]

A Church and Civic Servant

Dr. Hart was very active in the community among civic and business organizations. While pastoring in Washington D. C., some of his members and several of the citizens formed an organization called the National Organized Brotherhood of Afro-Americans. Dr. Hart was elected president; Charles Strother, secretary; and Nathan Bell, chaplain. Auxiliaries were to be formed all over the country with the General Headquarters at 236 New Jersey Avenue, Southeast. Research has uncovered nothing about this organization although we can make an assumption, judging from the name of the organization, that it was probably a community support group for black males. Most of Dr. Hart's affairs were recorded through the *Christian Index*, but there were other news media that took notice, such as *The Washington D. C. Daily Record*, which published this article:

Rev. R. E. Hart, pastor of Israel C. M. E., Church, will preach his farewell sermon next Sunday night and will then go up to the conference of his church which will convene at Lynchburg, Virginia to render an account of his work the past year.

It is our pleasure to say that no minister in Washington has impressed himself with his people as has Rev. Hart, and at a business meeting where over 300 members of his church were present, he was unanimously endorsed. The official board in its session last week endorsed Rev. Hart's work and will use their strongest efforts to have him returned for another year.

The church has prospered greatly under Rev. Hart's pastorate, both in way of finance and members.

Many of the old debts have been wiped entirely out while considerable improvements have been made.

As a citizen, Rev. Hart stands high in the estimation of his people of this city. No subject of interest to the race escapes his notice and as a platform orator, he has few equals in the community. His life and energy have won for him a host of friends, who with the members of his church, hope for his return to us one more year. [17]

Dr. Hart was a humble and suigeneris servant of God, which can be validated by the compliments expressed in this lengthy article by Rev. James W. Poe of the CME Church:

Rev. R. E. Hart, pastor of Israel C. M. E., Church, 1ˢᵗ and B Streets, Southwest, in this city, is one of the most erudite, unassuming, popular, eloquent, resourceful, and eminent pulpit orators in the nation's capitol city, which is not only becoming the center of national attraction, but which is rapidly becoming the metropolis of the world. Rev. Hart came here a stranger to our city and people but a short time ago, but his terse theological views, his clear logical reasoning's, his brilliant display of a classical mind, his irresistible eloquence, and his rare qualities as a forceful and powerful pulpit orator soon brought him to the front rank and made him an object of admiration, both to the clergy and laity of Washington. The Rev. Hart is still in the morning of his life, and is destined at no very distant time in the future to take and hold rank with the most eminent divines of the Christian ministry, who will deserve even higher promotion in his highly moral and religious sphere He is highly suited to preside over a Christian flock in a great and popular city like this, where the educational refinement of our religious audiences require such talent as is exhibited by Rev. Hart. He constantly finds himself environed with more invitations from local churches, irrespective of denominational lines, than it is in his power to comply with. This attest both his great popularity and ability as a minister of the gospel of Christ, and yet there might be a few who would not be pleased with all of his acts and who would not be completely suited with the most orthodox bishop of the Church, nor even with the divine Master himself, if he was here. Rev. Hart is a gentleman, a scholar, a theologian, a logician and an orator of fine attainments.

While I am a member of the A. M. E., Church, unfettered by prejudice in my desire to see the Master's" kingdom come." I am forced to publicly say this much in bestowing deserved praise upon an unassuming Christian gentleman.

His church is a modern improved brick structure, and is in nearer proximity to the capitol building, its beautiful grounds, the two branches of Congress, the Supreme Court of the United States, the National Congressional Library building and grounds, the Botanical Garden and the Garfield monument than any other Afro-American church at the nation's capitol. That is his field of usefulness, there let him remain. **[18]**

After reading Rev. Poe's article, one could conclude that Bishop Robert S. Williams played a very pivotal role in Dr. Hart's destiny, suggesting that he transferred Dr. Hart at a time when the South was becoming a "hot-bed" for spiritual change. Rev. Poe, at the end of his article, suggested that Rev. Hart should remain at the church in Washington; however, Bishop Williams had the final decision; or could it have been Dr. Hart's request to be transferred to the Tennessee Conference? I believe it was Dr. Hart's request to transfer to the South and to the Tennessee Conference. He would have been aware of the spiritual change that was taking place in the South, especially in Memphis and coming through the Sanctified Church. Dr. Hart's tendencies to accept invitations from other denominations and freely fellowship with them irrespective of doctrinal differences would eventually raise some serious issues between him and the bishops of the CME church and with one bishop in particular. His desire to be an open and transparent Christian, and not afraid to reach out to other denominations and go into their meetings, kept him "rooted" and "grounded" and in touch with his brothers and sisters in Christ. However, this practice later caused deep divisions between him and some leaders of the CME Church.

2

COMING TO TENNESSEE IN THE TWENTIETH CENTURY

Jackson, Tennessee was a most logical setting for the Organizing General Conference of the Negro members of the Methodist Episcopal Church, South. It is situated in Madison County about fifty miles north of the state line bordering Tennessee and Mississippi. In 1870 it was a small agrarian town rather accessible by good roads and railroads from all directions. Map 1 of the colored conferences and districts which had been organized by that time, show Jackson to have been almost the geographical center of what would be the new church. To the north was the well-organized Kentucky, to the west were the well-populated Memphis and the embryonic Arkansas, to the east and southeast was the strong Georgia, while the Alabama and Mississippi conferences were located respectively southeast and due south. Texas would, of course, lie to the southwest. [1] Jackson was an ideal setting also because of the strong influence of Methodism in Tennessee generally and the favorable attitude of white Methodists toward the colored Methodists. [2]

Isaac Lane was elected the fifth bishop of the Colored Methodist Episcopal Church eighteen days following his 39th birthday. He was born March 3, 1834, near Jackson, Tennessee. At the age of 20, Lane was converted and licensed to preach. In 1866 he was ordained a deacon by Bishop Robert Paine, and the following year ordained elder. Lane was appointed Presiding Elder of the Jackson District of the Memphis Colored Conference when that conference was organized in 1867, thus having the distinction of being the first "Presiding Elder" of what was to become the CME Church. At the time of his election, Lane was the Pastor of the Jackson Station (later known as "Mother Liberty") in Jackson, TN. [3]

Rev. Hart had already experienced a considerable amount of recognition and appreciation through the ministry as a rising leader of Methodism in the nineteenth century, and now the twentieth century was going to impact his life in a more "profound" way. Rev. Hart was transferred from Israel Metropolitan CME Church in Washington, D. C., and appointed pastor of Mother Liberty CME Church in Jackson, Tennessee, at the General Conference held in Lynchburg, Virginia, in 1899. He took charge of his new appointment on Sunday, December 17, 1899, under favorable and encouraging circumstances. On that day, a very large and enthusiastic audience greeted him; and at night, the church was packed for that service. Rev. Hart preached both the day and night services, and every one was well pleased with the new pastor. My grandfather, Dr. Samuel Henry Broome, and my grandmother, Eva E. Featherston, were likely in the audience. They weren't yet married; however, they were members of the church and probably attended both services. About four months later, they were married at Mother Liberty, which is the Mother Church of the CME denomination. Dr. Broome and Rev. Hart later became co-workers and good friends. My great-grandfather, Rev. Daniel Webster Featherston, (1856-1925) had been pastor of Mother Liberty from 1886-90.

The West Tennessee Conference of the CME Church

By 1882 the work in Tennessee had grown to the point that another conference, West Tennessee Conference, was created. The boundaries of the new conference were the Tennessee River, Mississippi River, and the boundary lines of the states of Kentucky and Mississippi. At the end of the century, the West Tennessee Conference was, numerically, the largest annual conference in the CME Church, reporting close to 14,000 lay members. [4]

The West Tennessee Conference of the CME Church wasted no time in introducing and involving Rev. Hart in their affairs. Memorial services in honor of Rev. R. T. James were held at Collins Chapel CME Church in Memphis, Tennessee, just days after Dr. Hart arrived in Jackson. He was asked to bring the message at the 7:00 pm service in the church auditorium before a crowd of hundreds. Collins Chapel boasted a membership of over a thousand parishioners and many of Memphis's African-American elite attended services there.

Charles Henry Phillips, Jr., welcomed Rev. Hart to the West Tennessee Conference, which was held in Memphis, Tennessee, at Collins Chapel CME Church in 1899, and he had this to say:

Rev. R. E. Hart was transferred from Israel Metropolitan C.M.E., church of Washington, D.C., and stationed at Jackson. Rev. Hart is one of the brainiest leaders of the race. He is a fine pulpit orator, a great financier, and a true upright Christian gentleman. He made the best report that has ever been given from Israel for the last eight years. Rev. Hart is a success wherever he may be sent. [5]

A few weeks after arriving in Jackson, Rev. Hart traveled to several surrounding towns and preached. He visited the North Mississippi Conference where he was well received and where he made an eloquent speech and preached a wonderful sermon. The people were "electrified" by his message and motivated to make these comments:

Rev. R. E. Hart, of Washington D. C., but now of Jackson, Tennessee, the last but not the least, our roommate, is a bright star, shinning in great illustration and splendor. He is a pulpit orator, a power behind the throne, a workman that needeth not be ashamed, a man (in our judgment) approved of God. [6]

Like many African-Americans during this period in our history, Rev. Hart was a loyal member of the Republican Party because Abraham Lincoln had freed the slaves and because Abraham Lincoln was a member of the Republican Party. Rev. Hart became engaged in political rallies in Jackson on Mondays at Court Square and was one of the favored speakers. James Franklin Lane, a son of Bishop Isaac Lane and President of Lane College from 1907-44, was present at one of the rallies before he was appointed President of Lane College. James Franklin Lane endorsed the speech made by Dr. Hart at the rally. His comments were submitted and published in the *Lane College Reporter*, the college newsletter:

The Rev. Dr. R. E. Hart, pastor of Liberty C. M. E., church, of this city, is one of the most eloquent speakers it has been our pleasure to hear for quite awhile. His extemporaneous speech made not long since at the Court House at a mass meeting of the Republicans of this county won for him much applause and distinction. Logic and eloquence characterized the doctor's address. Great is Rev. Hart, and masterly was his effect. [7]

Obviously, Dr. Hart was strongly supported by many white Republicans in the city, which enabled him to address fellow white and black Republicans from the steps of a segregated courthouse. The African-American community in Jackson enjoyed a short lived politically charged atmosphere in the early part of the twentieth century through the efforts of Dr. Hart. One local white Jackson resident in his memoirs complained, "The white folks ought to leave the Negroes alone and stop stirring them up. White folks should stay in their place and the Negroes in their place."

The First Lady Arrives

Mrs. Cornelia Triplett Hart, the wife of Dr. Hart, arrived in Jackson from Washington D. C., in March of 1900 about three months after her husband. She was accompanied by her close companion and adopted daughter, Miss Addie Robinson. The people of Jackson gladly welcomed Mrs. Hart into their midst and wished her a happy future home in Jackson. The Harts took up residence in the church parsonage, which was completely furnished and decorated. The church was able to provide such luxury because of its large membership. Many of its members were the black elite of Jackson. They soon found out that Mrs. Hart was an accomplished organist and soloist. She was an excellent organizer of church work and auxiliaries, a good example for the women of the church, and a leader of women.

Dr. Hart and his wife had tried several times to have children but had not been able to. It wasn't until after they had moved to Tennessee that a child had been born who had lived to see her first birthday. The *Christian Index* expressed its sympathy to Dr. and Mrs. Hart after the lost of their daughter:

*We take this opportunity to express our sympathy with **Dr. and Mrs. R. E. Hart** in their bereavement in the loss of their little daughter Robie C. Hart. She was born July 16, 1902 and died August 2, 1903. Her funeral was conducted by the pastor from Liberty CME Church at Jackson, Tennessee and a large congregation of friends was present. Little Robie is no more with us, the only child and daughter of **Dr. and Mrs. Hart**. We know that her dear mother and father greatly appreciate the prayers of the Church in this their moments of sadness.* [8]

I find it extremely extraordinary that Dr. Hart was able to conduct and deliver the eulogy at his daughter's funeral. After Robie's death everyone learned just how much of a difficult time Mrs. Hart endured trying to bare children. One week later a second article told of the many heart wrenching disappointments the Harts had experienced:

> **Dr. and Mrs. R. E. Hart** *lost their only child on the 2nd inst. It was not quite two years old. This is the eighth child to die in infancy. We extend the sympathy of the church to them in their hours of deepest sorrow.* [9]

One can only imagine how devastating it must have been to lose "eight" children in infancy. On their "ninth" attempt (two years after Robie's death), they were able to have a child that survived longer than two years. Their son, Robert Mason Hart (named after C. H. Mason), was born September 18, 1904, and survived, breaking the bondage of death in the family. Phyllis Elizabeth Hart (named after Dr. Hart's mother), was born in 1910 when her mother was forty-three and beyond the ideal child bearing age. Attempting to have a child at forty-three could have been very "risky," considering the time period and medical availability for African-Americans. Robert Mason Hart graduated from old South Jackson School in the Class of 1920, one year before his dad passed away. Also graduating in that class was Theodore Roosevelt White, better known to Jacksonians as Professor T. R. White.

Spring Revival and April Showers

Many African-Americans churches at the turn of the twentieth century had Spring Revival every year. Dr. Hart received large crowds at his first revival services at Mother Liberty and about thirteen converts were received into the church. Dr. Hart reached beyond his denomination and invited Rev. Charles G. Diggs, pastor of Bethel AME Church in the city, to carry on revival. Likely present at the revival was Brother E. M. Page, who later became one of the first bishops in the Church of God in Christ. He was living in Jackson at the time and a member of Bethel AME Church. Dr. Hart expressed, "I was much pleased with the members and friends who did all in their power to make the revival meeting a success."

The week following revival my grandparents were married at Mother Liberty Church. One of my grandmother's friends wrote and submitted this article to the *Christian Index:*

On Wednesday evening, April 11, 1900, promptly at 8 o'clock, quite a number of friends had gathered at Liberty C. M. E., Church to witness the marriage of Dr. S. H. Broome and Miss Eva Featherston. Bishop Isaac Lane officiated. The bride is the beautiful and cultured daughter of Rev. and Mrs. D. W. Featherston, a well known family of Jackson, and a member of Liberty Church. At eight o'clock, p. m. the sweet chords of the organ pealed forth the sweet strains, Mrs. Z. T. Robinson presiding. During which time, the bride's maid, Miss Rena B. Calhoun entering, marched slowly down the isle. Thence came the bride resting on the arm of her father. The groom and best-man, Rev. A. N. Steven, Pastor, St. Paul C. M. E. Church, entered the side door approached the altar where the ceremony was performed by Bishop Lane in his impressive and dignified way, as usual.

The bride was beautifully attired in white silk, trimmed in lace, pearls and ribbons and a veil which was tastily draped, becoming to the sweet face. The bride's maid wore a beautiful white organdy, neatly trimmed in ribbon and lace. The bride carried in her hand, a beautiful white bible presented by Miss Ida M. Lane.

The Church was tastily decorated with evergreen and flowers for the occasion. The groom is a practicing physician of Jackson, formerly of Brownsville, Tennessee having practiced there for three years. He is a graduate from Meharry Medical College, Nashville, Tennessee. After the ceremony, the bride and groom and host of friends gathered at the residence of the bride's parents, Rev. and Mrs. D. W. Featherston, on Berry St., where all things were in readiness. The table was laden with such things that were pleasing to the appetite. The invited guest seemed to have enjoyed themselves sumptuously until a late hour. After biding the bride and groom adieu and a sweet repose, one by one, they departed to their respective homes. The couple received a number of valuable presents. By a Friend [10]

Baccalaureate and Commencements

On the front page of the *Christian Index*, dated February 17, 1900, there was an editorial titled, "Our Schools and Degrees." The editorial, in general, complained that no school under the authority of the Colored Methodist Episcopal Church had ever conferred the "Doctor of Divinity" degree upon any of the men in the church. The editorial exclaimed, "In as much as the Baptists, the African Methodist Episcopal, and the African Methodist Zion's have schools that confer degrees, should not the CME Church have at least one school to do a similar thing!" The editorial was perfectly timed and didn't fall on "deaf" ears. Lane College's Commencement was only a few weeks away, and the perfect opportunity was presented to make history. The Board of Trustees at Lane College decided in favor of the desires of many men in the denomination and conferred upon eighteen ministers the Honorary Doctor of Divinity. Let the record speak for itself. Upon the first week of June 1900, Lane College became the first school under the auspices of the CME Church to confer the honorary Doctor of Divinity degree in the CME denomination. Nelson C. Cleaves, D. D., an alumnus of Lane College, was the commencement speaker and one of the recipients of the honorary degree. At the top of the list was Dr. R. E. Hart, who was already being addressed by the title; however, now it was going to be made official by an honorary diploma. Second on the roster to receive the diploma was my great-grandfather, Daniel W. Featherston, D. D., and the Honorary Doctor of Laws (LL.D.) was conferred upon Bishop Isaac Lane, founder of Lane College.

About two weeks before the Lane College Commencement in 1900, Dr. Hart was invited to deliver the baccalaureate sermon before the State Normal Institute, located on the campus of Rust College, in Holly Springs, Mississippi. The ceremony was scheduled on May 20 and was held outside on the lawn.

On Friday morning, June 8, 1900, the commencement exercises of the colored city schools of Jackson, Tennessee, were held at the old South Jackson school building. Dr. Hart delivered the commencement address to the graduating class, which consisted of eight pupils: six boys and two girls. Austin Raymond Merry, B.A., M.A., (1855-1920) was principal of the Jackson Colored Schools and an 1879 graduate of Fisk University. Professor Merry, a Kentuckian, was the first African-American to earn a college degree and settle in Jackson after graduating in 1879. He earned his Masters of Arts from Fisk in 1885; and from 1879-1920, he was principal of the Jackson Colored Schools. He died before he could see the first twelfth graders graduate in 1923.

A Master Sermon Writer

Rev. George Washington Stewart was the tenth man to be appointed a Bishop in the CME Church. He was so impressed with Dr. Hart that he was moved to write and submit this extensive article to the *Christian Index* entitled, Rev. R. E. Hart, D.D. Dr. Charles H. Phillips (later bishop) was editor of the *Index* when the following article was submitted:

With interest have I read the many comments in the Index relative to this distinguished divine. As a minister I have some hesitancy in expressing an opinion as to the qualifications and success of this man of God. Yet, as a lover of my church and a firm believer in its traditions and teachings, with my convictions deepened by a study of its cardinal doctrines and believing that the C.M.E., Church has a part with others of great Methodist family in redeeming the world, it is with no little satisfaction that I try to attest the worth of one whose works indicate the man. The Church is doubtless proud of her distinguished sons. I am not, however, of the opinion that **Dr. Hart** can lay preeminent claims of distinction for scholarship, his success as a pastor, or because he is desirous that the borders of the Church be extended and every interest strengthened. Measured by such standard there are others who might claim and merit equal distinction. All of these qualifications in this man, it seems to me, results from his conception of. "And if I be lifted up from the earth will draw all men unto me." In these times of higher criticisms, pseudo-scientific investigation of religious subjects, disregard of church laws and frequent worship of scholarship's its refreshing to know that in the C.M.E., Church there is a school of conservative yet aggressive, cultured and refined, but not effeminate preachers who believe that the gospel has power to save. They believe that the wisdom of this world, whatever is obtained through the medium of knowledge, furnished by books, investigation, or otherwise, must lead one, if it leads a right to the foot of the cross. In this circle is **Dr. Hart** modest, unassuming, affable, a humanitarian, he is easily popular; a lover of learning, he is studious, and an encouragement to whatever tends to improve the mind of fix his fellowmen for usefulness. I have suggested that as a preacher he stands out in bold relief. So he does. In his private life he is enviable; in the pulpit he is almost phenomenal. He has the power to draw and hold men while he tells in simple language the story that never grows old.

I have often wished to know how he prepares his sermons. Once I got a glimpse of his manuscript; it was only a skeleton. The sermon was a masterpiece, pregnant with though, apt illustrations, brilliant with quotations, and imagery effort that seemed to move the audience at the speaker's will and pleasure. It is at the height of sermonic effort that **Dr. Hart's** learning is displayed, perhaps unconsciously. Swinging around the circle of his own individuality he seizes whatever has become a part of his experience and hurls it only as one can who believes in the wilderness of the spirit. If the sermon fails to produce the desired effort he uses his gift of song and tunes and sentiments that come from the heart, reach the heart, and conspire to make men say "it is good for us to hear." Thus he combines the emotions and the intellect in reaching the wills of his audience.

From Wesley's time, Methodism has been vital. Free grace, repentance, justification, and perseverance in the faith have held mankind as can nothing else holds it. General atonement is taking the place of limited atonement in denomination whose dogmas were formerly arrayed against those which Methodism fosters and "salvation is *free to all," preached with so much success by our ministry, will eventually be the world doctrine. Ministers who preach this have little time for metaphysical dissertations or reviews of the latest literary products. They feel it their duty to exemplify: "Tis all my business here below to cry behold the lamb." Such a man is our subject. A Whitefield in eloquence, a Charles Wesley in song, a John Wesley in devotion to the doctrines he believes and preaches. He is a gospel preacher, worthy of emulation and honors. He is such a man that the connection can well put in any place of responsibility or trust.* [11]

The Twentieth Century Movement

The Colored Methodist Episcopal Church at the end of the nineteenth century adopted the idea and vision of the white Methodist churches across the country. They chose Bishop Robert Simeon Williams, D.D., one of the members on the general board of the CME Church, as the project General Manager, representing the CME Church. The project plan was to raise $25,000 in 1900 for education and missions in the CME Church with the idea being "dubbed" the Twentieth Century Movement. Several ministers were asked to prepare statements in support of the movement for publishing in the *Christian Index*. Dr. Hart responded with the following article entitled: "The Characteristics of the 19th Century Contrasted With What the 20th Should Be":

The though and spirit of the 19th Century have been materialistic, and such have permeated the nation, stamping their personalities upon all classes of men. Materialism has insinuated itself into our most responsible spiritual centers. A kind of materialistic philosophy has undermined faith in general. The spirit of avarice, inordinate pride, a desire for personal worship, and a general disregard of the rights of others have been embodied even in Christian systems. The results are everywhere apparent. Evil suspicion, popular unrest, and the consequent decline of the Churches. The M. E. Church with 16,490 ministers, 25,974 churches and 2,698,610 members, there was, in the year 1899 a reported decrease of 21,731.

Our own Church with a membership of 150,000, reports a decrease of 20,000. In her scramble and success in a financial way, let not God's Church forget her great mission of saving souls. Let the Bishops' cry for $25,000 be heeded; then let the Bishops issue another call for fifty thousand souls in 1901. Let there be a cessation of petty jealousies and strife-of the strong against the weak, of might against right. Let the pulpit, God's throne on earth, be a center of spiritual forces that the 20th Century imbibe and breathe an entirely different spirit; that it turn our eyes inward so as to enable us to *discover our inner splendors—the wealth of the soul; discover islands of spiritual beauty.*

May it be such a century of spiritual thinking as will push back the threshold of a more lofty plane of consciousness, that the sixth sense-spiritual detection-may be realized and recognized as the prime factor in solving the mysterious problems of life. **R.E. Hart.** [12]

You can formulate from reading Dr. Hart's letter that he was very much concerned with the state of the church, concerning saving souls and how materialism had crept into the church. I wonder what would Dr. Hart's letter say addressing the church of today if he though materialism was out of control at the beginning of the twentieth century. He didn't realize at the time (when he was talking about breathing in new souls and a new spirit in the twentieth century) that he was going to play a vital role ushering in and defending the greatest religious movement of the twentieth century.

Robert E. Hart: Founding Charter Member of the University of West Tennessee

Dr. Hart was a prominent man in the CME Church, and his gifts and talents would soon lead him into a new field. Dr. Miles V. Lynk, an 1891 graduate of Meharry Medical College, from Brownsville, Tennessee, started his medical practice in Jackson shortly after graduation. He decided that he needed a law degree to complete and accomplish his vision of starting a medical and law school. Dr. Lynk saw an urgent need for more and better trained Negro doctors and lawyers. After surveying the state for schools that trained African-Americans in higher education, his investigations revealed a shortage in the field; and he decided to do something about it. The following is an excerpt from his autobiography:

"I approached a few fellow citizens, to be exact, **Rev. R. E. Hart***, pastor of the C. M. E., Church, Mr. J. H. Trimble, postman, Drs. J. L. Light and S. H. Broome, all of Jackson, Tennessee. Together we applied to the State of Tennessee and were granted a charter of incorporation with liberal powers to conduct a school in the corporate name of "University of West Tennessee."* [13]

The Charter of Incorporation for the University of West Tennessee Medical College (UWT) was hand written by the Tennessee Secretary of State and filed with the state in Nashville, December 18, 1900, and in Jackson, Madison County, December 20, 1900. The following is an excerpt from the charter:

Be it known that by virtue of the general laws of the land that M. V. Lynk, J. L. Light, S. H. Broome, **R. E. Hart** *and J. H. Trimble, are hereby constituted a body corporate and politic with perpetual succession by the name and style of "The University of West Tennessee," for the purpose of giving instructions in the various branches of Medicine, Law, Dentistry, Pharmacy, and all other branches of science, art, and literature, with the additional powers to grant diplomas and confer degrees.* **[14]**

Dr. Lynk quickly realized he was busy engaged in his medical practice and didn't have time to leave home to pursue a law degree. Therefore, he devised a plan; and all he needed was the support of some key players. He first approached Bishop Isaac Lane with his plan, and the following is Dr. Lynk's account from his autobiography:

I first approached Bishop Lane, President of the Trustee Board at Jackson, Tennessee, and asked if we could institute a law school at Lane. My request met a cool reception. However, he finally consented that a law class might be taught under the auspices of Lane, if I would be personally responsible for all expenses. With this promise I consulted Mr. H. R. Saddler, LL.B., a prominent Memphis attorney, who consented to teach the proposed class. He outlined a standard three year law course. I then went about soliciting members for our class. The following was the class roster: J. F. Lane, Professor at Lane College, afterwards president; G. A. Payne, principal, Jackson Public Colored School; C. A. Leftwich, teacher at Lane College; **Rev. R. E. Hart, Pastor CME Church;** *Rev. J. W. Grant, Pastor AME Church; Mr. J. H. Trimble, U.S. Letter Carrier; Mr. C. R. Neely, Public School Teacher; Mr. Sanders Jordan, Industrialist; M. V. Lynk, the Writer.*

Regular study began June 1, 1900, with daily classes meeting either at Lane College or at my office. About the latter part of February, 1901, after nine months of study, Mr. Saddler, our teacher, announced that M. V. Lynk was about ready for examination, preparatory to admission to the Bar. Pursuant to this he made a motion before the Circuit Court of Madison County, asking, that in accordance with the statute, in such case made and provided, a committee of the Bar should be appointed to examine M. V. Lynk to ascertain whether he is fit morally and mentally for admission to the Bar. **[15]**

Mr. Saddler made recommendations before the court for Dr. Lynk in order that he might be confirmed as an attorney and he was likely present with Dr. Lynk when the following motion and order enrolling Dr. Lynk as an attorney was read:

Order Enrolling Attorney: "It appearing to the Court that M. V. Lynk has been duly licensed to practice law in the courts of Tennessee and having been sworn to support the Constitution of the United States, the Constitution of the State of Tennessee, and to properly demean himself. He is enrolled as attorney of this Court." **[16]**

Hart Earns a Law Degree

On February 16, 1901, three days after Dr. Lynk was enrolled as an attorney, Dr. R. E. Hart was issued his license to practice law by John M. Taylor, Circuit Judge and A. G. Hawkins, Chancellor of the State of Tennessee, becoming the second African-American to receive a license to practice law in Jackson, Madison County, Tennessee. Dr. Hart's plan at that time was not to practice law but to teach law at the University of West Tennessee where Dr. Lynk was the president. Therefore, it wasn't necessary for him to be enrolled in the courts as a practicing attorney. He waited several years before he went before the judges to be properly enrolled as an attorney to practice in the courts of Tennessee. However, for the immediate future he and Dr. Lynk had other plans as to where, when, and how their law licenses were to be used. At that point in time, if a person's ambitions were to practice law, he didn't necessarily have to earn a law degree from a qualified institution to practice. Many studied or "read" law as an apprentice under an already licensed attorney; and if they passed the bar, they were granted their license. Such was the law in Tennessee and a few other states in 1901.

Dr. Hart was recognized as a graduate of Lane College's law class in 1901. The editor and manager of the *Christian Index*, Dr. Charles H. Phillips, was present and submitted the following article to the *Christian Index* from the Trustee Board meeting at Lane College:

We attended the Trustee Board Meeting of the school for the first time in many years. Bishop Lane is President and Rev. E. W. Moseley, D. D., is the Secretary of the Board. The report of President Sanders was well received. The affairs of the school had been well conducted and the trustees were pleased with the report. The twentieth cen-

tury and the educational moneys gave the institution a pretty fair sum to further foster its interests. The Board decided to purchase a farm and appointed a committee to make a selection of a place, report to the Local Board, and authorized the latter to make the purchase. Some additions will be made to the girl's dormitory as more ample accommodations are an apparent necessity. One of the most noted discussions of the sessions was had on the question "whether the school had had a Law Department during the term," or "whether it would have in the future." Between May 1900 and May 1901, the local board of trustees allowed Hon. Mr. Saddler, of Memphis, to organize a Law Course as an appendix to the college. He would come over from the "Bluff City" at certain times; hear his class, and then go back to resume his practice of law. There were two members of this class recommended for graduation by Mr. Saddler. This gave rise to the introduction of the questions propounded above. At the morning session, held on the 29th of May, the General Board indorsed the action of the Local Board in recognizing a Law Department and voted to graduate the persons mentioned in Mr. Saddler petition. At the afternoon session of the same day some one proposed to elect a Dean of the Law Department. But the Board voted that they would have no such department in connection with Lane College. So the Law Department of this school, which existed too much in the mind and the imagination, and too little in reality, was duly abolished. In the mean time Mr. Saddler's candidates were recognized for graduation, and on Thursday, May 30, just after the other regular exercise had ended, **Rev. R. E. Hart** *and Rev. J. W. Grant, of the A. M. E., Church, delivered good orations and were graduated as Bachelors of Law. We heard Secretary Moseley read several applications from different persons appealing for the degree of Doctor of Divinity. No discussions were had, and no action was taken. It appeared to be the sentiment of the Board, though unexpressed to confer no degrees. And none were conferred. Lane College is doing a great work and its trustees are doing all they can to make it one of the best schools of the race.* [17]

M. V. Lynk vs. R. E. Hart

Drs. Hart and Lynk's friendship was temporarily jeopardized when they became "embroiled" in a dispute over money that was owed to Dr. Lynk by Dr. Hart for tuition. They weren't able to settle their differences out of court, and charges were filed by Dr. Lynk. Reluctantly, the case went to court on May 23, 1901, just seven days before the graduation at Lane College. Circuit Court papers documented the following compromise:

M. V. Lynk

vs.   Debt, Compromise

R. E. Hart

Came the parties in person, and in open court, and stated to the court that this case has been compromised. Thereupon cause the plaintiff and the defendant, and paid to the clerk of this court the cash of this cause. **[18]**

Apparently, Dr. Lynk and Dr. Hart settled their differences just hours or minutes before the case was to be heard. Keep in mind, Dr. Hart was Dr. Lynk's pastor; therefore, it was expedient for them to settle their differences.

Dr. Hart Appointed Law Professor at the University of West Tennessee

Dr. Lynk was acutely aware that he was the first African-American to practice medicine in Jackson; and having the oversight of developing a law class would assure him the same status in the field of law. There were four that graduated from the law class out of the eight enrollees, and the four appear to have been "hand" picked. Some disagreements arose between the members of the Board of Trustees at Lane College over whether to continue the law class. Also, there were suspicions as to the motives of Dr. Lynk and Mr. Saddler. Dr. Lynk knew that he alone could not represent a law department, and he needed someone to chair the law department while he administered to the daily needs of the college. Dr. Hart was the man Dr. Lynk had in mind and he asked him to chair the law department. Mr. John W. Grant and Professor Charles R. Neely were the only ones besides Hart and Lynk that graduated and were conferred degrees at the regular commencement exercise, which only fueled more suspicions. Dr. Lynk stated in his autobiography that the other members of the class simply gave up. The question is, "Did they give up because they felt something wrong was being perpetrated?" Mr. Saddler appears to have made the final decision as to who was ready for examination. Dr. Lynk was the first to receive his law license followed by Dr. Hart. They were the only two who were enrolled by the court in Madison County out of the four that graduated. Mr. Saddler or Dr. Hart had no idea at the time that they would later cross each other's path in the near future in a very "high profile" religious trial between two Black Holiness factions in COGIC.

About three months after classes began at the University of West Tennessee; Dr. Hart was transferred by Bishop Lane as pastor of Mother Liberty Church to Brownsville, Tennessee, as presiding elder of the Brownsville District. Relocating him with new responsibilities in the ministry shouldn't have compromised his duties at the college. Ernest W. Irving, M.D., (Meharry, 1897) Jacob C. Hairston, M.D., (Meharry, 1888) and Robert G. Martin, M.D., (Meharry, 1893) were already commuting from Memphis to Jackson and were members of the faculty at UWT. Dr. Hart and his wife didn't move to Brownsville but kept their residence in Jackson. He commuted from Jackson to Brownsville, making it easier for him to perform his duties at the university. He would sometimes make the trip by train; and at other times, by horse and buggy.

The University of West Tennessee (UWT) was organized at Jackson, Tennessee, in 1900 by Miles V. Lynk, M.D., (Meharry, 1891) Beebe Stevens Lynk, PH.C., (UWT, 1903) and Samuel Henry Broome M.D., (Meharry, 1897) as an institution of higher learning for black students. Dr. Lynk, a native of Brownsville, Haywood County, Tennessee; and Mrs. Beebe S. Lynk, a native of Mason, Tipton County, Tennessee; and Dr. Samuel H. Broome, a native of Oakland, Fayette County, Tennessee were the primary organizers of the University. Dr. John L. Light, M.D., (Meharry, 1898) James H. Trimble (postal carrier), and Dr. Robert E. Hart (CME, pastor) were the other Board of Directors. The university from the beginning established departments of medicine, law, dentistry, pharmacy and nursing. The college was one of fourteen African-American colleges that opened between 1868 and 1901 in the United States for the specific purpose of establishing a medical school for blacks.

The college hospital was the most important part of the university and was the first facility to offer sick bedding to African-Americans in Jackson. It furnished abundant clinical materials for the medical department and, at the same time, was of incalculable help to the poor people of Jackson and surrounding counties. Its wards included good boarding, nursing, medicine, medical and surgical attention was free to the poor. Because there were no endowments, government student loans, or organization contributions, the board of directors had to find other ways to raise money to meet the needs of the school before opening. One way they raised money was by sponsoring skating parties nightly at one of the community halls. Also, Dr. Lynk and his wife mortgaged their home and used the money to purchase the building and lot; plus, they added a third floor to the building and purchased other needed merchandise and equipment.

In an article appearing in the *Indianapolis Freeman*, newspaper, Dr. Lynk gave credit to Dr. Broome (my grandfather) for his contribution in helping establish the college:

> *Dr. Samuel H. Broome, the efficient secretary of the faculty, also comes in for special mention. He was with the university in its foundation, and shares no small credit for its success and progress.* [19]

Dr. Broome practiced medicine in Brownsville, Tennessee, from 1897-1900, and then moved to Jackson. His office in Jackson was located in the Isaac H. Anderson Building, which also served as the office and publishing house of the CME Church. When the building that was to be used as the university and hospital was finished after undergoing renovations, he moved his office into that facility; and the same month classes started. Entrance examinations started around September 15, 1901; and two days later, the regular medical lectures began. The university started in 1901 with a student body of about twenty-six pupils. Tuition was comparative with some schools and lower than others. Tuition was approximately $40 a session (seven months) plus a $10 graduation fee.

Medical Faculty

Miles V. Lynk, M.S., M.D., LL.B., professor of obstetrics, materia medics, surgery, clinical medicine, and electro-therapeutics, President of the University. Walter F. Rochelle, M.D., (white) professor of gynecology and clinical gynecology. Samuel H. Broome, M.D., professor of anatomy, physiology, hygiene and pathology, clinical lecturer and secretary of the faculty. Ernest W. Irvin, M.D., professor of the theory and practice of medicine and clinical medicine. John T. Herron, M.D., (white) professor of the diseases of the eye, ear, nose and throat. Jacob C. Hairston, M.D., professor of diseases of children and clinical lecturer on gynecology. Mrs. Beebe S. Lynk, Ph.C., professor of chemistry and assistant to the chair of materia medica. Robert G. Martin, M.D., instructor in physical diagnosis. Willie Cason, (white) instructor in medical Latin and botany.

Pharmaceutical Faculty

Miles V. Lynk, M.S., M.D., LL.B., president and professor of materia medica and microscopy. Mrs. Beebe S. Lynk, Ph.C., professor of chemistry, botany and assistant to the chair of pharmacy. Samuel H. Broome, M.D., professor of hygiene and demonstrator in chemistry. Willie Cason, instructor in Medical Latin.

Law Faculty

Miles V. Lynk, M.S., M.D., LL.B., Dean of the Law Department and Robert Eber Hart, B.D., LL.B., D.D., Professor of Law and Medical Jurisprudence.

The First Graduates

Dr. Hart had the honor of recognizing the first student to graduate from the university out of his department. On February 22, 1902, the University of West Tennessee (UWT) had its first annual commencement exercises at Berean Baptist Church, located on Royal Street in the city of Jackson, Tennessee. The students came from six different states and spent in Jackson for tuition, boarding, and books over two thousand dollars. There were no graduates from the medical department and only one from the law department. Marshall L. Morrison of Tishomingo County, Mississippi, was conferred the Bachelor of Law. The first medical students graduated in 1904, and they were Willie Cason of Weldon, Ark.; F. E. Christopher of Gregory, Ark.; and Edward W. West of Little Rock, Ark. There were thirteen students that graduated from the medical department before the removal of the college to Memphis in 1907. Six graduated in 1905, four in 1906, and three in 1907.

Relocating the University

The rapid growth of the school made it necessary that we move to a more metropolitan center, where the greatest clinical facilities and a strong teaching force could be secured. Accordingly, in the spring of 1907 the Trustees decided to locate the school in Memphis, Tenn., a city of over 200,000 inhabitants and business and manufacturing interests that will easily make it the commercial mistress of the great Mississippi Valley. Well situated geographically and environed by a friendly and progressive community, we believe that the high ideals early set by the founder of the University may be worked out to their ripest fruition. The colleges of Medicine, Dentistry, Pharmacy and Law are in successful operation. Memphis furnishes a wealth of clinical material second to no city in the South. **[20]**

3

THE HART CONTROVERSY BEGINS

For about two years, June 1901 through June 1903, there were no articles placed in the *Christian Index* concerning Dr. Hart, although he was still teaching at the university and presiding elder of the Brownsville, Tennessee District. I believe it was about this time Dr. Hart began visiting holiness meetings in Memphis and in other towns in the area. About this time he would have met Bishop Mason and their fellowship as well as their friendship was well under way. For this reason, I believe articles mentioning Dr. Hart in the *Christian Index* were purposely excluded by Dr. Charles H. Phillips who was editor of the *Index* at the time and was in 1902 elected a bishop.

George Atlanta Payne, who had been an enrollee of the law class at Lane College and a classmate of Dr. Hart, was now enrolled in the UWT law class and a student of Dr. Hart. He graduated from the UWT in the spring of 1903 with one other person. Professor Payne served as assistant principal of the Jackson Colored Schools and later served as Professor of Mathematics and President of Miles Memorial College in Birmingham, Alabama. There were no enrollees for the fall session of the law class in 1903 at the University of West Tennessee; and consequently, Dr. Hart's position in the law department at the university was no longer needed. Also, this was about the time the rumors and controversy surrounding Dr. Hart's "infidelity" to the denomination started. Although Dr. Lynk was a "staunch" Methodist, his reason for dismissing Dr. Hart around this time may seem suspicious; however, it likely had nothing to do with the Hart controversy that was "brewing" in the CME Church.

Oblivious to Dr. Hart, nevertheless, 1903 was going to be a year of major trials and tests in his life. They would lose their only daughter; and afterwards make it public that this was their "eighth" child to die in infancy or by miscarriage. Dr. Hart survived a severe attack of malarial fever. Surprisingly, the next attack that came was the most "severe," and it challenged his integrity, faith, and faithfulness to the doctrine of the CME Church. It came from a newly elected bishop, a "giant" in the CME Church, and a lover of Methodism.

Hart Accused of Heresy

The first session of the West Tennessee Conference of the Colored Methodist Episcopal Church was held in Jackson, Tennessee, November 1882, with Bishop William Henry Miles presiding as president. From 1902-05, Bishop Charles H. Phillips was president of the West Tennessee Conference, having been elected the eighth bishop of the CME Church at the Annual Conference held in Nashville, Tennessee, in December of 1902.

It was Bishop Charles Henry Phillips who delivered the most "severe" attack against Dr. Hart at the Annual Conference held in Dyersburg, Tennessee, in December of 1903, when he was accused by Bishop Phillips and held up before the Conference as a preacher of "false doctrine." This so-called false doctrine was Bishop Phillips indictment against Dr. Hart for preaching and teaching sanctification as it was taught and believed by the sanctified church, and not by the CME Church. Dr. Hart was suspended at this conference, until the spring of 1904 when the case would be tried at the conference in Trenton, Tennessee. The vast majority of mainstream Methodist believed and accepted the doctrine taught by John Wesley, which said entire sanctification, was the second work of grace and had the power to destroy sin; however, the work is a life-long process. However, some Holiness and Sanctified Churches believed and taught that entire sanctification could come as an instantaneous transformative experience. This is where the Methodist, Baptist, Sanctified Church, and other denominations differed on the Holy Scriptures at the beginning of the twentieth century.

The Doctrines and Discipline of the CME Church in America

Revised in 1910, the Doctrines and Discipline of the Colored Methodist Episcopal Church in America in part one of their manual was very brief in their Articles of Religion on the Holy Trinity, Holy Ghost, justification, and speaking in tongues; however, there was nothing on sanctification. In essence, it offered very little toward a comprehensive understanding of the denomination's doctrines. The following articles are from their 1910 manual:

[Article1.] Of Faith in the Holy Trinity.
There is but one living and true God, everlasting, without body or parts; of infinite power, wisdom, and goodness; the maker and preserver of all things, both visible and invisible. And in unity of this Godhead, there are three persons of one substance, power, and eternity-the Father, the Son, and the Holy Ghost.

[Article IV.] Of the Holy Ghost
The Holy Ghost, proceeding from the Father and the Son, is of one substance, majesty, and glory, with the Father and the Son, very and eternal God.

[Article IX.] Of the Justification of Man.
We are accounted righteous before God, only for the merit of our Lord and Savior Jesus Christ, by faith, and not for our own works or deserving's; wherefore, that we are justified by faith only, is a most wholesome doctrine, and very full of comfort.

[Article XV.] Of speaking in the Congregation in such a Tongue as the people understand.
It is a thing plainly repugnant to the word of God and the custom of the Primitive Church, to have public prayer in the Church or to minister the sacraments in a tongue not understood by the people. **[1]**

Some CME's Testify of Sanctification and Receiving the Holy Ghost

Ten years before Dr. Hart was accused of heresy, some members of the West Tennessee Conference of the CME Church posed serious questions of doubt surrounding the work of sanctification in the believer's life, but Rev. W. J. Adams of the Georgia Conference gave this testimony in full support of sanctification in this letter addressed to the editor of the *Index*:

Please give me space on the witness stand to testify. My testimony is: "With the heart, man believeth unto righteousness; and with the mouth, confession is made unto Salvation." Romans 10:10. Glory to God I am saved and sanctified. It has been one year since the Colored Holiness Convention of the Georgia Conference was organized at Griffin, Ga. We organized with preachers and twelve lay members in the experience of Christianity.

Hallelujah to God, we have now 15 or 20 traveling and local preachers with a hundred and fifty laymen in the experience of full Salvation. And Oh! Glory to God, for Bishop Holsey to head the list of the Army. The Lord hastens the day when the dead churches shall be resurrected; this would soon come to pass if the traveling preachers of the Methodist churches would come up to their vows.

Every preacher in full connection from Wesley's day, to the present, taking an oath that he would get sanctified, Oh, Brethren how much longer shall the church wait on you? See discipline page 75.

Brethren this is the will of God, even your sanctification. First Thessalonians 4:3. My dear brethren let Jesus do the work for you at once and then get on the throne with him and reign forever. [2]

According to Rev. Adams, before the Discipline Manual (doctrines) of the CME Church was revised in 1910, there existed an article on sanctification in which the minister was encouraged and in some cases, took an oath that he would get sanctified. It appears that the CME Church revised its manual on the doctrines and disciplines of the church at the end of the first decade of the twentieth century. Did the controversy surrounding Dr. Hart and the sanctified church cause the CME Church to revise its manual, and purposely exclude a section on sanctification?

Lucius Henry Holsey, D. D., was born in Columbus, Georgia, July 3, 1842, and was the fourth man to be elected to the office of Bishop in the CME Church in 1873; and he was a man whose convictions led him to believe, "No man shall see God without holiness." It was under his jurisdiction in the great State of Georgia that the Colored Holiness Convention was organized in Griffin, Georgia in 1892. At the beginning of the twentieth century, the convention was still organized and growing. In 1900, the following proceedings of the convention were published in the *Index:*

The Holiness Convention convened at the CME Church in Fort Valley, Ga., May 24-27, 1900. The meeting opened about mid-day Thursday, May 24, with a praise service, in which the spirit of the Lord was not by no means absent. On the afternoon of the same day there was another service led by Rev. M. D. Spencer, pastor of the M. E. Church in Macon, Ga. The 12th chapter of Romans was read and explained by him. The explanation was helpful to all who were present. The first part of the night service was converted into praise service. The 1st Psalm was read; "I love thy kingdom, Lord" was sung. Then Rev. Spencer discoursed from 2 Peter, 3:18 in a very instructive and beneficial way. After the sermon we had a few words from Revs. Adams and Haygood, who did not arrive until the meeting had begun. Then there was an altar service and the Holy Spirit was greatly manifested.

Friday morning the Sunday school gathered at the church, from where they marched to the picnic ground to the celebration of the Sunday-school. This gathering took the place of our regular praise service. The 11 a.m. service was held directly after their departure. Rev. Spencer preached an affecting sermon from Ephesians, 19:22, which united us closer together. By request of the President all Christians assembled around the altar for reconsecration; and they all seemed to be greatly benefited. We adjourned to meet at 3 o'clock for Bible instruction, which were given by Rev. Haygood and others. All were requested to bring their Bibles. Through the instruction there were many perplexing questions asked by ministers who were not in full possession of the Holy Spirit and their constituencies. The privilege was given every one to ask any question they desired. But they who asked those perplexing questions acknowledged to have received light on the word before the close of the meeting. Rev. Adams closed by a sketch of the beginning of the Holiness Convention. After which an invitation was extended to all who wanted more power with God to come to the altar and have those who were filled from on high pray for them. Many came, and among those who came were Revs. O'Neal and Lowe, who surrendered entirely their all to God during this altar service. A great number seemed to have been endowed with the Holy Spirit in this meeting.

The night meeting opened with praise service. After entering into the second part of the meeting Rev. Spencer read from John 5th chapter. Then Rev. Haygood preached a wonderful sermon from Romans, 6:6, and there was a great outpouring of the Holy Ghost on the whole church. Rev. Adams conducted the altar service, from which there were a great many who professed to have received the fullness of the Holy Spirit. At the close of the service Friday night Rev. Spencer was compelled to leave the town to attend to some official business of his church.

The meetings Saturday were not so well attended by the citizens on account of making preparation for Sunday. Sunday was the Pentecostal day to the Convention. At 11 o'clock Rev. Haygood preached a soul-stirring sermon from Matthew 11:11. There was an altar service as usual. Those who came seemed to have been anxious about their souls. The 3 o'clock p. m. service was conducted by Rev. Adams. He preached from John, 17:16-17. It is naturally supposed by all who have heard Rev. Adams that his discourse was accompanied by the Holy Spirit. On Sunday night Rev.

Haygood preached from Isaiah, 3:5. This sermon came as a burning light right from the altar, and it being demonstrated with such force until sinners quaked and trembled and the saints of the Lord rejoiced at the wonderful omnipresence of God. At the close of the meeting Sunday night, Rev. Adams conducted the altar service. Many anxious ones came and were baptized with the fire and the Holy Ghost. And a multitude of those present arose and explained how they had been blessed by the presence of the Convention. There were workers from about all the following places and ministers as follows: Rev. Adams of Jones County, Rev. Spencer of Macon, Rev. Haygood of Elberton, Rev. O'Neal of Fort Valley, Rev. Cobb of Columbus District, Rev. Patterson of the Fort Valley, Rev. Gray of Macon, Rev. Coggins of Concord, Rev. Lowe of Fort Valley, and Rev. Turner of Macon. Rev. W. J. Adams, President, Rev. N. F. Haygood, Vice-President, and Mrs. E. A. Sears, Secretary. [3]

The only testimony that seemed to be missing from this extraordinary service was the evidence of speaking in tongues. God's presence was there, and the people felt His power; but the Holy Ghost with the evidence of speaking in tongues wasn't testified of as part of the service.

Misunderstanding Sanctification

Prior to the West Tennessee Annual Conference held, December of 1903, there were very few articles in the *Christian Index* that discussed sanctification, sanctified people, and their churches. Beginning in 1904, articles to the *Christian Index* on sanctification were possibly submitted because of the "surmounting" controversy surrounding sanctification and Dr. Hart. Or maybe it was because of the Sanctified Movement in general that was taking place throughout the South, particularly in Memphis led by C. H. Mason and in Mississippi led by Charles P. Jones. The first article came from the Memphis District Conference of the CME Church:

Several splendid papers were read and discussed. The one on the advance work of the Church and sanctification claimed most attention. The paper on sanctification overshadowed all others in importance. Several dozen questions were asked as to whom this second blessing is obtainable. One brother said it does not come until one is ready to pass into the unknown world, another said it is like an apple and soon as it gets ripe it falls, and as soon as sanctification is obtained death comes. Another held that it takes ages before sanctification can be had. There were tenable objections to all these diversified opinions given.

Sanctification is the old doctrine of the Methodist Church and not a new propaganda as many suppose. If the first opinion given was valid it would destroy the force of the Scripture, for it says be ye holy and sin not. Then again it admits that God requires of his children to be what he knows they cannot.2nd. If it were an age proposition, then those who die before old age is unsanctified and lost, and are practically debarred by the statute of limitation. All these varied opinions as introduced were refuted. Memphis is the headquarters of the Sanctified Church, much street preaching is done to decoy the members of other churches. They have had some notable recruits and are more aggressive than others.

Our church has suffered some, but after all a few disgruntle here and there might cast their lot with them, but the great body of Colored Methodists will remain on the old line and true to the church of the fathers. [4]

The second article, an editorial by an unnamed writer came from the same dated paper criticizing the sanctified church:

There never was a graver mistake than what some professed sanctified people are making. They think because they are sanctified they must sever their relation with their church. The Methodist Church is not inimical to sanctification and really her sanctified members should make better members and help their fallen brethren to obtain that grace. There is plenty of room in the church for sanctified people and we see no reason why they should not occupy the front seats, but for hypocrite sanctification there is no room whatever for it in the Colored Methodist Episcopal Church. They are simply wolves in sheep's clothing preying upon the ignorant for the fleece they get. We urge all our members to live holier lives and emulate the example of Christ. [5]

War of Words

Dr. Hart was held up before the West Tennessee Conference for preaching a false doctrine supporting full sanctification. It was a doctrine contrary to the way Methodists believed. This set off debates throughout the ranks of the CME denomination in opposition to Dr. Hart's position as well as in support of him. It took only a few days for Dr. Hart to response to the action taken by the conference in this letter addressed to the *Christian Index* entitled, "He Dropped the Mask He Wore":

Editor Christian Index: David, though an ancient king, was right when he said: "He that ruleth over men must be just, ruling in the fear of God; for any other kind of ruler or ruling will tend toward disruption of good government and provoke not only the humble to rebel but may drive the meek and quiet to a vigorous resistance.

It has been well said that one truly wronged and throbbing heart may rend an empire. If a ruler is truly just his errors will not be charged to an evil heart but usually to an illy formed head. But if it be apparent of all that the ruler is unjust and unfair and pursuing a policy that will pour vengeance upon his formerly supposed rivals and opponents, that ruler will be held under great suspicion by the brave and loyal. If the decisions and rulings of such a governor be the outburst of deep seated prejudice or envy, or long standing jealousy or a strong desire to get even with, or an inordinate craze to show his power to make strong men crouch at his feet or an exhilarating delight to see those who have heretofore occupied front seat, "go way back and sit down," that ruler will stand before every man brave enough to think convicted of corrupting right government by a bad use of entrusted power. The latter is the position in which Bishop C. H. Phillips has placed himself before our great Church. If the following facts be carefully considered they will clearly demonstrate the fact that Bishop Phillips in this sinful and degenerate age is taking a position that will discourage the pure aspirations of both the Ministry and Church.

The idea that a free man can't go into a holiness meeting because it exposes an immoral preacher! His arguments before the Conference to show the improbability of freedom from sin in this life were unworthy of the great office he holds. In proof of his above proposition he appealed to the patriarchs. After a glowing description of the glory that encircled Moses head, and near approach to God, finally concluded that he was a great sinner. Thereby ignoring the advantages of the Christian dispensation. Let us here consider the facts in detail. In answer to my groaning after perfection the Holy Ghost sanctified me. As I had professed my regeneration, being moved by the Holy Ghost I thought it consistent to profess my sanctification, Matthew 10:32-33. Afterward I was moved to preach this great and full salvation which delivered me. I was not disobedient to the heavenly vision. This glorious truth was mighty through God in setting my district on fire; not only so but surpassed its former financial record by over two hundred dollars bringing it round except $64.00.

But at the Annual Conference at Dyersburg, Tenn., I was held up before the Conference by the Bishop as a preacher of false doctrine. When I called upon him to explain before the vote was taken what the false doctrine was he boldly announced that it was the second blessing of sanctification. He vigorously maintained that the second blessing was not taught by Charles or John Wesley. Consequently the motion for my condemnation prevailed; therefore, I was removed from the district. But how

strange! The next morning while receiving some young men into full connection, and inquiring after their holiness of conversation which means matter of life the Bishop asked these questions: "Are you going on to perfection? Are you groaning after it?" Here the Bishop paused, and so far forgot his former ruling as to explain to candidates that "the term perfection here meant sanctification," and continuing said "we do not get this blessing in regeneration," that is why we have to go on unto it. Of course all knowing Methodists differ from the Bishop as to regeneration. We believe that in regeneration we get the elements but not the fullness of the blessing. But granting that it is not received at the time of regeneration and that it is a blessing to be sought and groaned after, why when it is received, it must be in some respects a second blessing. Now it can be clearly seen that the Bishop in his first position against me is not only contrary to the history and doctrine of his Church, but actually reversed himself in his last position. In his constant change of base the Bishop shows that neither did he not know what Wesley had taught concerning this cardinal doctrine or he desired to seize that opportunity to play upon the prejudices of those who did not know until he could dispose of me. Either cause was unworthy the great place he occupies in the Church."
Bishop Phillips after denouncing me without allowing me the time to reply, urging my men to be brave, speak out and had promised publicly to make a new presiding elder, got a few sin loving men to testify that they did not enjoy my sermons. But suppose he had have asked the congregation who were free from pulpit jealousy?

Granting that there were a few who did not like to hear sermons on the purity of Christian life, should that prompt a chief pastor in this degenerate age to change the preacher. Is it becoming the office of a Bishop to gratify the sinful heart in its rebellion against the pure word of God? In so doing does the Bishop inspire the young man who is longing for perfection to go on? Will his conduct nerve the modern prophet of righteousness to declare the whole counsel of God, or the conscientious to continue to preach righteousness in the great congregations? The age and the Church are calling for a Holy ministry.

Bishop Phillips dares him to show his head. He is not a lover of good men if they are fairly intelligent and in the least degree gifted. He is "soon angry" now a days. After his constant scathing insinuations that draw humble and quiet men to their feet to explain his usual growl and storm of words he refuse to allow them to reply.

He is given to "filthy lucre," for he publicly announced that after he would take me down he would give me some kind of an appointment, but that he knew that I would not succeed financially preaching that kind of doctrine—the doctrine of purity. Should a Bishop teach that the doctrine of purity must be withheld for lucre's sake?—Titus 1:11. The apostles require it.-Titus 1:8.

He declared before the conference he was not sanctified. Before he was made Bishop and after his spell of sickness he professed to me and many others that he had received the second blessing of sanctification. I can prove by hundreds that since my sanctification he preached sanctification at Milan. Now, how strange that a Bishop should preach what he is not, but denounce a man for professing what he is. The good Bishop smiled when he told the conference that the people thought he was sanctified. Now it is no secret that the Bishop kept the people thinking it until his election. But since he has been placed beyond the reach of all powers to depose, like Caesar on the sea of Tiberius, he now throws aside his holy ermine, and policy of legerdemain to stand in clear view as to what he really is. Trenton, Tennessee. **[6]**

It took only one week for the preachers of the West Tennessee Conference to response to Dr. Hart's letter to the *Christian Index*, entitled "He Dropped the Mask He Wore." In that letter, he was highly critical of Bishop Charles H. Phillips, and in the opinion of many brethren, he was very disrespectful and a liar. The preachers replied with the following article of their own in the *Index:*

In the Index of January 9ᵗʰ, there appeared a very remarkable and unbrotherly letter from **Rev. R. E. Hart** *concerning Bishop Phillips and conference matters. He enviously and unjustly makes misleading statements concerning Bishop C. H. Phillips's lectures, advices and rulings of the Conference.*

The Bishop had nothing to do with **Rev. R. E. Hart** *and action of the Conference with reference to his case.*

As the attack on the Bishop was unjust and uncalled for, and not a semblance of truth in his statements, we the following signed elders and preachers of the West Tennessee Conference, feeling it our duty in defense of the Bishop to make the following statements, as it occurred in the Conference. There has been a class of people in this part of the State of Tennessee who professed to be sanctified and holy. In certain parts of the Conference they have by their persecution, done considerable harm in Jackson, Memphis and many other parts. Many of our members have professed Sanctification, and as soon as they make the above named profession they withdraw from their Church and the record of their influence is against the Church they formerly belonged to. They denounce all our preachers in general and the Methodist Bishops in particular.

Now there came a time when **Rev. Hart** *professed Sanctification. He then allied himself with so-called holy people. He visited their meeting in Jackson and Memphis, Tenn., and perhaps other places. He associated with and preached to that class of people. Now as they were fighting his Church and ministry, this put the* **Rev. R. E. Hart** *in an awkward position before the people, upon which a number of his preachers in his district and in the Conference made complaint against him. When his name was called in the examination of the preachers' characters there was considerable discussion over the matter, after which,* **Dr. Hart** *was called by the Bishop to reply, which he did. When he had finished his reply, a motion was made by the Conference to locate him. But the Bishop would not put the question for his location and he was saved from the local rank.*

Then the Conference passed the following resolution, condemning the proceeding of **Dr. Hart.** *On motion of Rev. E. W. Moseley: resolved, first, that we the ministry and members of the West Tennessee Conference, do hereby condemn all acts of* **Dr. R. E. Hart** *in being allied with the following and preaching for the above named people. Signed: E. W. Moseley, A. N. Stevens.*

The Bishop in his lecture said he did not believe in Sanctification as a second bless-ing theory. But he did believe in the doctrine taught by the Methodist on Sanctifica-tion. Bishop Phillips is not a Caesar nor a boss but a gentle born leader of men.

It was the Conference that would have given the Doctor the back seat, and not the Bishop. Therefore, we in defense of the Bishop condemn the article as a whole. First, we disapprove of the motive of the paper. Second, it seems to be more from the hand of an enemy of the Bishop, than a friend. Signed: W. H. Daniels, P. E., J. W. Harris, P. E., W. P. Greer, P. E., R. L. Coleman, P. A. Walthall, H. McKinney, Wm. Payne, L. E. B. Rosser, W. H. Barham, J. T. Strayhorn, A. Allison, B. Herron, Secretary; T. A. Tyus, W. W. Levels, D. J. Murphy, G. W. Wiley, J. T. Bradford, M. D. Partee, G. W. Morgan, C. C. Townsend, G. W. Burney, N. B. Smith, and A. E. Young.

There are scores of other ministers who will be and are witnesses to the facts of the above named mortal facts, and acts of the old West Tenn., Conference of 1903. Sub-scribed by me this the 9th day of Jan. 1904. W. H. Daniel [7]

The conference ministers were reluctant to publicly denounce and publish in the *Christian Index* the names of the sanctified preachers in which Dr. Hart had been affiliated and for whom he had preached. What reason or fear could they have had not to publicly publish the names? Out of all the articles published in the *Index* on the subject of sanctification and Dr. Hart's affiliation with the sanc-tified church, they never mentioned the name of any sanctified preacher. With-out a doubt, C. H. Mason was one of those preachers.

Hart on Trial for Heresy

The twenty-second session of the Annual West Tennessee Conference convened at Johnson Chapel CME Church in Dyersburg, Tennessee, December 15, 1903, with Bishop C. H. Phillips serving as president of the conference. It was at this conference that the case against Dr. Hart was heard and tried with this article later published in Rev. T. H. Nichols's book in 1909:

> *The committee appointed to try the case of **Rev. R. E. Hart**, reported that he was not guilty. On motion of D. W. Featherston, **Dr. R. E. Hart** was located. Thus one of the readiest men that West Tennessee had ever listened to was dropped from the itinerancy. We have spoken of him in another chapter, only partially, as we have here. All that was done may be right and best, but God will reveal everything at the judgment, at the last day. When angels, men and devils will stand before him and "Hear the conclusion of the whole matter."* [8]

Rev. Daniel W. Featherston (my great-grandfather) motioned that Dr. Hart be located (which meant to assign Dr. Hart to a post in the district) since he was found not guilty. However, Bishop Phillips didn't allow the motion to be carried, and he didn't assign Dr. Hart to a post. As a consequence, Dr. Hart was temporarily without an assignment and consequently dropped from his duties. Dr. Hart went back the next day and demanded a trial after finding some discrepancies in the way the signatures appeared on the document that they had signed in protest. His request and inquiry temporarily reversed their decision in his favor for the time being, and he was reassigned to the Trenton District as pastor after having served as presiding elder of the Brownsville, Tennessee District, pending a trial. It was a personal "gigantic" sigh of relief for me to see that my great-grandfather's name wasn't listed among those that signed the resolution in protest against Dr. Hart. He had done nothing wrong and was simply an ecumenist at heart, but adopting the doctrine of full sanctification wasn't going to be tolerated by strict adherents of the Methodist doctrine. The majority of the 119 traveling preachers and 193 local preachers present at the conference didn't sign the letter. Many of the signatures were later found to be forged after Dr. Hart went to the office of the *Christian Index* and demanded to see the documents.

War of Words Continue

Dr. Hart responded with another letter addressed to the editor of the *Christian Index*, after having such a bad experience at the conference in Dyersburg. His letter was given an editorial title by the paper, Dr. R. E. Hart, Again. The *Index* didn't hesitate but continued to follow the controversy by printing the following letter:

The only answer to that fair and unbiased statement of facts in my first article that could resemble an exoneration from the charges made must have been a flat denial of those facts, therefore I was confident that a man who had not destroyed his conscience or had any respect for the truth or any regards for the recollections of so many lay and clerical eye witnesses at Dyersburg could not afford to make such a denial. It is clearly seen that the Bishop was not just prepared to make such a sweeping denial. But who can be found that is already prepared to commit the deed? Are all those whose names appear in that list prepared? Not all of them. The majority of them live in Jackson. I have been to see the most of them who are resident members, and they positively deny both their consent and signature to such a statement. Here I would give their names; but I don't care to mark them to slaughter, I found only one that had given his name. He told me that when he thought of the fact he went and demanded in vain that his name be dropped. Others who refused his solicitations are now indignant. Now as to the parties that are out of the city, they are so far away, I know they could not have seen the statement to which their names were attached. Some of them I have called over the phone; they declare they know nothing of the article and have not as yet read it.

Of course I will admit that some of those parties whose name appears in that list would write and sign anything that the Bishop would request. But as a matter of fact the great majority has not signed. Now to make the matter short, on demand, the Editor, very reluctantly showed me the manuscript and just as I had suspicion, I found that all those names had been affixed by the same handwriting that composed the article which brazenly denies a truth that the public will uphold. Now who is so blind that he cannot see that the writer of this article has committed a clear case of "forgery?"

Now I believe in loyalty and reverences to our superior officers, under a trial of persecution that the fact was clearly demonstrated. Bishop Phillips just the other day complimented my coolness and courtesy to my superiors, now a days, but here is a man, Rev. W. H. Daniels who has committed a crime, not in the defense of the Bishop, but just to hold the place he now occupies. This is the man and that is the means by which a preacher of holiness is to be disproved and done away with. By whose authority does he act? By who is he backed? I wonder if he is a fair specimen of the sin loving few in the West Tennessee Conference who are so bitter to Sanctification, which stand for a clean life. He certainly does not represent that great majority of gospel preachers in the West Tennessee Conference, who would certainly have killed forever any resolution to locate me for being sanctified or going into holiness meetings. He certainly cannot be representing our Bishop in his spirit and methods.

No; he is a Pseudo Episcopes; and since the world knows that Bro. Daniel is meddling, I shall have to rap him a little. Now stop that shaking! Get you a backbone and stand up like a man. I am going to handle you carefully. I know how tender you are. If I can't find a well place on you, I won't strike you at all, for I fear I may bring bruises, blood, or peel the skin off places already blistered. Now come out here, Daniel! Put your foot down, pull off that coat, bend across that barrel; now I guess you will tell me why you could not go back to the district over which you had presided only five or six months? Keep your mouth Covington; hold your peace Trenton; sit down over there Halls, and let him speak for himself. Now it is useless for me to reassert what was done in the Conference. I told you in the first article on the 9th. It contains a truth that no bread and butter article can erase. The public knows that if I had some districts to give away, why Brother Daniel would get me up a paper and commit forgery to contradict some other man's statement.

Must I abandon the doctrine of Methodism because a class of people who fight sinful preachers profess it? But few members if any left my churches on my district since my Sanctification: for I argued by precept and example that a man could live a sanctified life and stay in the Methodist Church. On investigation I found that wherever there was a clean pastor who was a lover of good men and women the sanctified members did not leave the church, but on the other hand wherever there was a sin loving-holiness hating-sanctification fighting preacher the sanctified members were forced to leave just as soon as they would rise and testify that they were sanctified. It is a relief to his sin loving conscience to get rid of me as they did some of the sanctified members. But not so, I am still on board with a living testimony and a red hot gospel; glory!

The holiness people did sometimes denounce those preachers who were haters of Sanctification: such preachers are haters of Methodist doctrine. No wonder they can't hold a charge six months.

"Now there comes a time when the **Rev. Hart** *professed Sanctification." My! Won't Sister Daniel and the Humboldt district shout when the time comes that Elder Daniel is sanctified. "Now as they were fighting his church and ministry, this put the* **Rev. Hart** *in an awkward position." Whenever they fought my Church and ministry proper I fought back, but when they fought the sins of my Church I held my peace, but promised God I'd do my best in helping to remove the cause of attack. Let every sin*

loving preacher do the same, and then he will not have to fight the doctrine of his own Church in self defense. In that great Bible Meeting called by the holiness preachers to which Bro. Daniel was invited: **Bro. Hart** *was the only CME preacher to fight our battle of doctrine. Where was Bro. Daniel who is so dead in love with the members of our Church when there were those who held false views of holiness and churches as man made institutions on the streets in Jackson around who the members of Liberty Church flocked like sheep that had no shepherd; who took the street and spoke one hour in defense of his Church? It was* **Rev. R. E. Hart.** *Where was Daniel the great lover of our membership? I now go into holiness meeting because I enjoy them and because I have a conscience void of offence toward man and God. But for some strange cause Bro. Daniel is as scared of a holiness sermon as a coward man is of a pointed gun.*

That written resolution was an after trick, and the question of location never came up until I came back the next morning and demanded a trial. In fact the whole bundle of tricks in that article is wrapped by a man who could commit forgery to contradict my statements. **[9]**

Harsh Judgments

Dr. Hart's former district was "outraged" over the articles he submitted to the *Christian Index* entitled, "He Dropped the Mask He Wore," and "Dr. R. E. Hart Again," criticizing Bishop Phillips and the Conference for the way they had handled his affairs. They submitted the following resolution from the Brownsville Station Quarterly Conference of the West Tennessee Annual Conference to the *Index:*

A resolution from the Brownsville Station Quarterly Conference of the West Tennessee Annual Conference:

Whereas, there has been an audacious assault made upon the West Tennessee Annual Conference and our worthy Bishop C. H. Phillips, D. D., by one **Rev. R. E. Hart,** *of Trenton, Tenn., through the columns of the Christian Index, under the following subject: "He Dropped The Mask He Wore" and Whereas, this being a part of the territory wherein the said* **R. E. Hart,** *by public and private admonitions, did disseminate doctrine contrary to our faith and practice; and attempted to do our Methodism much harm; therefore, be it*

Resolved, that the Quarterly Conference of the Brownsville Station, now assembled, condemn the communication and its publication in the Christian Index. Be it further,

Resolved, that we denounce the writer, **Dr. R. E. Hart**, *and recognize him as an imposter, unworthy of the confidence that has been placed in him by our great and growing Methodism.*

Resolved that a copy of these resolutions be spread on the minutes and published in the Christian Index, the official organ of the Church.

Done by order of the Quarterly Conference of the Brownsville Station, this 11th day of January, 1904. **[10]**

The Hart controversy set off a "firestorm" of discussions and arguments in the CME Church centered on sanctification. Some of the members, to say the least were very defensive toward their Methodism, concerning this new revelation about the "old" doctrine of sanctification. Rev. G. W. Spearman, B.D., was present at the conference and trial of Dr. Hart and was somewhat "mean-spirited" in the following letter he wrote to the *Index* expressing his opinion on the matter:

The poet of Sierras has given us in the above lines the strongest kind of a hint to be charitable in our judgment of men. Men are not always as bad as their acts, though there are some people who are forever and eternally drawing the line on somebody, somewhere and thanking God that they themselves are different. This is particularly characteristic of some of the black and colored race. The sanctified men and women in our race if we are to judge of them by their own testimonies in respect of their virtues and personal goodness are almost as the sand of the sea, or the vallombrosa. The scriptures some where tells us to "Mark the perfect man, behold the upright," but these prefect and Sanctified people are increasing at such a fearful ratio that no poor sinner is equal to the task of either marking or beholding them; for he would find it a most tiresome job to mark and behold all the perfect and Sanctified men who testify of themselves. The sight would blind him. A clergyman once made a declaration in course of a sermon that God made all things perfect, and a very smart man in the congregation, a hump back solemnly arose at the close of the sermon and looking very wise, serious and certain asked; permission to say a few words. He was absolutely certain that the clergyman's theology was faulty, and he felt that he owned a duty to the human family to show the obscurity of the statement that God had made all things perfect. So clearing his throat and throwing back his little head to an angle of forty-five degrees he emitted the following question after which he struck an attitude and waited for an answer, feeling reasonably certain that no answer could be given.

If, said he God made everything perfect what think you of me? (Pointing to the hump on his back.) The minister eyed him for a moment and then solemnly replied

"My dear brother I think you are the most perfect hump back I ever saw." Then the congregation sang a hymn and went out. Some of these Sanctified people who are always prating about their personal goodness and drawing the deadly parallel and comparing their religion with the religion of somebody else are the most Sanctified hypocrites and Pharisees in the Church or out of it. They are the people who form close co-operation in Christian churches and are worthless and lived a dog's life, who draw a line of demarcation in the church and tell who is fit and who isn't fit for salvation. They know the pedigree of everyone in the church and just how much grace this one or that one is capable of holding.

Christ Jesus came not to call the righteous, but sinners to repentance. Are these exclusive Sanctifies quite right in their methods? Have they the spirit of Christ or the spirit of the devil? The spirit of Christ says to every man, "Come and drink of the water of life." The Sanctified Christian so-called is generally narrow between the eyes and in his intellectuals. He is a selfish, bigoted, intolerant man whose mental vision is obscured by the big "I" which is ever before him. When he looks in the mirror he sees a giant. When God looks at him, he sees an infinitesimal pigmy, a mere speck on the face of nature. Someday somebody is going to get a scraper and scrape them all into the heated, hence so that sinner for whom the church exists will have a chance to get a little grace and enjoy the blessing of free salvation. As soon as any congregation becomes sanctified it is ready to be translated into the upper air. The sanctified Christian when they discover that they are not as other men is sometimes prone to hug themselves in a little corner and to take on a feeling of exclusiveness.

They will not mingle with bad men, but only with their peers. Holy men will not strive to lift up their fallen sisters, but will rather let them journey on down the path of destruction. Some real nice sanctified Christians are ashamed to be seen in the churches of today. They are so good, so perfect, so holy that they actually afraid of themselves. Now it seems to me that this is entirely out of harmony with divine teaching, out of harmony with all that makes for the uplift and regeneration of the human race. If the religion which Jesus lived and taught is not fit for the poor, despised, outcast of society, if those who profess to have it are too proud and holy and exclusive to go among sinners and to the church, why let me be excused. Brownsville, Tennessee. [11]

Freedom of Speech Denied

Robert Turner Brown, B.A., M.A., M.D., D.D., was the thirteenth man to be elected to the bishopric of the CME Church in 1922. Earlier in his career, he was appointed and served as editor of the *Christian Index* from 1902-10, following Dr. Charles H. Phillips. Several complaints came to the office of the *Index*, when

Dr. Brown was editor, concerning the Hart controversy. Some complained that their freedom of speech was being denied because their letters addressing the Hart controversy were not being published in the paper. This prompted Rev. Dr. Brown to response to their grievances with the following article entitled, "Freedom of Speech Not Denied":

*The Editor of this paper has taken no interest in the West Tennessee controversy respecting **Dr. R. E. Hart** and others. He has simply held his hands off. And neither is he responsible for the views of **Dr. Hart** nor other contributors of this paper. We regard all contributors as being honest and truthful, and will write what they know is true. If any should falsify themselves, it is with them and their God.*

However, the columns of this paper are open to all contributors of our Church. It is not the organ of a fraction or select few, nor will this Editor use it to crush any man in the Church-be he small or great. There are none in the Church outside of the legitimate pale of criticism. It cannot be used as a battle ground between contending parties; but when a brother thinks he has been unjustly dealt with, and wants to be heard, we shall not close the "door of hope" in his face. We shall not suppress free speech-which is one of the cardinal principals, not only of the Church but of the government. The man who holds office may expect criticism.

Under no circumstances will any communication be published which reflect on the moral character of any one. We have received several letters of too personal nature for the columns of this paper. The contributors ought to be able to draw the line between official character and moral character. It is the official character alone that will be dealt with and none other. Since there are none perfect (?) all are liable to be called into question for their actions.

If you stifle legitimate criticism in Church or government you destroy the last vista of reformation in Church or State, and open wide the flood gates of tyranny, despotism, and corruption.

The New York Christian Advocate, edited by the erudite Dr. J. M. Buckley, said: "The Christian Advocate is not a forum to shield any officer in the M. E. Church, not even its editor from criticism."

*The sagacious and conservative will face criticism like a lion and be profited thereby. A great many from several conferences have written communications respecting the **Hart** and West Tennessee controversy, but we have absolutely refused to publish them. Some of them condemn the controversy while the others compliment it. There are some who seldom write but seize such opportunities as this to strike back at those against whom they have had grievances for years.*

When two parties are engaged in a wordy war it has been our policy to play "hands off" and let them have their say.

While the diplomat, the schemer, the trimmer, and the insidious parties who seeking notoriety or a place of emolument (or preferment) rush to register a protest or extend a compliment for something of which they know nothing, there are monstrous hypocrites these days who would make Judas blush. Brethren, be plain, simple, and honest, and God will make all things right. [12]

Support for Dr. Hart

Before and after Dr. Hart claimed full sanctification, he defended Methodism on the streets, in the pulpit, and at holiness meetings when invited by the brethren. It was widely known that Dr. Hart was very defensive when it came to the Methodist doctrine on sanctification. His position was that one could profess sanctification, (a holy and clean life), which was the "second blessing doctrine," and become sanctified, meanwhile remaining true to the Methodist denomination. He took it a step further when he proceeded to teach, preach, and spread full sanctification, and the holiness doctrine to his Methodist congregation. This is what brought him into serious conflict with the leadership and some laity in the CME denomination. There was a moderate amount of support for Dr. Hart among his fellow colleagues, such as this preacher (Rev. J. C. Coclough) hiding behind the pseudonym: "The Stork" who was from Dr. Hart's home state of Georgia. He submitted this statement to the *Index:*

*When the "Stork" read of **Dr. R. E. Hart** being sanctified, and professing sanctification stood by himself on Jackson, Tennessee's streets defending the doctrine of the Colored Methodist Episcopal Church, which doctrine was being assaulted by other sanctifications, I thought my! What a contrast between now "and in those days when" this same man preached all day Sunday and lead the political crusade on Monday until his cohorts yelled themselves hoarse, like the silly peasants returning from a repast of the gods. And "is Saul among the prophets"? But listen: Now, come out here Daniel, put your foot down, pull off that coat, bend across that barrel, keep your mouth Covington, hold your peace Halls, sit down over there Trenton, and let him speak for himself. Goodness! What "a hot time in the old town." [13]*

Suspended Until Trial

Dr. Hart ignored the warnings from the committee that was appointed to hear his case at the Annual Conference held December of 1903 at Dyersburg, Tennessee. I believe it was punishment rather than gratitude that the bishop appointed Dr. Hart to pastor a small church in Trenton, Tennessee, after Dr. Hart having pastored some of the most desirable charges in the denomination. As soon as he took over the pulpit at the Trenton church, he began to preach holiness and the second blessing doctrine when the disturbances got out of control, and the following article made the front page of the *Trenton Herald-Democrat* newspaper:

*The Colored Methodist Church in this city seems to be in a bad way. The last conference sent **Rev. Hart** here as pastor. The new preacher had hardly been installed when he commenced a vigorous prosecution of the "holiness," or "second blessing" doctrine. Many of his members accepted his doctrine freely, but some dissented. Things grew so warm in Colored Methodist circles that finally a petition was circulated and numerously signed, charging that the divine was preaching a doctrine at variance with the accepted tenets of the Methodist Church. This brought on a church trial before the presiding elder, which commenced here Wednesday morning and closed sometime before day yesterday morning. The trial resulted in a suspension of the preacher until the meeting of the next annual conference. The proceedings at times were very lurid and the presence of an officer was required to keep the peace. It is pretty generally believed that the Colored Methodist Church here is hopelessly rent asunder. [14]*

Hart was suspended until the convening of the Annual Conference held December 1904 in Trenton, Tennessee when his case would be heard. Until that time, Dr. Hart continued to preach holiness and sanctification wherever he could. There is no doubt at this point whether Dr. Hart had met C. H. Mason. To have named his son, Robert Mason who was born September 1904 after C.H. Mason, there was a friendship established between Mason and Hart earlier than I had originally suspected. He had already admitted to attending holiness meetings in Memphis, and other holiness services in surrounding towns. About seven months after his suspension, Dr. Hart held a "sanctified" tent revival in Jackson that lasted for weeks and the *Christian Index* described it this way:

*Several weeks ago, **Rev. R. E. Hart, D. D.,** held a sanctified meeting not very far from where we live in this city. They held services late at night trying to sanctify strag-*

gling souls. They failed to make any headway in this city. The colored Methodism is well fortified, and the Baptist together has the city. The intelligent element refuses to follow strange gods, and continued in the even tenor of their ways. This sanctified element has a large stock invested in abusing and misrepresenting other denominations. It will be a long time before it will ever gain popularity among the Negroes. The pharisaic methods of decoying the people are becoming gradually exposed. Strenuous efforts have been put forth in this part of the State to retard the rapid march of colored Methodism. But all in vain, our people have given it little thought. A few irresponsible persons have deserted the fold for sinister motives but their places have been filled by hundreds of others. There is too much exterior sanctification and not enough interior; there are few men who are adept, adroit, and self-seekers are leading the movement. Our membership is undisturbed and without a ripple on the waters. [15]

At this point, Dr. Hart was not occupying the pulpit in the CME Church, but he was still officially one of their preachers; pending trial. However, he was carrying on services in the Sanctified Church and taking in members from the Methodist denomination. This posed a unique problem for the leadership in the CME Church due to the notoriety of Dr. Hart and the growing popularity of the Sanctified Movement.

The Trial of Dr. Robert E. Hart

The following editorials appeared in the *Christian Index*, and it is a description of the proceedings from the trial of Dr. Hart at the West Tennessee Annual Conference, held at Trenton, Tennessee around December 10, 1904:

*There was an unusual interest manifested in the **Hart** case, and several conjectures were made as to the final outcome. **Brother Hart** was present and attended the session of the conference, paid his Missionary dues along with other members. A great many of his Sanctified associates were present, came to see what disposition would be made of the man who had affiliated with them, and wanted to retain his membership in the Colored Methodist Episcopal Church. To all who witnessed the proceedings, it appeared to be a conundrum.*

*Bishop Phillips had instructed Bishop Lane to appoint a committee to try the case and to appoint a chairman of it. A committee of nine was appointed to try the case, and Rev. J. S. Smothers was appointed to the chairmanship. **Dr. Hart** had been tried and suspended during the intervals of our Church and had re-baptized several members and washed their feet; and had taken fourteen members of the church he was pas-*

toring and received them into the Sanctified Church. It was a dual pastorate of two different denominations at the same time, differed widely in doctrine, trying to ride two horses at the same time, and they going in opposite directions.

The gossip afloat that he was tried for being sanctified is refuted. It is false to the core. The Methodist have always believed in sanctification; taught it, preached it and defended it. Mr. Wesley, the father of Methodism advocated it. There are many sanctified members in the Colored Methodist Episcopal Church loyal and true, and are really living that higher life. But this fanaticism in this patent sanctification of the conference by presiding elder **R. E. Hart** of the Trenton District during last spring. He has become sanctified and affiliated with an element that was opposed to Colored Methodist. He has grossly misrepresented the elation which forces a man to leave his wife, and a woman to desert her husband is not what we Methodist believe in. There was no objection to **Dr. Hart** being sanctified, but when it comes to dividing our flock, sowing dissension and intervening against our doctrine, and then it is time for the Church to defend itself. During the preliminary trial at Trenton last spring, the trial of **Dr. Hart** continued for two days and nights. The church was densely packed day and night with white and colored. Lawyers, doctors, sheriffs, bankers, merchants, preachers of both races attended the trial. The excitement ran high. They were informed that some intimidation was to have been used, and seven hundred persons were present to see what would be done.

Dr. Hart defended himself and Rev. G. W. Morgan defended the Church. The committee brought in a verdict of guilty and **Hart** was suspended until conference.
[16]

In Defiance of the Law

He refused to abide by the suspension and continued to preach with his sanctified crowd. He came to this city and held a camp-meeting for weeks. We have been reliably informed by several who attended the meeting that he grossly misrepresented our Church, and made villainous attacks on several prominent men. He made a confession of the sins he had committed since he had been called to the ministry. The crimes as described were horrible and to offensive to appear in a decent newspaper.

When the case was called in the annual conference, **Dr. Hart** did not want his case tried before a select committee as the law directs, but he wanted it to be tried in open conference. Bishop Lane refused to accede to his request and sent the case before a committee. There were quite a number of his sanctified army bearers from Jackson in attendance who went there to help defend the great apostle of modern sanctification. From Jackson to Trenton is about twenty-eight miles. It was apparent to all casual *observers that **Hart** wanted a display before the conference to sway the crowd. He is an orator, eloquent, forceful speaker, clear and logical, adroit and knows how to attack the weak points of his opponent. He knows how to play upon the prejudice of a crowd. There are few who can cope with him in a debate.* [17]

Tried Before a Committee

*We were present on Saturday night at a private house when the case was tried. All visitors who were not preachers were excluded from the room. Two of **Hart's** disciples and brother preachers wanted to remain, but the committee objected to their presence. They did not consent to leave until **Hart** had given the word to leave. The hall and veranda were crowded with the sanctified "brothers and sisters." It was a cold night and how they stood it for more than five hours is a mystery to us. They flocked around the door and windows to hear what was being said. We remained until twelve o'clock until after the pleadings of the attorneys had left the sanctified element still waiting for their leader. Their curiosity was aroused and they went there to defend him. Rev. G. W. Morgan defended the Church, while **Dr. Hart** pleaded his own case.*

*Morgan is an able attorney, a powerful speaker and makes it warm for an opponent. **Dr. Hart** spoke more than an hour, and while Morgan was speaking he interrupted him several times. The chairman had to call him to order. He is yet irritable and cannot stand a fusillade of criticisms, although sanctified. The indictment was very defective and not legally drawn up, and from the indictment, a conviction could hardly be had.* [18]

The Committee Exonerated Dr. Hart

*In the trial he said that he wanted to retain his membership in the Colored Methodist Episcopal Church and did not want to be expelled. Why did he want to retain his membership in our Church and lead the sanctified element in another church is a mystery to us? What was his motive of being a member of two churches? These are unanswerable interrogatories except by **Hart** himself. If he had decided to live in the sanctified church, he ought to have the courage and manhood to withdraw from the Colored Methodist Episcopal Church and become a full-fledge sanctified apostle. It was his privilege to do so, and really there was no objection.*

*On Sunday night they passed **Hart's** character and located him without a dissenting voice. If **Dr. Hart** had have pursued the course he did when he first came to the West Tennessee Conference he would have divided Liberty Street church and built an* *independent church of his own, and thus would have given us much trouble. But he has lost grounds among the brethren and people and they refused to follow him.*

*He will not be able to do our Church any serious injury. Colored Methodism is a compact in this part of the State. The West Tennessee Conference is to be commended for the able manner in which it conducted the **Hart** episode. There is no harm done to our Methodism, and it glides sweetly on with her banner unfurled and floating in the breeze. Owning to the prominence of the defendant, we decided to give in detail a part of the trial. We apprehend no danger to our Methodism in this country. It is greater than any one or more of its constituents, and any man who attempts to destroy our Zion will go like all other transgressors.* **[19]**

After Dr. Hart was exonerated, he was relocated to the Trenton district where he continued to pastor the CME Church and preach for the sanctified church. This was definitely unusually strange to allow a minister to pastor in two different denominations at the same time, taking members out of the Methodist Church and rebaptizing them and washing their feet in the sanctified church. They (the Methodists) seemed to have felt from a previous statement (the people would not follow Hart and his "strange" God) that their Methodism was strong in this part of the state, and there was very little to worry about. Just left alone, this new revelation about an "old" doctrine would just die out; and Dr. Hart with it. Well, that didn't happen; and Dr. Hart, under much pressure walked away from his first love, the Colored Methodist Episcopal Church in 1905.

The West Tennessee Conference of the CME Church Criticized

Before and after Dr. Hart's trial, the *Christian Index* received several letters for and against the Hart controversy; but very few were published because, according to the editor, most of them improperly addressed the issue. The letters received from other conferences after the trial of Dr. Hart were said to be "unjust" in their criticism of the West Tennessee Conference for the way they handled the Hart affair. This prompted a statement from Rev. Edward W. Moseley, D.D., who addressed it to the editor of the *Index:*

*The West Tennessee Conference has been very unjustly criticized by some of the brethren of other conferences, respecting the **Rev. R. E. Hart's** affair. No minister was ever treated more loyally than **Rev. Hart** by the entire clergy of the West Tennessee Conference. When he could stay no longer in the Virginia Conference, Bishop R. S.*

*Williams transferred him to this conference and appointed him one of the best charges in the State, and when he could serve no longer, he was given one of the best districts. During his second year on the district, he professed reformation and misnamed it sanctification. For it is evident that no human being could attain sanctification in the matter that **Hart** claimed he got it. Some how or other we feel that we can take care of the West Tennessee Conference all other opinion to the contrary notwithstanding.*

The West Tennessee Conference is composed of more than one man. Your review of the case was fair and impartial. [20]

This was the last article that appeared in the *Index* that mentioned Dr. Hart for almost three years. The next time his name appeared in the *Index* was an opportunity for the paper to exploit their former pastor and the Sanctified Church for what was clearly an unnecessary and embarrassing situation.

Daniel W. Featherston, D.D., (my great-grandfather) was the presiding elder of the Memphis District and president of the West Tennessee Conference of the CME Church in 1924 when he invited and introduced Bishop Mason to the conference on Saturday, December 13th. The conference secretary recorded the following:

Rev. C. H. Mason the great apostle of the Holiness Church was also introduced and among the many things he said was that "I am praying that I will come unto you until we will know no divisions." [21]

Can anything be learned today from Bishop Mason's vision of tearing down the walls of separation between different denominations by continuing to fellowship with our brothers and sisters in Christ until there are no divisions? There will be differences in doctrine and how we worship but we should be ecumenical in spirit toward other Christian denominations first.

Walking Away From the Old

Something else transpired between Dr. Hart and the West Tennessee Conference of the CME Church; however, the *Christian Index* didn't publish anything else surrounding the Hart controversy, nor did it publish when Dr. Hart officially left the denomination. However, Rev. T. H. Nichols, in his book, *History of the West Tennessee Conference of the CME Church in America*, published in 1909 on page 39 stated, "Dr. Hart withdrew from the CME Church rather than being forced out." The next time we hear from Dr. Hart, he had joined the Sanctified Church. He was attending one of the holiness conferences in Jackson, Mississippi, held January 14-21, 1906, at Christ Temple AME Church. Everything to this point has been about the life and ministry of Dr. Robert Eber Hart in the Colored Methodist Episcopal Church; however, now he had to prepare to move into a different spirituality and face greater challenges with a new experience in the Sanctified Church.

Dr. Hart was a man of gifted abilities and was well liked within the CME Church. I'm sure he was going to be missed. Maybe it was destiny that was in control; therefore, all that had transpired was out of everyone's control and understanding. There is no doubt, at this point, Dr. Hart was allied with C. H. Mason and the sanctified movement of the nineteenth and twentieth centuries. To quote from Rev. T. H. Nichols's book, "All that was done may be right and best, but God will reveal everything at the judgment at the last day when angels, men, and devils will stand before him and hear the conclusion of the whole matter."

Stepping Into the New

The Azusa Street Revival in 1906 was the beginning of modern Pentecostalism in America. William J. Seymour, a plain and simple self educated man was the overseer of the greatest move of God which had been poured out on his people since the day of Pentecost. From this movement practically all the black and white twentieth century Pentecostal-Holiness denominations were birthed in this country and around the world. From this experience, humble men of God were filled with the Holy Ghost and with the evidence of speaking in tongues and empowered to preach the gospel and do mighty exploits for the Lord!

The men that attended the revival such as Charles H. Mason, David J. Young, and John A. Jeter, not only took the Pentecostal message back to their churches but also, under the power and anointing of the Holy Ghost, preached and laid hands on the people in order that they might receive the promise. A large measure of the Spirit was poured out on C. H. Mason in order that he could accomplish the calling that was upon his life. His calling was to a down-trodden group of people, many of whom had been slaves and the children of slaves and were despised by a government and world system that was only interested in their continued oppression. In the process, many men and women of other races were drawn to the anointed preaching and teaching of C. H. Mason. He showed himself to be friendly to all men. He was not their Deliverer but was sent by the Deliverer to give them hope through the preaching of the gospel and receiving the Holy Ghost.

When Mason began to walk in his new spirituality, Dr. Hart was willing and committed to the doctrine of sanctification and holiness the way Mason received and believed it. Exactly when Dr. Hart received the baptism of the Holy Ghost isn't known and I haven't seen any evidence that suggests he attended the Azusa Street Revival. However, through one article in the *Christian Index* entitled, "A Sanctified Fight" in chapter five, the writer mentions that Dr. Hart had found the "new tongue," which suggests Bishop Mason likely laid hands on him and imparted the Holy Ghost after he returned from California. Hart recognized the power and anointing that was upon Mason's life; and he submitted to that calling, becoming a believer and supporter of what God was going to do through Mason. Hart chose not to start an independent church after he had left the CME denomination but chose rather to walk with Mason and together along with others to support Mason in reorganizing COGIC beginning in 1907. They "dramatically" increased converts into COGIC and spread the Pentecostal-Holiness message throughout the South first, then throughout the country and sequentially in many nations.

4

CHARLES HARRISON MASON AND SIBLINGS

Author's Note

After following the progress of Bishop Mason's siblings for decades through the census, I have seen no evidence from research of their connection with the Church of God in Christ. However, this doesn't mean that there wasn't any. There weren't any questions asked on any of the U. S. Census concerning church affiliations; however, being raised in a Christian family would likely assure that all of them would be involved in church at some level. Whether some of them later joined COGIC after finding out their brother, Bishop Mason founded the denomination could probably better be answered my knowledgeable family descendants.

Charles Harrison Mason

Charles H. Mason was born September 8, 1866, on the Prior Farm, located in Shelby County and in Civil District #7, known today as Bartlett, Tennessee. Mason's parents, Jeremiah (Jerry) and Eliza Mason, were slaves on the Prior Farm. Jerry Mason was born in South Carolina in 1825 and Eliza in Virginia in 1835; however, these dates are probably slightly inaccurate. Mason's siblings in 1870 were Israel S. Nelson, age eighteen, a half-brother and the son of Eliza; Joe was sixteen; Eliza (Elsy) was six; Mary was twelve; Jeremiah (Jerry) was four and Robert was two-months old and born in April. [1]

When Charles or Charley as he was sometimes called was about twelve, he and his family were forced to leave Memphis because of the yellow fever epidemic that broke out in August of 1878 and killed over five thousand people in Memphis and Shelby County. They moved to Howard, Conway County, Arkansas near Plumersville and lived on the farm of John and Cinderella Watson, who were cotton farmers. Mr. Watson and all his family were born in Tennessee and there is a possibility that Jerry Mason knew him before the Masons moved to Arkansas, which would explain why they chose his farm on which to settle. The Watson's were already living in Howard, Arkansas, early as 1870. All of the Mason's children moved to Arkansas with the exception of Mary and Joseph (Joe). Joseph married and moved away from home before the yellow fever epidemic outbreak in Memphis, and Mary presumably did the same.

In 1880, Jeremiah (Jerry) Mason was still alive. He was sixty-six years old and his wife, Eliza was fifty-six years old. Five of the seven children were still living at home. Eliza was sixteen; Charles, fourteen; Jeremiah, twelve; Robert, ten; and Israel S. Nelson was twenty-nine years old. Some historians and researchers have mistakenly pronounced Jerry Mason's demise one way or another prior to 1880; however, this was simply not true. Although we don't know how or exactly when he died we do know he was still alive in 1880 according to the U. S. Federal Census. Also, in 1880, no one in the family could read or write. Charles learned to read and write between 1880 and 1890. He was able to sign his own name on the marriage license in 1890 when he obtained it to marry Alice R. Saxton.

After closely examining the 1870 United States Federal Census Record of the Jerry Mason family, I discovered that C. H. Mason was possibly two years older than he thought. One of his parents and likely his mother reported his age to be five. The family was enumerated on June 24, which meant on September 8; Charles would turn six years old. This suggests, if the census is correct, he was, in fact, born in 1864 instead of 1866. It wasn't uncommon during this period of time for individuals to lose count of their correct age. While we can now examine the census and other records, they didn't have that option; and public records such as birth certificates, hospital, state, and death records didn't exist for black or white citizens in the United States in 1870. In most cases, parents couldn't read, write, or count; therefore, it wasn't uncommon for some people to be slightly off by a couple of years or more. Some people didn't have any idea how old they were when they came out of slavery.

Traveling Preacher and a Struggling Marriage

Mason and his family attended church services at the Mt. Olive Baptist Church near Plumersville, Conway County, Arkansas where Mason's half-brother, the Rev. Israel S. Nelson, baptized him. Mason went throughout southern Arkansas as a lay preacher, giving his testimony and working with souls on the mourner's bench, especially during the summer camp meetings. [2]

Despite being licensed and ordained to preach in 1891 at Preston, Arkansas, Mason held back from full-time ministry to marry Alice Saxton, a daughter of his mother's best friend. To his great disappointment and distress, Alice bitterly opposed his ministerial plans and divorced him after two years. Mason fell into such grief and despair that at times Satan tempted him to take his own life. Mason remained unmarried while Alice was alive. [3]

Charles H. Mason married Alice R. Saxton on Wednesday, January 15, 1890, in Faulkner County, Arkansas. He was twenty-three and she was nineteen. [4] They were married by Minister J. W. Cunningham (white). P. C. Claridy (black) was the man that accompanied Mason to the courthouse as his witness to purchase the license, and he was likely the best man at the wedding. Their licenses revealed that he and Alice lived in Preston, Faulkner County, Arkansas, where it is said, Mason was first ordained as a minister.

Alice R. Saxton was probably the same person as Alice R. Sexton (spelling difference) found in Walker, Faulkner County, Arkansas, in the 1880 U. S. Federal Census. Alice was the daughter of Stamie and Mary Saxton. It is difficult to determine which spelling of the name is correct because the mistake could have been made either by the census taker or the county court employee; however, I chose *Saxton* because a marriage license is a legal document, and *Saxton* was more than likely the correct spelling on the marriage license.

Stamie was born in Maryland about 1831 and Mary in Virginia about 1840. He stated his father was born in Africa, and his mother in Maryland. They had eight children and all of them were born in Tennessee, which leads me to believe that the Saxton and Mason families possibly knew each other before moving to Arkansas. Eliza Mason and Mary Saxton were said to be the best of friends. It is possible both families could have come from the Prior Farm or the Saxtons from a neighboring farm, fleeing Memphis during the yellow fever epidemic of 1878.

The distance between where the Mason family lived in Howard, Conway County, and where the Saxton family lived in Walker, Faulkner County, was only about fifteen miles.

Joseph Mason

Joseph (Joe) was the oldest child of Jerry and Eliza Mason. He was born into slavery in 1854 on the Prior farm in what is now Bartlett, Tennessee. He married Margaret (Maggie) White when he was twenty-four years old on November 15, 1878, in Nashville, Davidson County, Tennessee. [5] After marrying, they moved to Topeka, Shawnee County, Kansas, possibly to get away from the yellow fever epidemic or to find work. He left home before Charles, Jerry, and Robert (his younger brothers) were able to really get to know their older brother. The first two years of their marriage, they were blessed with two children, Anna and Lucy. They were living at 361 Monroe Street in Topeka. Joe was a day laborer while Margaret kept the house and raised the children.

Joe and Margaret moved from Topeka to Lincoln, Oklahoma County, Oklahoma, around 1891 and had eight more children. They were Frank, Maude, Otie, Oscar, Fay, Blanche, Alfred, and Johannah. Otie and Oscar were twins. Anna and Lucy were grown and out of the house at this point. Shortly after moving to Oklahoma, they were able to purchase a house on a farm. All the children were required to work on the farm. In 1890, Joe and his family were enumerated in the Kansas state census where he was listed as a mulatto. If this is true, then Joe's father could have been their white slave owner or the mixed ancestry could have come from Jerry or Eliza Mason side of the family. This would certainly add a new twist to the family pedigree.

In 1900, Joe was the only one listed as being employed. He was a farmer. By 1910, all of the children were out of the house except Alfred and Johannah. Joe was still farming and had a second job and Alfred and Johannah helped on the farm.

By 1920, Alfred was twenty-six years old, unmarried, and the only child left at home. Joe was still farming at sixty-six years old. Margaret was sixty-two and still a faithful housewife. Joe died between 1921 and 1929. Afterwards, Margaret went to live with her son Otie, the twin to Oscar. Margaret lived out her days in Lincoln, Oklahoma.

Robert H. Mason

Robert was the youngest child of Jerry and Eliza Mason. Born in April of 1870, he and Eliza, Charles, and Jerry were the four children born free of slavery after the signing of the Emancipation Proclamation, January 1, 1863. At ten years old, he was already working beside his siblings on the farm.

In 1900, he turned thirty years old and had recently married Elnora in 1899. She was also born in Tennessee and had a son named Rice Phillips, who was six years old when she married Robert. They were living in Louisville, Jefferson County, Kentucky, and he worked as a barber in a white owned Barber Shop but was only allowed to cut the hair of blacks. By 1910, they purchased their own home, and he changed jobs. He was now working as a janitor at a buffet restaurant. Elnora was unemployed and stayed home, while Rice, now seventeen, was employed as a janitor at a movie theater. Robert and Elnora couldn't have children, or they decided not to.

Between 1910 and 1920, Robert switched jobs again and went to work as a waiter at a hotel. They were now home alone and Elnora was still unemployed and a housewife. Elnora passed away July 24, 1932; and Robert couldn't be located in 1930, although more research probably will reveal what happened to him.

Israel S. Nelson

Israel was the oldest child of Eliza Mason and the stepson of Jerry Mason. He was born in August of 1852 in Bartlett, Shelby County, Tennessee, where he worked on the farm and was likely in charge of the other children. Israel was born into slavery and carried his biological father's surname. He was never reported in the census as being a mulatto, which meant his father was probably not a white slave owner who had fathered a child with Eliza.

The family was members of Mt. Olive Baptist Church near Plumersville, Arkansas, where their brother the Reverend Israel S. Nelson was pastor. This is the same church in which it is said, he baptized little Charles Mason a few days before his fourteenth birthday. Since Israel baptized Charles, he likely baptized some of the other children also.

Israel was about twenty-eight years old in 1880 and had not yet married; however, all that changed on February 19, 1885, when he obtained a marriage license from the Danville, Yell County, Arkansas Courthouse to marry Easter Cole. [6] Easter, a mulatto, was born in May of 1863. She was a native of Arkansas. The couple made their home in Yell County for several years, later moving to Van Buren, Crawford County, near Fort Smith, Arkansas, sometime before the year 1900. Their marriage license stated that he was twenty-seven years old when they married; however, that was probably incorrect. Usually you could depend on such documents as being factual but in this case I believe it was incorrect. He was about thirty-three years old, and she was twenty-three. This is another example that demonstrates how blacks, who had been slaves, had a very difficult time keeping up with their correct age.

By 1900, Israel and Easter had three children: Velva was twelve years old; Callie was eight years old, and his son, Aldon (possibly misspelled) was five years old. Between 1900 and 1910, they moved to Dardanelle, Yell County, Arkansas, probably because he was elected as pastor of a local Baptist church. They rented a house on 4th Street in Dardanelle; and while he became acquainted with his new parishioners, Easter began taking in laundry. She reported in the 1900 U. S. Census to have been married twice, and to have had six pregnancies in the twenty-five years she was married to Israel, but only three children survived.

In 1910, Israel was fifty-eight years old; Easter was forty-seven years old and living with them were Aldon and his sister. Callie was now married with a two year old son named Darnell. She was employed as a cook for a private family, but her husband wasn't listed as living in that household. Their oldest child, Velva, had probably married and moved away. Israel apparently passed away before 1920.

Eliza and Mary Mason

Eliza and Mary Mason, the sisters of C. H. Mason proved to be impossible to locate at this writing because of limited information and because their names changed after marrying, making records even more difficult to locate.

Jeremiah (Jerry) Mason

Jerry was named after his father and probably was a junior; however, the title junior in those days was rarely used or written. There were only two years difference between Charles and Jerry's ages, and they would have likely bonded more than any of the other siblings. Jerry worked on the family farm until he was old enough to marry and move away. Before Jerry married Polly Kennedy, something "extremely" ironic took place. Another gentleman with the same name as Jerry's married Georgia Ann Kennedy, the sister of Polly Kennedy, July 3, 1884, in Ouachita County, Arkansas, four years before Jerry married Polly. [7] They were indeed two different persons; I made sure of that through my research.

Jerry married Polly Kennedy on September 23, 1888, in Ouachita County, Arkansas and they made Smackover, Union County, Arkansas, their home. [8] Ouachita County was likely the home of Georgia Ann and Polly. The distance between the two counties was only about twenty miles with both counties lying in the extreme southern part of the state. Jerry and Polly seemed to have been prosperous, meaning that they purchased a house before 1900 at the corner of Eldorado and Camden Road in Smackover. Between 1888 and 1900, Polly was reported to have had seven pregnancies; but only four children survived; however, they ended up having six in all. Their names were Willie (girl), Rube (son), James, John, Jessie, and Susan. Polly did laundry and Jerry worked as a type of wheelman in a saw mill.

By 1910, their oldest daughter, Willie Mason-Gaskin, had been married a few years but came back to live with them along with her two children, Minnie and Pollie. Her husband may have died or they had gotten a divorce because he wasn't living with them. Jerry and Polly had another daughter named Susie, who was born in 1904. Their oldest son, Rube, was now seventeen years old and working at the saw mill with Jerry. Jim, the next to the youngest boy, was thirteen years old and working on a farm away from home.

Jerry and Polly had another son, Jessie, who was born in 1911. Between 1920 and 1930, Jerry was blessed with a better job working as a laborer for a crude oil company; and Polly worked as a laundress for a private family. Their second oldest son, Jim, had moved back home with his wife Annie and their son Leon. Jim was also employed by the same crude oil company where his dad worked. Jerry and Polly Mason lived in Smackover all their lives. He passed away on April 25, 1942, at the age of seventy-five.

5

BIRTHING PAINS OF A NEW DENOMINATION

Mason traveled to Los Angeles, California, with David J. Young and John A. Jeter at the urging of Charles P. Jones. They went out to investigate the rumors of a phenomenon that was spreading across the country and world of a spiritual outpouring taking place in Los Angeles. Prior to going to Los Angeles, Mason had never spoken in tongues; however, a few members of his church and a visitor from St. Louis were reported to have spoken in tongues before he visited Los Angeles. These accounts were told by church members under oath during the taking of depositions.

Approximately one year after Mason returned from California, he was asked in his deposition taken during the legal battle between him and the Jones faction to explain how he received the Holy Ghost while visiting the Azusa Street Revival. He "cleverly" tried to avoid the questions, not wanting to spiritualize the hearing further, but the complainants' lawyer was very persistent in his cross examination. Mason had to eventually tell his account and this is how he explained it:

I received by faith. I gave up to God, believing his word, believing that He was going to baptize me with the Holy Ghost. I was sitting with my legs crossed just as I am looking at you. It was daytime and several others were present. I sat there after I had surrendered to the Lord, believing that he would baptize me with the Spirit, and after a while my very soul began to cry to God just like a pump without a sucker, and after a while you catch the water and the man is strong, even physically, so, after a while my desire seemed to become intense within me, and every breath seemed to become heavier as I looked to God. I sat there a while and I heard a sound just like the sound of wind, a great wind. I heard the sound like in the Pentecost. I heard it just as real. I sat there, some on my left, some on my right, and I gave up to God, not resisting him; I determined not to resist him, and after a while I went through a crucifixion, and after I had gone through that I was completely empty; my mind was sweet, at rest; my flesh was sweet, at rest. I sat there a while giving up to God. The anthem of Heaven seemed to rise then; I felt myself rising out of my seat, without any effort. I though at first it was imagination; then I saw it wasn't imagination. Well when I was drawn to my feet there came a light in the room above, the brightness of the light of God. When I opened my mouth to say "Glory to God," a flame touched my tongue and my English left me, and I said "Glory" and then my hands was moved by the power of the Spirit of God. He had complete control of me. Now when this was over I was filled with the presence of God. I didn't move a foot; I sat there just as I am sitting now; I knew everything going on; the people even talking in the room; I was looking at them just as I am looking at you. God didn't knock me out. I saw others that were knocked out. [1]

What a powerful, anointed experience and testimony of how he received the baptism of the Holy Ghost! Glory to God! Mason was questioned extensively about speaking in tongues after he had explained his "upper-room" like experience of how he received the baptism of the Holy Ghost. His testimony and experience at the Azusa Revival is very similar to the actual New Testament account of tarrying for the Holy Ghost on the Day of Pentecost in the Upper Room. What a powerful testimony from our founder and apostle, Charles Harrison Mason. Much of the questioning during the deposition was about speaking in tongues. Mason tried to avoid any attempt by the attorney to probe into his personal spiritual life, but his efforts were unsuccessful. However, notice how calm Bishop Mason seemed and how he used his God-given wisdom to answer the questions asked by the Attorney on speaking in tongues:

Q. How many languages can you speak?

A. I don't know; He gives divers tongues.

Q. I am not examining the Spirit, but you. How many can you speak?

A. He gives divers.

Q. Haven't you boasted you can speak four hundred and five?

A. I haven't boasted.

Q. Haven't you stated?

A. Yes, sir, I have counted after him about four hundred.

I can tell from the questions asked that the attorney was "fascinated," and he could sense the power and the anointing that was on Bishop Mason's life. Questions and answers continue:

Q. How can you tell that the Lord has spoken to you in four hundred languages?

A. You see you can tell a different utterance when you hear it.

Q. Yes, but can you tell which is a language?

A. You can tell it is an utterance. The scripture says you may be voiced of many tongues.

Q. My dear Sir, I am not asking what the Scripture says but what you say.

A. If they speak to one another and they don't understand, they are speaking to God; they was not speaking to one another. [2]

The Washington-Mason Nuptial

The founder of the Church of God in Christ, Charles Harrison Mason of Memphis, Tennessee, was a man of integrity and believed strongly in the institution of marriage. Two years before he founded and reorganized the Church of God in Christ denomination and first Holy Convocation, he was united in Holy Matrimony to Miss Lelia Washington; and together they faced the challenges of the ministry that were before them. She was the daughter of the late John and Indiana Washington. The wedding took place on Wednesday, October 18, 1905. [3] Wednesdays were popular days to plan weddings during this era because the saints made plans to attend church anyway. Almost all the members of the church would have shown up for the wedding ceremony.

Deacon William Roberts accompanied Elder Mason downtown to the courthouse on Tuesday, the day before the wedding, as a witness to obtain the marriage license to marry Lelia. Deacon Roberts signed his name under Elder Mason's name as a witness. The courthouse clerk or employee wrote "Col'd" in the left corner of the license signifying their race. There was a space provided for the name of the minister or Justice of the Peace that performed the marriage rites and a space for the date when he returned to the courthouse and documented that he successfully carried out the marriage rites.

The next day was Wednesday and a beautiful day for a fall wedding, with clear skies in Memphis and a daytime high of 87 degrees and a low temperature of 75 degrees. Late Wednesday evenings was ideal times to have weddings since each Wednesday was mid-week worshiping night, which assured them of a good attendance. Lelia's mother, Indiana, would have made sure that the church was tastefully decorated and that all things were in readiness before the chosen hour. At the appropriate time, Elder Mason probably would send one of the finest fully enclosed horse drawn carriages to transport Lelia to the church. When the driver opened the carriage door to help Lelia up into the coach, there would probably be numerous fresh cut flowers methodically placed on the inside, which would release a "sweet" fragrance that would fill the compartment of the carriage. On the seat beside her would probably be a beautiful white box inlayed with a gold-colored material in which her bouquet would be located. She would carry a gorgeous wide smile on her face and one of the flowers in her hand all the way to the church. Accompanying her in the carriage on the ride to the church would be her mother and her matron of honor.

Excitement among the ladies would be very high as they would help Lelia with all the final touches and as they would prepare themselves, giving attention to every detail. All the ushers, deacons, and trustees would be on their post to aid in whatever way they could. When the time was right, the word would be given and through the back or side door would enter Elder Mason with his best man, Deacon William Roberts. Both men would be immaculately groomed and dressed in black tuxedoes. Already positioned on the platform looking "handsome" and "dignified" would be the minister of the Gospel who would to perform the wedding ceremony, Elder Charles Price Jones.

If there were an organ, after the soft cords would erupt, the bride would enter. She would be beautifully attired in a white dress with a veil tastefully draping the gorgeous sweet face. Lelia likely would be escorted by one of her uncles, Professor Charles J. Neal, her mother's brother or Robert Washington, her father's brother. Her father had passed away several years before. Elder Jones would have performed the wedding in an eloquent and dignified matter; and after about twenty or thirty minutes, they would have been pronounced husband and wife. After the much anticipated kiss, they would have then turned to face the audience as Elder Jones presented them to the attendees as Elder Charles and Lelia Mason.

After the ceremony, the bride and groom would have invited the host of friends that attended the wedding to the residence of the bride's mother, Sister Indiana Washington, where the table would have been spread with many things that would be pleasing to the appetite. The guests would have enjoyed themselves until a late hour; and then one by one, would bid the bride and groom adieu and would depart to their respective homes.

The wedding ceremony just described wasn't an actual published account of the way it happened, but rather the author's depiction of possibly the way it could have been. However, the characters were real; and the parts they played were real, and I almost forgot to mention, the weather report was real.

Before they married, Elder Mason lived on Williams Avenue for about five years. After he and Lelia were married, he moved in with Lelia and her family who had been living at 609 Stephens Avenue since about 1893. A few months after the trial started between the Mason and Jones factions in 1908, they moved to Lexington, Mississippi, where Mason temporarily took over as pastor of St. Paul COGIC. He, the officers, and congregation of Saints Home COGIC in Memphis were barred from the church (temporarily) by an injunction. At the time, Mason had no idea how long the injunction would last.

Saints Home COGIC:
The First Church Founded and Built
by Bishop Mason in Tennessee

Bishop Mason's first church in Memphis, figuratively speaking, was inside himself; and he preached on the streets, under tents, from house to house and wherever else he was received. There was no specific place or house of worship until he was able to buy a tent and erect it on some rental property. Mason was in and out of Memphis as early as 1889, gathering followers and organizing a few faithful saints that would become his future church body. Other historical accounts have mistakenly overlooked his presence in Memphis at such an early period. He can be placed in Memphis as early as 1889 by two statements made under oath in 1908 during the taking of a deposition from Dee J. Smith, a trustee at his church. This was during the case, Avant vs. Mason, in the legal trial between the Jones and Mason factions.

Basically, as far as preaching the word and gathering followers, Elder Mason was accomplishing both in Tennessee and Mississippi at the same time; however, there is evidence that suggest he may have started in Memphis first. He was given the name Church of God in Christ by divine revelation from the Lord in 1897 while visiting Little Rock, Arkansas; however, long before then, he was preaching and teaching on the streets of Memphis. He had several followers, and they were worshipping from place to place without a specific building in Memphis.

Beginning in 1895, Mason and Charles Price Jones began to communicate and work closely sharing in the Word of the Lord. Jones, at the time, was pastor of St. Helena Baptist Church in Jackson, Mississippi. They were joined by two other Baptist preachers, John A. Jeter and William S. Pleasant, who helped them organize what they called holiness meetings with the first one held in 1897 in Jackson. Jeter was pastoring in Arkansas, and Pleasant was the pastor of the Damascus Missionary Baptist Church in Hazlehurst, Mississippi.

In comparison, back in Tennessee, the Lord had given Elder Mason a vision in 1900 to purchase property and prepare to build a church. On October 22, 1900, a contract was made by Dee J. Smith, Edward Loveless, Charles Liddell, and Jim Murphy (all trustees of the church) on a piece of property located on the east side of South Wellington Street. The property was owned by Thomas Ripley Farnsworth and his wife Eula, owners of a real estate company, located on Central Avenue in Memphis. In the beginning they first rented the property and then purchased the lot and erected a tent until they were able to start the building process. The price agreed on was $750 for the lot and $50 was paid in hand to Mr. Farnsworth in cash. The balance was paid in eighteen promissory notes with payments of $37.50 per month and a final payment of $25.00. [4]

During the taking of Mason's deposition on April 25, 1908, he was asked by the attorney, "How long have you been pastor of this church?" He replied, "Oh,

I have been pastor of this church about seven years; I think it was in 1900, about that time, I was pastor, just a little before I was thinking about a building. That has been built about seven years, but I was pastor before it was built." According to Mason's statements, it would have been in 1901 when the forty foot by sixty foot frame church was erected on the property for approximately $4000. It was a plain wood structure with a rubber roof and there wasn't even a cupola on the roof to distinguish that it was a church. There were no partitioned rooms inside, only one very large sanctuary, and the floors were carpeted as well as the pulpit area.

As the church was growing, this edifice proved to be very inadequate and too small to hold the crowds that gathered for both local and national meetings. As a consequence, the frame structure was torn down and a new brick building, 40 by 100 ft., with a balcony, dining room, kitchen, two rest rooms and a pastor's study, was constructed. **[5]** The church was named Saints Home Church of God in Christ, although most people referred to it as the Sanctified Church.

Mason himself, from his statements made in his deposition, established the fact that Saint Paul COGIC (built in 1906) located in Lexington, Mississippi, wasn't the first church built from the "ground-up" by Mason. However, the saints in Lexington probably were the first group of believers organized under the name Church of God in Christ. It's important to understand that any church that was founded by Bishop Mason after the Lord gave him the name Church of God in Christ would automatically become part of COGIC body of believers and later denomination. I haven't found any evidence that suggests Jones and Mason quarreled over the use of the name Church of God in Christ, but there is positive evidence from the deposition of C. P. Jones that the name, Church of God in Christ, wasn't adopted by the Convention or Convocation at Jackson, Mississippi, until 1906; one year before Mason was excommunicated from the group.

I couldn't find any legal action taken in the State of Tennessee by Charles P. Jones that suggests he was interested in extracting the name Church of God in Christ from Bishop Mason. Jones was given by revelation, or had chosen on his own, the name Church of Christ Holiness, which he tried to convince his congregation in 1898 at the Mt. Helm Missionary Baptist Church in Jackson, Mississippi, to change the name of the church to Church of Christ Holiness. Jones was met with much resistance, and they went to court over the matter. The Jones faction lost the case. Jones held on to that name and later applied it to the new denomination that he founded, the Church of Christ (Holiness) U.S.A. after he and Mason went their separate ways. This is important because it demonstrates Mason had full rights and control of the name without any legal action by C. P. Jones over its use. What is more important, but probably impossible to exactly know at this point, is where Bishop Mason first applied the use of the name Church of God in Christ. We have a marvelous and miraculous history; but the truth of the matter is, we really don't know whether Bishop Mason stopped in Memphis first on his way back from Little Rock and gave the name Church of God in Christ to his group of followers there or proceeded first to Lexington, Mississippi. Either way the denomination can still proclaim that its history began in 1897.

In 1906, Elder Mason had the second largest ministerial staff of the convention with Elder Jeter of Arkansas having the largest. Ministers on staff under Mason were Elders Sam Davis, Henry Scott, (assistant pastor) Isaac L. Jordan, R. Mangum, Robert Davis, Isaac Jacobs, Milton Sanders, M. B. S. Clayton and E. R. Driver. Henry Scott, Isaac L. Jordan and Robert Davis later defected from Mason's church over speaking in tongues after Mason was excommunicated by the convention in Jackson, Mississippi.

Mason Pastored a Church in Conway, Faulkner County, Arkansas

There is enough information and evidence available to know without a doubt that Mason was at one time pastor of a church in Conway, Arkansas, before he founded the church in Memphis. It was likely between 1890 and 1900 when he was pastor of that church. During his deposition, he was asked if he had a church in Conway, Arkansas. He replied, "Yes sir." Charles P. Jones and his faction filed litigations against that church around the same time charges were brought against Mason's church in Memphis. Remember, he and Mason were close confidants; therefore, Jones would have known about all the churches under Mason's influence. When Mason decided to leave Arkansas for good, he gave the pulpit up to Elder Justus Bowe; therefore, he wasn't directly involved in litigations when they were filed by the Jones faction. Mason probably had very little oversight in their affairs although their doctrinal beliefs would have been the same as Mason's. Elder Bowe was one of the supporters of Mason after he was excommunicated.

The Memphis Meeting Called By Mason

Mason had no other choice but to organize his supporters after he was excommunicated from the council in Jackson, Mississippi. He knew without a doubt that he had been baptized with the Holy Ghost with the evidence of speaking in tongues, and he had no plans of denying what he knew was real. He sent a letter to his closest contacts in the ministry and to those who he thought would accept this New Testament "upper room" twentieth century manifestation of the Spirit. His letter might have read something like this: "If you are a minister of God's Word, and you are willing to walk by faith believing that the baptism of the Holy Ghost, with the evidence of speaking in tongues was poured out on me and many others in Los Angeles just like on the day of Pentecost in the Bible, and if you can trust God and believe in him, then meet us in Memphis, Tennessee, on Wednesday, September 4, 1907, at 7:00 pm at my church, Saints Home COGIC on Wellington Street."

Along with the ministers that attended this meeting, there was also the congregation of Saints Home COGIC present when the following letter was read before them, written by the secretary of the church, and certainly the words of Bishop Mason dictated to her:

September 4, 1907. The General Assembly or majority of members having removed Elder C. H. Mason and under those heads he put the matter square before the saints. He said: "We are preaching Jesus blood cleanses; His spirit sanctifies, and Jesus baptizes with the Holy Ghost." The preliminaries were to the extent that as in the years gone by, to not be cramped, but be frank in their conviction. And all stood save about five or six." [6]

Elder Robert E. Hart took the lead at the meeting along with Elders Eddie R. Driver and David J. Young; all three were college educated and close confidants of Bishop Mason. A resolution was drafted by Hart, Driver, and Young that were consentaneous to all that were present at the meeting. They supported Mason and condemned what the convention or council of elders had done in Jackson, Mississippi. This is the resolution that was drafted and read before the General Assembly:

"Whereas it is reported in "The Truth" that Elder C. H. Mason, dealt with by a convention called together in Jackson, Mississippi, on Thursday, August the 29th,

1907, his finding was the withdrawal of the right-hand of fellowship, and whereas the Holiness Assembly of the Churches of God, composed of representatives from all of the churches of God, did meet in the month of January, 1906, and elected Elder C. H. Mason one of the chief pastors or overseers. And Whereas, the committee assigned no true reason from their heads and unconsidered action, we the ministers of the Church of God, assemble in Memphis, this the 4th day of September, 1907, do re-affirm his election as declared by the Tennessee Assembly of all the Churches of God, which met at Jackson, Mississippi, in January, 1906. All of which we respectfully submit. Signed by **R. E. Hart**, *E. R. Driver, and D. J. Young.* [7]

Before the Memphis meeting adjourned they made plans for their first convocation to be held in Memphis, Tennessee, about two months later in November of 1907. The ten congregations that attended the first Holy Convocation and National Meeting comprised the whole Church of God in Christ at that time. Two of the three congregations from Tennessee were pastored by Elder Hart, one located in Jackson and the other in Trenton, Tennessee. Elder Hart was appointed Overseer of Tennessee; Elder Justus B. Bowe Sr., was appointed Overseer of Arkansas and Elder Mason, Overseer of Mississippi; for this was the extent of the church body at this time.

After attending the Convocation and the first General Assembly Meeting of COGIC, Elder Hart returned to Jackson, Tennessee, and was immediately confronted with opposition from the Jones faction. Jones stated that he was against the brethren taking the matter to court; however, the deacons preferred to handle the matter in the courts. After a few weeks, Elder Hart gave up fighting the Jones faction and with a few members, he founded a new church under the new denomination, the Church of God in Christ, adopted and approved by the General Assembly, September 4, 1907, in Memphis. With a small group of followers, he succeeded in renting a small lot where they erected a tent that was used as their first church home. In 1908, the Jackson city directory listed the Church of God in Christ as being located at the corner of Madison and Totten Streets with R. E. Hart as pastor. A specific name for many years wasn't given to the church; it was simply listed and known as the Church of God in Christ, or the Sanctified Church.

The 1918 Holy Convocation Cancelled Due to the Spanish Flu Pandemic

Bishop Mason moved back to Memphis in 1917 and bought or rented a house at 755 Williams Avenue. He and his family lived there for a little over a year, and he then purchased the residence of Dr. John and Ruby Rauch, at 1121 Mississippi Boulevard. Dr. Rauch was a veterinary surgeon who owned the American Veterinary Remedy Company in Memphis.

The *Commercial Appeal* newspaper reported on September 25th that Dr. Neuman Taylor, head of the Memphis Health Department, admitted, "A few cases of the Spanish flu have been reported in the city, but there is no cause for alarm." On September 25th, the Spanish influenza was reported to have officially arrived in Memphis; and on September 26th, the flu claimed its first victim. On November 6th, amidst all the growing cases of the flu, fear, and death, Bishop Mason and Lelia pressed their way and sealed the deal on their new house. Mason didn't have any other choice but to cancel the Holy Convocation planned for 1918. The Health Department closed schools, churches, and all places of amusement, including theaters, dance halls, and moving picture houses. Even funerals were canceled, and only graveside services were permitted; for there were no church services. Any usual or large planned gatherings were not permitted. Families were encouraged to pray and gather in their homes and conduct private church services. Memphis resembled a "ghost town" at the height of the crisis.

The Health Department reported that Memphis had seen 5,617 cases of the Spanish flu with exactly 493 deaths. In New York City, over 33,000 died; and in Philadelphia, over 7,000 died in two weeks. Nationwide the death rate average was about 5 percent among those that contracted the disease; however, in Memphis, the death rate was about 9 percent. Worldwide the Spanish flu killed some 25 million people, and some researchers placed the death toll as high as 100 million. The United States lost somewhere between 500,000 to 650,000 people. [8] Although weakened, the Spanish flu returned to Memphis in 1919; and for several years after, it managed to kill several hundred in Memphis as late as 1923. My great-great grandmother, Malinda Featherston Parker, (1840-1923) died from the dreaded disease at her home in Capleville, Shelby County, Tennessee, February 27, 1923. [9]

Holy Convocations and National Meetings

The first Holy Convocation and National Meetings were held at Saints Home Church of God in Christ located at 392 Wellington Street near Vance Street in the city of Memphis. In the early years, the address was 306 Wellington Street; and as the neighborhood grew, the address changed. Up until 1925, with the exceptions of 1908 and 1918, the National Meetings were held at 392 Wellington Street. When the National Tabernacle was built and completed at 958 Fifth Street in 1925, the Convocations and National Meetings were moved to that location until the tabernacle was destroyed by fire in 1936.

Mason and his family moved to Lexington, Mississippi, in 1908 when the litigation started between him and the Jones faction. Lexington is probably where the Holy Convocation and the National Meetings were probably held in 1908. Mason and his congregation were read out of the church by an injunction in 1908. When Bishop Mason returned to Memphis from Mississippi in 1917, he was reinstalled as pastor of the Saints Home COGIC on Wellington Street.

The property for the National Tabernacle was purchased in 1922 at a cost of $40,000. After the National Tabernacle was completed in 1925, Bishop Mason and his congregation became excited and visualized a new edifice for themselves. Their vision was realized in 1931 when they purchased Tabernacle Baptist Church, at 672 South Lauderdale Street from Dr. Sutton Griggs, (black) pastor of the congregation. The church was built by Pastor Griggs in 1914 and opened on Easter Sunday before World War I broke out in 1914. It was built with a swimming pool and was intended as a community center for the neighborhood. For years it was the only swimming pool for blacks in the city. Bishop Mason renamed the church, Temple Church of God in Christ. Temple COGIC burned to the ground on Thursday, February 13, 1958. Given the racism and hatred against blacks and the sanctified church, it was likely no accident. Bishop Mason was very saddened over the lost of the church and an old bible given to him by his father. On Friday, February 7th, a week before the church burned, a cross was burned at 1:35 am in the yard of Bishop Mason's home at 1755 Glenview Street, which backed up to the African-American houses on Parkway; however, the rest of Glenview Street was white. When the National Tabernacle burned in 1936, the Holy Convocations and National Meetings were held at Temple COGIC until 1945 when Mason Temple was completed; and then they were able to move the convocations and all the national meetings to Mason Temple.

In 1934, Bishop Mason paid $394 to have the Saints Home COGIC on Wellington Street moved to Bartlett, Tennessee. This was a historical decision made by Bishop Mason to memorialize the area where he was born by moving the first church he founded and built in Tennessee back to his "roots." After it was relocated, an addition $1,560.45 was paid for labor and materials, plus $134 for small bills and $210 plumbing cost. **[10]**

Church on Fire

Prior to Bishop Mason returning from Los Angeles, April of 1907, the Holy Ghost had already gone on before him "declaring the works of the Lord" and preparing the people at his church for what had taken place in Los Angeles. The *Commercial Appeal* newspapers in Memphis ran a front page article titled, "Negro Houseboy Makes Funny Talk At Police Station." The following is what the paper stated that took place at Elder Mason's church just days before he returned from California:

"Iggy Gik wok, muggy ung chugaloo. Iggy gluk aqua pura dub is ferique uggy blok."-Prayer, Chief O'Haver says F. C. Ford, Negro religious enthusiast, offered up when released from city prison where he was placed because his exuberance was mistaken for a form of Americana dementia.

Twenty-four hours in the darkened recesses of a prison cell failed to cool the religious ardor of F. C. Ford, 22, negro houseboy, employed by Major Eldridge E. Wright, 688 Jefferson Av., but it served to stop a flow of strong language which Ford and others claim he became gifted with as the result of baptism in the Apostolic Faith movement. He says he has religion. His employer says he has lost a job.

Ford was arrested yesterday morning on complaint of his employers. His living quarters on the place were unoccupied Sunday night, but Monday morning he showed up for work about 7 o'clock. He refused to speak to other servants on the place except through paper and pencil in English and addressed himself verbally by utterances which, according to the maid, sounded very much like "O-pala, O-pala," at the same time raising his hands high towards heaven. Becoming alarmed, the police station was called by phone. Patrol Driver Jack Klinck and Acting Turnkey Heckles responded. They say that on the way up to headquarters Ford attempted to convert them by signs of praying, uttering strange noises all the time.

Tuesday morning a peculiar sight presented itself in the private sanctum of Chief O'Haver, who called Ford in for investigation. At about the same time G. A. Cook and L. P. Adams, who say they are preaching the Apostolic Faith movement, appeared on the scene. They greeted Ford with outstretched hands and a three-corned conversation in language which sounded like Esquimaux looks in print, took place. Chief O'Haver looked on in mild wonderment until the Negro, his face wreathed in smiles, turned to shake hands with him.

"What's the matter with you," inquired the chief showing some animation and Southern resentment at the brotherly greeting."

"Ford found his tongue. "Dey ain't anything, boss; I'se got ligon," he declared. Cook, who claims to be a former printer, and says he became a convert to the Apostolic Faith when it was started 11 months ago by W. J. Seymour at Los Angeles, Cal., told this story to a reporter of The Press: "The Apostolic Faith movement is based on the powers of the Holy Ghost and centers around the gifts infused by Him into the apostles at Pentecost, when He descended upon their heads in forms of fiery tongues from heaven and filled them with the spirit. They went forth and preached the gospel to every man in his own tongue. That is what we do. "By laying hands on one's head we baptize and he is filled with the power to speak unknown languages."

Here Cook paused long enough to show his powers in speaking Hindustani and Chinese. No proof to the contrary being present he proceeded.

"We came to Memphis last Friday. Sunday afternoon we held services in the colored church on Wellington St. and Ford became filled with religion. He fell on the floor in a stupor and remained lying there from Sunday afternoon until Monday morning. He spoke a strange language-what it was I do not know, but it was not gibberish."

Cook asked Chief O'Haver to release Ford. When he was again brought out, Sergeant Hayes dared to speak English to him.

"If you don't stay away from Mr. Wright's house, we'll land you in the county workhouse," he said with beautiful simplicity.

"Glory be ter Gawd," shouted Ford, again lapsing into plain United States. He left the station house with Cook, who says he may make a preacher out of the Negro. Ford has lost his job as Major Wright's house boy and may be open to an offer.

"I'm from the north and do not discriminate between white and black in preaching," said Cook, "but I do respect the southern ideas of racial equality and am not here to settle any such questions. Neither do I say that unless a man follows our ideas he will be lost. Let every man follow his own light, but I shall do my best to make converts."

G. B. Cashwell of Durham, N. C., M. M. Pinson, formerly a Methodist minister of Nashville, and L. P. Adams, Cumberland Presbyterian minister, who says he has been in Memphis five years, say they hold meetings afternoon and night on Trigg av., near Mississippi Av. [11]

In the early years, Saints Home COGIC was a target for everyone that was skeptical or felt threatened by the holiness doctrine of the Sanctified Church, especially speaking in tongues. Lies and rumors of every sort were spread around Memphis and across the country. One such rumor circulated was that a person was going to be "hanged" as an act of faith and brought back to life. Local newspapers such as *The Commercial Appeal* mocked and joked about the kinds of services that were carried on at the church through the following article published about six weeks after Elder Mason returned from California:

After five weeks of speaking in the "holy tongue," the sanctified negroes at the Sanctified Church, on Wellington street, near Vance avenue, have decided to vary the performance to "treading the wine press," which diversion will be practiced until June 6, when the supreme test of faith will be made by hanging a half dozen blacks who have expressed the desire to shout off in midair if their faith is not strong enough to ward off death by the hangman's noose.

Strange things have been going on at this church for the pass five weeks and if the authorities do not interfere some lives are sure to be sacrificed to the fanatical spirit which has been controlling that congregation for the past month.

Some time ago the pastor, one Rev. Mason had a "visitation of the Holy Spirit," and began to speak the language used by the "Spirit" during his interview with the prominent member of the Holy Trinity. The test then came. If the members of the church could not speak and understand such language they were not sanctified, and could not be saved. This gave rise to one of the most remarkable religious fervors that has ever struck even the superstitious Negro church. The pastor pretended to speak the language of the Spirit and the wise ones of the congregation got on to his curves and began using a strange, idiotic jargon, which was alike meaningless to them and the preacher. As a matter of self-defense both the minister and the "wise ones" of his congregation pretended to understand each other and the result was the language of the Spirit, which all understand and which is meaningless to all.

The minister would exclaim, Hicks, hicks," and the congregation would answer back," Sycamore, Sycamore, Sycamore," and such insignificant words, which lifted the congregation to the highest point of ecstasy, showing what has been contended for years that the Negro religion is sound instead of sense.

But the supreme act of folly is to be committed June 6, when six Negroes have agreed to be hanged in the church to show their faith. Unless they weaken, as did a candidate Sunday night, and some one does not interfere, death to one or more of the faithful is likely to occur. A rope is to be thrown over one of the beams in the roof and will hang low enough to reach the neck of the victim standing on a box. When the hangman's noose is adjusted, the box is to be kicked out and the martyr left hanging in the air. If his faith is sufficient, he is supposed to be insensible to the pressure of the knot, but otherwise death will come to him like it does to ordinary individuals when hanged.

This test was made Sunday night when a Negro named Parker was led to the noose. After the noose had been adjusted and the box was about to be kicked out from under him, Parker lost his grip on faith and called out to hold a moment. This was taken as an evidence that he was not sanctified, and he was taken down in disgrace. Parker is the same Negro who preached the destruction of Memphis a short while ago in connection with a crazy woman from Arkansas. He was sent to the penitentiary a few years ago for one year for shooting a Negro in compliance with the instructions of the Holy Spirit. After his failure to stand the test, it is said Parker left the Sanctified Church and has joined the Church of the Living God.

Until the frenzy of the members has reached its highest pitch it will be impossible to predict what the "treading of the wine press," will amount to. It should be a matter for the police. Certainly, if the authorities do not interfere, some one will be killed by this frenzied congregation sooner or later. The services last from 7:30 p.m. to 6:30 a.m. every day, and the Negroes are beginning to be crazed by such tax on their endurance.
[12]

Some passed on other rumors that told of how people when slain in the spirit would be carried outside of the church and laid on "quilt pallets" to be revived. Another rumor was spread of how fine china and dishes were brought to the church by parishioners because they planned to stay several days and would need something to eat out of.

Holiness Meetings in Jackson, Mississippi: 1897-1907

Beginning in 1897, Charles Price Jones, Charles Harrison Mason, John A. Jeter, and William S. Pleasant were the founders and primary organizers of holiness meetings convening in Jackson, Mississippi. All of them were former baptist preachers who had become increasingly disenchanted with the baptist doctrine and their baptist brother's refusal to embrace the Pentecostal-Holiness message. They tried to schedule a summer and winter conference every year. The meetings were open to pastors, elders, and ministers from every denomination, even the white brethren. The name, Church of God in Christ, was given exclusively to C. H. Mason from the beginning by divine revelation, and divine circumstances later permitted him to use the name Church of God in Christ to identify a new body of believers. However, the name wasn't officially adopted by the Ministerial or Elders Council of the Holiness Meetings in Jackson, Mississippi, until 1906.

The Ministers and Deacons Institute was birthed out of the Churches of God in Christ's Holiness Meetings in 1906 or before and was intended to give guidance and training to experienced as well as inexperienced ministers and deacons that were involved in ministry. The training they received through the Institute help put them on one accord with the pastors and elders. The following meeting took place in 1906 close to Jackson, Mississippi:

The ministers and Deacons' Institute will be held at the Church of God at Canie Creek, April the 27, 28, and 29. The church is six and a half miles South of Jackson, Miss., and one mile from Sigers on the I. C. R. R. first stop from Jackson.

Come, dear brethren, and let us lift up Christ together. Bring your Bibles. Come fasting and praying that we may have the same mind and mind the same things. Luke 24:48, 49. F. S. Sheriff, Chairman, G. H. Funches, Sect. [13]

Charles P. Jones, Charles H. Mason, Robert E. Hart, and Eddie R. Driver along with others met at the winter convention of 1906, in Jackson, Mississippi, to give their input in the "Rules of Government" for the Churches of God in Christ, which was written by Charles P. Jones. The introduction for the convention was also written by Charles P. Jones, the chief overseer and chairman of the convention. They would also be voting on whether or not to adopt the name, Church of God in Christ, as the official name of the group. The following was the introduction to the convention:

To the Churches of God in Christ greeting: In the fear of God, and as we pray and hope, in the Spirit and mind of Christ, as president of the Convocation of the Church of God in Christ, it is necessary that I now have printed in book form those rules adopted among us as to church government agreeing with the pattern of the New Testament as the Lord made us see it and agree to it in Elders Council assembled.

The government of the churches up to this time was congregational with certain brethren exercising a sort of unofficial oversight. On account, however, of young preachers taking advantage of their influence as among the weak dividing the flocks, drawing disciples off after themselves, the brethren decided to make this apostolic over-sight official and regular; which was officially done by voice of the Elders counsel, the ruling part of the Convention.

The call having been made thru TRUTH, our organ in such matters, published at Jackson, Miss., that the brethren come up to settle the matter of the general govern-ment of our work in Christ, the following brethren, (ministers) with others were present. Jan. 14-21, 1906.

*Elders present at the Convention held as called: Charles P. Jones, C. H. Mason, J. A. Jeter, **R. E. Hart,** W. S. Pleasant, J. L. I. Conic, J. C. Cartwright, Daniel G. Spearman, R. H. I. Clark, Wm. Washington, George Robinson, G. W. Cooper, A. J. Scarborough, H. R. McKinnis, L. J. Brunson, L. W. Lee, John Hicks, E. Thomas, Jas. Waddell, L. C. Cobbins, R. A. Morris, H. Blackman, R. Randall, A. T. Rucker, E. M. Bennett, W. J. Johnson, J. C. Nichols, T. J. Hardy, Johnnie Vance, Geo. Funches, D. W. Welch, R. A. Garrison, Justus Bowe, I. B. Pleasant, John Brewer, James Brewer, A. J. Williams, J. W. Curry, E. M. Huey, Robert Stewart, Mack McQueen, W. H. Smith, G. L. Bogan, S. B. Bogan, E. D. Tyner, J. A. Armstrong, Thomas Sanders, F. S. Sheriff, E. D. Sheridan. Besides these a number of unordained preach-ers and deacons and other workers were present.*

Elder W. S. Pleasant acted President pro tem of the meeting. Elder D. G. Spear-man was scribe of the occasion.

*The following ministers were appointed a committee to draft resolutions for consid-eration: Elders J. A. Jeter, **R. E. Hart,** C. H. Mason, J. C. Cartwright, W. S. Pleas-ant and C. P. Jones. C. P. Jones was recognized as Chairman of the committee.*

The first resolutions drafted were considered too stringent and were modified to the substance of the rules following in this book.

May the Lord God of Israel grant us unity and peace. May He lift up His counte-nance upon us and bless us continually and grant that as He hath begun a good work in us He will carry it on till the day of Christ. Charles P. Jones, Chief of Convocation.
[14]

It was at the winter convention of the Church of God in Christ held in Janu-ary of 1906, that C. H. Mason was appointed State Overseer of Tennessee. The following year Charles H. Mason, John A. Jeter, and David J. Young visited the Azusa Street Revival in March of 1907. Mason was in Los Angeles about five weeks and returned to Memphis before the first Sunday in April, baptized in the Holy Ghost with the evidence of speaking in tongues. Eager to spread his Azusa Street Revival experience, he made plans to meet with his friends and associates in the ministry. John A. Jeter, Charles P. Jones, and William S. Pleasant disagreed with Mason about his Pentecostal experience at the revival. They strongly urged him to retract his statements and forget about what he experienced, which Mason didn't do. That is what eventually led the Ministerial Council in Jackson, Mississippi, to take the following action against Mason:

In our last convention at Jackson, which is headquarters of the work, our brother C. H. Mason was found heretical, he having departed from the faith we at first preached, and having taken up with a rank heresy from Los Angeles, California, which heresy he has propagating to the hurt and confusion of the people, and which he refused to cease to preach and teach. He was withdrawn from, he and all who affiliated with him in any way as aiding the propagation of this awful delusion. Elder John Hicks was appointed by the chief of the work, C. P. Jones, to do Elder Mason's work in Tennessee. [15]

Mason, Driver, and Hart were present at the convention in 1907, when the Ministerial Council met with the three of them and a few others twice, trying to get Mason to abandon his teaching, preaching, and speaking in what they called a "false doctrine of tongues". He refused and that is when the right hand of fellowship was withdrawn from him and all who associated and affiliated with him by the council. There were several ministers within the council that agreed with his testimony about his Pentecostal experience. There was present at the convention CME, AME, Methodist Episcopal Church, Missionary Baptist, and Adventist Baptist. Robert E. Hart, Eddie R. Driver, and David J. Young were among his strongest supporters. There has never been an exact number given as to how many left the convention at the same time Mason left; however, it has been said, it was about half of the convention, but that was probably a gross exaggeration of the actual number.

Hot Tempers

Attitudes got very "hot" among the brethren over this so-called "rank" heresy from Los Angeles, California, that C. H. Mason and others were accused of spreading to the hurt and confusion of the people and preachers. I'm sure what was very confusing for C. H. Mason and David J. Young was John A. Jeter's lack of faith and unbelief concerning their experiences at the Azusa Street Revival. If he received anything at the revival, he most likely got a strong rebuke from C. P. Jones and W. S. Pleasant. At that point, he had to decide whether he would believe in his experience or listen to them. He chose the latter. His decision to reject what he saw and experienced at the Azusa Street Revival later caused a lot of trouble for Mason and the other preachers who believed in their Pentecostal conversion.

Sent to the Penitentiary

Dissemination from the ranks of supporters and followers of Charles P. Jones to follow C. H. Mason proved to be very "disastrous" for the Recording Secretary of the convention, Elder Daniel G. Spearman. Elder Spearman was born in Nokomis, Montgomery County, Illinois, to Esow and Elizabeth Spearman in 1879. He was the youngest of three children. Elder Spearman was part of the Little Rock, Arkansas, affiliation of ministers under Elder Jeter and the Council of Holiness Meetings at Jackson, Mississippi. Charles P. Jones, John A. Jeter, and other supporters of their faction had Elder Spearman committed to the Brushy Mountain State Penitentiary in Morgan County, Tennessee, for following the Mason faction and getting under what Elder Charles P. Jones, called the "tongue" affair. They directly took out their angry and frustrations on Elder Spearman and made an example out of him. The false accusations made against Elder Spearman were that he had gone "crazy" seeking the tongue, and they had him sent to the Penitentiary from Memphis. How do you get a man committed to prison for speaking in tongues? My opinion is that they probably framed him and told the local and state officials that Elder Spearman had simply lost his mind while claiming to have "religion" and the "tongue." With several witnesses, it wouldn't have been difficult to get a black man that was speaking in tongues and claiming full sanctification in 1907 committed to prison. He was just another free laborer for the Brushy Mountain coal mines. Elder Spearman was about twenty-eight years old and a married man when he was locked away in prison for five years. After his release, he relocated to Atlanta, Georgia, and was working as a printer in a print shop although without his wife. [16]

A Sanctified Fight

Hot tempers continued to "boil" over from the after effects of the convention withdrawing the right hand of fellowship from C. H. Mason. Elder John Hicks was appointed to represent Tennessee as overseer in place of C.H. Mason after he was excommunicated from the group. Elder Hicks and Dr. Hart may have had a few words before leaving the convention since it was no secret that Elder Hart was allied with Mason. Dr. Hart had a short period of time to prepare himself and the church for what he probably realized was coming next. Dr. Hart was a powerful preacher and physically a fairly large man with an uncanny way with words. He knew there was going to be trouble; and it erupted on Sunday night, September 8, 1907, in Jackson, Tennessee, about ten days after Mason was excommunicated from the group and four days after Elder Mason called the "urgent" meeting at his church in Memphis. The *Christian Index* ran this story:

On last Sunday night in this city the Sanctified Church had quite a disturbance. **Dr. R. E. Hart** *is the pastor. There were several blows passed and the doctor was in the mix up. On Monday morning* **Dr. Hart**, *Hicks and a great many more who were in the melee were in the Mayor's office. They were fined and some were put under bond. It is said that Rev. Hicks had been elected pastor instead of* **Dr. Hart**. *The sanctified brethren have made frequent visits to the Mayor's office, and the worse has not yet come.* **Dr. Hart** *is a fighter whether sanctified or unsanctified and is hard to down. He has learned the new tongue while he has had the old tongue for many years.*

In the melee, we presume that both tongues found employment. Will sanctified people who are sinless fight? Can they strike a brother with a deadly weapon? There are some who have believed that the sinless saints are angels and can not fight. They should visit Jackson and see these pugilists. They have practiced their deception a long time and the mask has been removed. It was Abraham Lincoln who said; "You can fool some people all the time, and you can fool all the people some time, but you can not fool all the people all the time."

This hypocrisy practiced among these sanctified brethren is gradually being exposed. They are helping in a financial way to support the city courts. See! See! See! [17]

A Few "Brushes" With the Law

On Monday, the next day following the disturbance on September 8, 1907, an affidavit for arrest was issued on Dr. R. E. Hart. Augustus (Gus) Hicks, the brother of Elder John Hicks (newly appointed overseer of Tennessee by C. P. Jones), filed the complaint and made the statements. There were six persons subpoenaed as witnesses for the State against Dr. Hart. From the statements given, charges of disturbing public worship were brought against Dr. Hart that stated, "He did feloniously, willfully and unlawfully take possession by violence of the pulpit in the Church of God or the Colored Sanctified Church." He not being the pastor or having any privilege in said church." After having stood before the court and after all the statements and evidence were presented, the court was satisfied that the offence was committed and there were reasonable grounds to believe that Elder Hart was guilty of the charges. Dr. Hart denied all charges and asked for a trial; but since the Chancery Court Grand Jury was in session, the judge transferred the case to Circuit Court to be heard by the Grand Jury of that court. Madison County Circuit Court did hear the case and thirteen grand jurors found Dr. Hart guilty of unlawfully and willfully disturbing and disquieting an assemblage of persons meeting for the purpose of religious worship by noise, by profane discourse, and by rude, indecent, and improper conduct against the peace and dignity of the State. Dr. Hart couldn't make bond in the amount of $250 as required and was jailed. Elder John Hicks was not arrested, but a complaint was filed by Elder Hart and the State brought the same charges against Elder Hicks. He was found guilty by the Grand Jury in Circuit Court of the same charges. His brother, Gus Hicks, made his bond of $250 for him; and he was released from custody until trial.

The *Christian Index* eagerly took advantage of the opportunity to report the news concerning an embarrassment to their former pastor and the Sanctified Church by publishing all accounts of any disagreements and altercations that occurred between the sanctified church and Dr. Hart. It is certainly interesting to notice how that Dr. Hart and not Elder Mason became the first pastor and congregation that the Jones faction filed a lawsuit against. The following article was released through the *Index:*

> *A new chapter was added to the church row of the Madison Street Colored Church of God yesterday, when a writ of injunction was filed in the Chancery court by seven of the deacons and trustees of the church against **Rev. R. E. Hart**, the former pastor.*
>
> *Those praying the injunction are E. D. Chester, L. Fuqua, James Davis, Isaac Fry, Albert Mayo, Isham Coleman, and Gus Hicks.*
>
> *The bill alleges that **Rev. Hart**, as pastor, preached well to the church for more than a year past until about five months ago, when he commenced to preach what the deacons, trustees, and most of the members call false doctrine and heresy and contrary to the teaching of the church. The bill further alleges that the deacons and trustees met about six weeks ago and preferred charges against said **R. E. Hart** and turned him out of the church, and that the church ratified their action. They state that he still persists in trying to preach in the tent used as a church house, and that he attempted to preach there on Sunday night, September 8th, when several fights occurred. He still says he is going to preach hence this application for injunction to restrain him from taking part in the affairs of the church.*

*Judge Woods granted the application upon complainants executing bond or taking the pauper's oath. Bond was executed and the injunction served on **Rev. R. E. Hart**, who had announced his intention of preaching at the tent last night.* [18]

This was the last mention of Dr. Robert E. Hart found in the *Christian Index.* The rest of his years in ministry were spent in the Church of God in Christ, working beside Bishop Mason as a close legal advisor and confidant and helping structure the church during the formative years. From this point forward, Dr. Hart shall be referred to as Elder Hart.

Elders Gus and John Hicks: Members of the Jones Faction

Elder Gus Hicks in the beginning was part of the C. P. Jones, faction and fought Elder Hart's ministry all the way to court. After Mason's expulsion from the group, Elder C. P. Jones and Elder John Hicks had Elder Hart voted out of the church in Jackson, Tennessee, and replaced him with Elder Gus Hicks, John's brother. Elder Gus Hicks was very active in litigations against the Church of God in Christ in Jackson, Tennessee, during its formative years. Several years later he resigned his membership with the Church of Christ (Holiness) U. S. A. and joined COGIC, later becoming the pastor of Allen Avenue COGIC in Jackson, Tennessee, around 1932. [19]

It wasn't Elder John Hicks's first "brush" with the law. An affidavit and warrant was issued for his arrest on August 9, 1906, for accessory to commit murder in the 1st degree. The affidavit stated, "On or about the 31st day of July 1906, the offense of accessory to an attempted murder in the 1st degree was committed in said county, (Madison) and believes John Hicks guilty thereof; that the said John Hicks did feloniously, willfully, and unlawfully and premeditatedly conspire with, influence and encourage one Clyde Hicks, to lay in wait with a pistol and assault and shoot one Ben Gill with deadly intent, against the peace and dignity of the State." He made bond in the amount of $500 and was released until trial. [20] Apparently he didn't get a jail sentence from the charges. Clyde was Elder John Hicks's brother and was probably a sympathizer of the C. P. Jones faction.

Madison Street COGIC: Jackson, Tennessee

Elder Hart had the privilege of organizing and pastoring the first Black Pentecostal-Holiness church that he organized in Jackson, Tennessee around 1903. During this particular time he was also attending the Council of Churches Holiness Meeting, headquartered in Jackson, Mississippi, and was still a pastor in the CME Church. Elder Hart left the meeting after Mason was excommunicated in 1907, and he later attended the meeting Mason called in Memphis. After attending this meeting he later traveled to Jackson, Tennessee; and a few days later, he was voted out as pastor of the Church of God in Christ after an altercation with the deacons and some of the members of the Jones faction. According to Charles P. Jones, in a statement given in his deposition, he traveled from Mississippi to personally unseat Hart as pastor of the Church of God in Christ and install the new pastor. Elder Hart was replaced by Elder Augustus (Gus) Hicks, the brother of Elder John Hicks, the overseer of Tennessee that was appointed by Elder C. P. Jones in place of Elder Mason, after he was excommunicated. Elder Hart along with a few faithful followers were forced to start another congregation under the Mason faction, reorganized as the Church of God in Christ, adopted by the first meeting of the General Assembly of COGIC held in Memphis, September 4, 1907. Within a matter of months, Elder Hart was listed in the Jackson city directory in 1908 as pastor of the Church of God in Christ, located on the corner of Madison and Totten Streets.

C. H. Mason Faction
vs.
C. P. Jones Faction

Two years after the initial Hart and Hicks controversy in 1907, charges were filed, December 1, 1909, by the Trustees and pastor (Elder Hart) of the Church of God in Christ at Jackson, Tennessee, against the C. P. Jones faction of the Church of God in Christ. Those named in the suit for the plaintiffs (COGIC) were Jesse West, Si Witherspoon, Granville Hudson, Tom Miller, Walter Wright, Michael Holmes, Bonnie Lee, Fletcher Flake (a former member of Mason's church in Memphis), Buck Thomas, Jim Wilson, John Aaron, and R. E. Hart. Those named in the lawsuit as defendants and supporters of the Jones faction were Lark Fuqua, and Edward Chester. Several depositions were taken in the case from members of the Jones faction. Also, a subpoena was issued to the First

National Bank of Jackson; and a deposition was given by one of the bank officials in the case.

A decision by the Chancery Court of Madison County wasn't handed down until almost three years later on June 15, 1912, which stated:

> *Be it remember that this cause came to be heard before the Honorable E. L. Bullock, Chancellor etc. on this day upon the bill and answers of the defendants, exhibits and proof, when the Court was of the opinion that the defendants are justly indebted to the Complainants in the sum of $111.93 together with the sum of $20.07, interest thereon from the 22nd day of May 1909; but that the defendants the said Lark Fuqua and Edward Chester are primarily liable for said amount.*

> *It is therefore ordered, adjudged and decreed that the Complainants, Jesse West, Si Witherspoon, Tom Miller, Walter Wright, Michael Holmes, Buck Thomas, Fletcher Flake, and Bonnie Lee, as Trustees for the use and benefit of the congregation known as the Church of God in Christ, have and recover the sum of $132.00 and all the costs of this cause, to be collected in the first instant, if the same can be done, out of the defendants Lark Fuqua and Edward Chester, for which execution may issue.*

> *It is further ordered on motion of Biggs and Spragins that a lien is hereby declared upon said judgment in their favor for reasonable attorney's fees for services rendered in said cause.*

> *From which decree the defendant First National Bank prays an appeal to the next term of the Court of Civil Appeals at Jackson, Tenn., which is granted upon said bank giving bond and security as required by law and for satisfactory reasons and on appeal of said Bank it is given 30 days within which to give said Bond. The other defendants also pray an appeal from said decree and judgment which is granted upon their giving bond and security as required by law and they are given 30 days within which to give said bond or take the oath provided for poor persons; the appeal being granted in said court also.* [21]

Church of the Living God, Christian Workers for Fellowship

Bishop Mason was already preaching sanctification and holiness in Memphis; however, he was preaching without a specific building or church when an early associate of his, William M. Christian (1856-1928), moved from Texarkana, Arkansas, to Memphis around 1895 and established a holiness church on Winchester Road. A former Baptist preacher born in Panola City, Panola County,

Mississippi, to Oliver and Clarissa Christian, he was the founder of the Church of the Living God, Christian Workers for Fellowship, (CLGCWFF) organized at Wrightsville, Pulaski County, Arkansas, in 1889. In 1900, he was living with his wife Sarah and six children on Lula Avenue in Memphis. [22] The church was located at 159 Winchester Road.

The denomination managed to establish only three churches in Memphis up until his death; however, they did see a considerable amount of growth over the years in other locations. Elder Christian remained chief overseer and kept his resident in Memphis until his death on April 11, 1928, from arteriosclerosis; popularly called hardening of the arteries. [23]

Reverends C. J. Smith, W. E. Bowen, Edward Banks, Robert B. Burl, and Adam D. Cartmon were among several that served as pastors of the Church of the Living God congregations in Memphis, often referred to as the "Do Rights." Rev. C. J. Smith, for an unknown period of time, was manager of the denomination's official publication called the *Church Review*, edited and published at their headquarters on Woodlawn Avenue.

Elder Christian's son, William A. Christian, was employed by COGIC and might have later joined COGIC. At the 34th Holy Convocation in 1941, the Board of Elders made several recommendations during the board meeting. The last recommendation submitted was the following:

We recommend a Custodian for the Fifth Street Property of the Church of God in Christ to see after the upkeep of the property and report such financial revenue as may be available. We recommend Mr. W. A. Christian of Memphis, Tennessee; such reports to be made to the National Convocation. [24]

6

MASON'S INNER CIRCLE

Author's Note

With the exceptions of R. R. Booker, L. P. Adams, and I. S. Stafford, there are eight other saints mentioned in this chapter that were members of Bishop Mason's congregation in Memphis, Saints Home COGIC. These eight people are whom I refer to as Mason's "inner circle." They are referred to as his inner circle because they were the closest to him in the ministry, and they were trustworthy and faithful. Three of them stayed humble and were later the first men consecrated to the office of Bishop in COGIC. They were E. Morey Page, William M. Roberts, and Eddie R. Driver. Elder Roberts started out as a deacon, and Elder Page was elevated through hard work and dedication. Elder Driver joined the church having already served as a pastor in another denomination. Saint Samuel was elevated to Elder, then to National Evangelist, and later to pastor. Mother Coffey worked her way from a young convert and was later elevated to an evangelist, then to National Evangelist, and from there to Assistant Supervisor of Women, then to National Supervisor of Women. Mother Washington stayed faithful and was appointed Church Mother. Minister Hightower was elevated to elder and then State Overseer. Deacon Jackson Prophet was a tremendous help to the church and involved himself in many areas of the church. These godly men and women were the first generation leaders of our church whom God used to birth through them what he wanted to do in the earth. They all ran the race and endured to the end and were faithful to God and Bishop Mason. Their dedication and labor of love for the ministry helped organize and structure COGIC during the formative years.

By no account are these all of the men and women that could be classified as trustworthy and faithful to the work of the Lord under Bishop Mason. However, they were chosen because they began following Mason during his early ministry and were members of his first church in Memphis. I find it "amazingly" ironic that three of the members of Bishop Mason's church had names that complimented the ministry in such a unique manner as **Saint** Thomas Samuel, **Noah** Deberry, and Jackson I. J. **Prophet.** These men were faithful brothers in the ministry.

Randolph Robert Booker

Randolph R. Booker was born June of 1869 and was one of six children born to Randolph (Randell) and Malinda Booker of Aberdeen, Monroe County, Mississippi. His siblings were Grace Ann, Josephine, (Josie) Riley, Mary Louise, and Samuel. Like most black families living in the South in 1870, they were farmers; and when the children became of age, they too helped in the fields. Between 1871 and 1879, the family moved to Okolona, Chickasaw County, Mississippi, where they continued to farm. There is a possibility that the Booker family and Bishop William M. Roberts's family knew each other; since both families were living in Okolona at the same time. Elder Booker was about ten years older than Bishop Roberts.

By 1900, Randolph, or Randell as he was sometimes called, relocated to Lexington, Holmes County, Mississippi, where he probably heard C. H. Mason preaching the sanctification and holiness doctrine. After hearing the gospel preached, he was saved and became a follower of Mason. He then joined Mason's church and eventually was elevated to elder. He was not listed on the roster as an elder that was present at the Churches of God in Christ convention held at Jackson, Mississippi, in 1906 (which was published in the *Truth* periodical) but he could have been at the meeting held in 1907 when Mason had the right hand of fellowship withdrawn. Elder Booker has been named as one of the elders that answered Bishop Mason's urgent call for all ministers who believed in the sanctification doctrine to meet him in Memphis, September 4, 1907, at his church, Saints Home COGIC, on Wellington Street. Although few in number, this was the first meeting of the General Assembly of COGIC.

Elder Booker was probably the first to pastor a COGIC church in Memphis after C. H. Mason founded the Wellington Street Church. This can be validated by the 1905 Memphis city directory in which Elder Booker is listed as pastor of the Church of God located at the corner of Italian and White Avenue. This was the first listing for this particular church and it's possible the church was founded by Elder Booker as early as 1904 or before.

He married Carrie L. Person in 1908, and they moved to Jackson, Tennessee, where they labored in the work of the ministry under Elder Robert E. Hart. There is no evidence Elder Booker became the pastor of a church after moving to Jackson; however, he certainly would have been a minister on staff at Elder Hart's church. They lived in South Jackson at 321 Institute Street, a very popular and thriving African-American section of town. Living with them in 1910, was their adopted son, Oscar E. P. Thomas, who was four years old and three of his sisters-in-law, Georgia, Hattie, and Farrah Person, and a niece, Emma Person. All of his sisters-in-laws did laundry except Georgia, and she was a cook.

Elder Booker resided in Jackson a few years, receiving training and helping Elder Hart. Bishop Mason later appointed him Overseer of Missouri, and he and his family relocated to St. Louis. He was later appointed Overseer of Kentucky where he served most of his years. After the death of Elder Hart in 1921, Bishop Mason sent Elder Booker back to Jackson as interim pastor until someone could be appointed. During that time, he resided near midtown at 227 E. King Street. Elder Booker was familiar with the ministry, having labored there several years earlier.

By 1930, Elder Booker relocated to Indianapolis, Indiana; and was renting a house at 2809 Shriver Avenue. He and his wife were now living alone; and although he was living in Indiana, he was still Overseer of Kentucky. Elder Booker was a strong leader and a tremendous gospel preacher.

Ector Morey Page

I find it intriguing that several years of Elder Page life was spent in my hometown of Jackson, Tennessee. He was listed in the phone directory, which illustrated his employer as well as his home address. While living in Jackson, he resided at different times on two very popular streets in the community. In 1896, he lived at 317 Beasley Street in South Jackson; and in 1900, at 624 Highland Avenue, several blocks north of Beasley Street near downtown in an all white neighborhood. He probably was a member of Bethel AME Church, located on Cumberland Street in the city, since he was a member of the African Methodist Episcopal denomination before leaving Mississippi. His pastor in Jackson would have been

Rev. Charles G. Diggs; and it's possible he was present when Rev. Diggs was the guest revivalist for Dr. Hart shortly after Dr. Hart was appointed pastor of Mother Liberty CME Church in 1899.

Elder Page moved to Memphis in 1903 and joined Bishop Mason's church around 1905; afterwards he was baptized with the Holy Ghost in 1907. Elder Page's wife, Mollie and his daughters Ruthie and Ruby were part of the approximately 150 member church. Elder Page was one of Bishop Mason's faithful members at Saints Home COGIC that later received a prominent but "extremely" challenging appointment in the Church of God in Christ. With the assistance of Elder Page, the progress of the Church of God in Christ during the formative years greatly increased, especially in Oklahoma and Texas where he was appointed overseer.

The life and work of Elder E. Morey Page was written by him and submitted to be recompiled in 1924 along with other biographies that were republished and copyrighted in 1977 by Rev. T. L. Delaney in the book, *The History and Life Work of Elder C. H. Mason, Chief Apostle and His Co-laborers from 1893 to 1924.* This is his story and testimony:

I was born in Yazoo County, Miss., May 19, 1871. I stayed on the farm until I was twenty-three. My father's name is Richard Page and my mother's is Polly Ann Page. I was converted in 1884 or 1885. At this time neither of my parents was converted. Yet they always taught us to pray night and morning, go to Sabbath school and also to go to church. I belonged to Union Paradise A. M. E., church in Yazoo County, Miss. Elder Mose Bailey was pastor. Not hearing a full gospel I soon realized that I had backslidden from God. I often wondered why the joy and happiness that I once possessed had vanished.

Being the oldest boy, I had to work on the farm, and I was deprived of my education. In 1894, I left Mississippi and went to Jackson, Tenn., where I lived until 1903. When I arrived in Jackson I knew no one, and had but a few dollars. I got a cab and went to Mr. Lancaster's boarding house on South Liberty St., where I spent one night. The next day I walked up town where I met a man by the name of Jeff Robinson, who lived on North Royal Street. As I talked with him I found that one of my playmates from Mississippi had roomed with him while attending Lane College. He said "Come go home with me, if you are a friend of Hilliard's you are mine, too." I went home with him and met his sweet little family. He made me so welcome that I said, "I have only a few dollars, but I will pay you when I get work." He said, "Eat *every time the table is set, money or no money." That made me feel good. In my feeble understanding, I thanked the Lord. I knew it was His hand. This was during the great Pullman strike. Work was scarce, so I hired to Mr. Robinson to work his truck farm for $10 a month and board. I worked seven months, at the end of which he owed me sixty dollars.*

On October 18, 1894, I secured a permanent job in the Illinois Central Railroad shop. I soon worked myself up to car inspector and repairer. My record today in service for that company is without mark against me.

In 1902 God stirred my soul to pray. I served as an officer in the A. M. E., for years, but my soul desired a greater and deeper experience. I prayed and sought the Lord. He showed me a vision. I saw a man and a woman coming from the east with a Bible in his hand. He said: "I'm Preaching the ever lasting gospel," and took his hand down. In a short time a man and his wife came to Jackson and preached Holiness in front of my door. I believed it from the first. In October 1902, I received the experience of sanctification. This Bro. Milan preached a clean life, divine healing, but not the full gospel. But it was so much richer than any I had ever heard, I accepted it. In 1903 I went to Memphis, Tenn., were I met precious Elder C. H. Mason. His teaching was quite different from what I had heard. Bro. Milam did not believe in water baptism, sacrament nor foot washing. In fact, he did not believe in any ordinances of the Bible. I shall not forget the first sermon I heard Bro. Mason preach on Virginia Ave., Memphis, Tenn. His text was, "He has translated us into the kingdom of His dear Son." It seemed like heaven had come down to us. In 1907 the Lord baptized me with the Holy Ghost and fire. Amen. Before I received the baptism I realized my call to the ministry, and when He baptized me my heart was made willing, and I said yes to God.

In 1911 I left the job that paid a good salary to preach the gospel. I could not see how I could support my family and five children, but I took God by faith. I preached in Mississippi for days and weeks with no income. I met with all the discouragement a young minister could meet with, but God bade me press on. Sometimes my brethren said to me, "Bro. Page, you had better get a job and go to work and take care of your family." That would hurt my heart. I would ask the Lord, "What shall I do?" My trousers were worn and patched, my shoes had holes in them, and my family was in need. God moved on the hearts of some one and they sent me eight dollars, which I sent to my wife. I prayed and waited on God until He turned the hearts of the people. They began to bless me and to supply my needs. I had the test of my life in the beginning of my ministry. My life was threatened and I was shot at, but the Lord wonderfully took care of me.

In January, 1914, I was called to Texas to take charge of the work at Dallas, which was in a backslidden state, being without proper attention. In July met my first state convocation in Texas, which was in Houston. This meeting was quite a coming together of the Lord's people. The spirit, through our chief apostle, appointed me as State Overseer. Thank God, I can say I have not caused him to regret the appointment. These five years I have endeavored to prove my works. In 1914, we had twenty-five missions in the state and not one church house in the whole state that was worth anything. In five years we had about eighty churches and missions and about thirty-five or more creditable churches. The church property at Dallas and Houston is worth $20,000. All glory to our blessed Christ. Pray for Brother Page, that I may keep in the center of His will. [1]

Elder Page was the typical COGIC communicant in the early years, meaning that he was from the South, lived on a farm and came from a very large family (in his case, a family of fourteen). His mother gave birth to sixteen children; however, she lost two. His last job was one in which he worked for the railroad in Memphis; and by faith, he resigned and went into full-time ministry. His hard work, dedication to God, and a desire not to disappoint Elder Mason were the reasons behind his promotion from a lay member to elder, then to state overseer, and from there to the bishopric. What a wonderful testimony to the glory of God!

In 1933, he and four other overseers were the first to be consecrated to the office of bishop in COGIC. He had been a member of COGIC about twenty-eight years. In 1944, the General Assembly of COGIC held a Memorial Service at the 37th National Holy Convocation in honor of Bishops E. Morey Page, Edward R. Driver, and several of the saints who had passed away that year.

Saint Thomas Samuel

Saint Thomas Samuel's parents had to have been saved to have given their son such a name. He was born to Daniel and Martha Samuel of Memphis, Shelby County, Tennessee, in August 1879. His father was born a slave in North Carolina in 1834, and his mother was born in Mississippi in 1841. He was the youngest of eight children. His siblings were Cherry, Henry, Ada, James, Francis, Margaret, and John. He was twenty years old when he married Hattie Ayres in 1897, and she was nineteen. In 1900, Samuel worked as a porter, and Hattie was a housewife. They rented a house on Broadway Street in Memphis. Mary Parker, a twelve year old boarder, lived with them and went to school.

Elder Samuel was an affiliate minister with the Churches of God in Christ, headquartered in Jackson, Mississippi, before Mason was excommunicated from the group. He was ministering in Mississippi; and after Mason's expulsion from the group, he allied with Elder Mason and went back to Tennessee and joined Elder Mason's church on Wellington Street. He was one of the ministers on staff at the church. His signature was on the roster that was circulated throughout the church, demonstrating his support for Mason to remain as pastor of the congregation during the Jones-Mason conflict. When the first court papers were filed in 1907 marking the beginning of a legal battle between the Jones and Mason factions, Elder Samuel was automatically named as one of the defendants in the case because he was an officer of the church.

Elder Samuel was captured in a rare group photograph taken on the steps of a COGIC church believed to be the second Saints Home COGIC constructed by Bishop Mason in Memphis. In the photograph was C. H. Mason, David J. Young, Randolph R. Booker, Ector Morey Page, W. B. Holt, William M. Roberts, Justus B. Bowe, Richard H. Isaac Clark, Edward (Eddie) R. Driver, Charles H. Pleas, John H. Boone, and Robert Eber Hart, just to name a few of the "worshippers" and "praisers" that shook the early church. What I noticed in the background of the photograph was a brick church. Which COGIC congregation in Tennessee might have been the first to erect a brick edifice? The Wellington Street church was the first to be erected, but it was a frame structure. Elder Hart was in the photograph, which means it was taken before his demise in 1921. According to Bishop Charles H. Pleas, in his history of COGIC written in 1956, the Wellington Street church became too small and was torn down and replaced with a new brick structure, which means Saints Home COGIC was likely the first brick church constructed by the denomination in Tennessee.

In the late 1910's or early 1920's Elder Samuel was elevated to Traveling Evangelist in COGIC and he was the first to head the Department of Evangelism in COGIC. He was mightily used of God. Bishop Mason sent him to Virginia, South and North Carolina, and other places mainly up and down the East Coast to evangelize and use his gift of healing. He would often carry his trumpet under his arm to church and blow it in Zion when the service was filled with God's presence. Elder Samuel was later appointed and served as pastor in the 1930's of

Lane Avenue COGIC in Memphis, where Elia V. Sparks was the church mother and editor of *The Whole Truth*, the official publication of COGIC. During this time, Pastor Samuel and his wife resided at 820 Alma Street in Memphis.

In 1934, at the age of fifty-eight, Elder Samuel became seriously ill. A notice appeared on the front page of *The Whole Truth*, asking the saints to fast and pray for three days that God would heal his body.

Jackson I. J. Prophet

Jackson (Jack) I. J. Prophet was "performing the duties of a deacon before he was actually appointed to the position." Those were his words describing the position he held at Saints Home COGIC on Wellington Street to a lawyer during the taking of his deposition in 1908. He was a student at Lane College in Jackson, Tennessee, before moving to Memphis in 1900. [2] He reported in the 1900 census that he was twenty-five years old and was born in Tennessee, November of 1874, and was single. Between 1900 and 1910, he married, but later was reported to be a widower in the 1910 census. He rented a room from church member, Lula Walker, at 566 Wicks Avenue but moved around 1910 and rented a room from sixty-five year old Fannie Webster at 424 East Butler Avenue in Memphis.

When Bishop Mason and the church were in litigation with the C. P. Jones faction, Deacon Prophet was one of the defendants in the case. He signed the supplemental answer of depositions for all the defendants in the case, Avant vs. Mason, March 4, 1908, and was questioned "extensively" during the taking of depositions in the case. The most significant statement made during his deposition in the case was, "There were some who had spoken in tongues before (Mason returned from California) that time, but not as many as there are now." When the case was appealed to the Tennessee Supreme Court, his name along with others was on the Appeal Bond.

His occupation was mainly a gardener and yard man for private residences, and he sole "junk" as a supplement to his regular income. Deacon Prophet stated in 1908 that he had no family; the saints were his only family.

Noah Deberry

Noah and his wife, Josie, were born in Tennessee; however, he had no idea of his age or where his mother and father were from. Josie was twenty-three years old in 1900, and they were the parents of one child, Aline, (possibly misspelled) their two year old son. They were members of Saints Home COGIC on Wellington Street. Noah was one of the ministers on staff at the church.

Elder Deberry changed jobs about every two years for a while. In 1895, he worked as a porter for the George H. Monsarrat Company, a wholesale flour and molasses business on Main Street. In 1897, he went to work for Gladden Lumber Company; in 1899, he went to work for John M. Hays & Company, a cotton warehouse. By 1900, he was working for himself as a "huckster" and selling merchandise out of his wagon. He was successful enough from working hard and running his own business that he was able to support his wife and purchase a house on Ingle Avenue in Memphis.

Elder Deberry was one of the officers from Saints Home COGIC named in the lawsuit filed by the C.P. Jones faction; however, at the time the lawsuit was filed, they didn't realize Elder Deberry had passed away. Prior to Elder Deberry's death, his wife was unemployed and a housewife. After his death in 1907, she began taking in laundry at home to support herself and Aline. I assume they remained members of Saints Home COGIC.

William M. Roberts

William (Willie) M. Roberts was born May of 1876 to Willis and Lydia Roberts. His father was born in Mississippi, January of 1843, and his mother in Virginia, January of 1850. In 1870, the family lived in Aberdeen, Monroe County, Mississippi, where Willis farmed and Lydia kept house. There were only two children then: Billy was seven years old and Austin was three. Between 1870 and 1880, they moved to North Okolona, Chickasaw County, Mississippi, where William was probably born and his siblings were Austin, Andrew, Johnny and an adult half-brother, Caledonia, lived with them. Caledonia was Willis's son and all of the Roberts' children were boys.

By 1900, Willis and Lydia Roberts and their son William and his wife Mamie moved near Tupelo, Lee County, Mississippi, and lived only two doors apart.

William and Mamie married in January of 1900, and he and his father owned the houses in which they lived. Like most black families living in the south, they farmed.

William and Mamie moved to Memphis, Tennessee, around 1901. He worked as a teamster until he went into business for himself. In 1900, a teamster was one who drove a wagon with one or more teams of horses pulling a load of merchandise from one point to another, similar today the way modern day tractor trailers serve our society. He owned his own wagon and later used his teamster's experience to start a grocery business out of their home at 623 E. Stephens Avenue. Mamie and the girls probably managed the store while he made wholesale purchases and deliveries for the store and to customers. Their business was advertised in the Memphis City Directory under "Groceries Listings" in 1907 and 1908. William later worked as a "huckster" after starting their own business instead of as a teamster, which allowed him to negotiate his own prices and sell his products directly from his wagon.

The Roberts joined Saints Home COGIC on Wellington Street in 1903, and he was appointed a deacon in 1904 when he was about twenty-eight years old. He was later appointed a trustee in 1907. On December 12th of the same year, Bishop Mason laid hands on him, and he received the Holy Ghost with the evidence of speaking in tongues.

William and Mamie made up for what his parents couldn't have—Girls! From 1901 to 1910, they had six girls. The youngest was three months old when Mamie was only twenty-eight, which meant she was still young enough to have more babies and she did. His sister-in-law, Katie Roberts, who was likely the widow of Austin, his oldest brother, lived next door to William in 1900 while they were living near Tupelo. She moved to Memphis in 1901 upon the invitation from her brother William. She accepted and joined Saints Home COGIC with their two children, Julia and John Holt Roberts.

In 1910, William and Mamie had church members as neighbors on both sides of them at their Stephens Avenue residence. Living at 621 Stephens were General (Jim) and Julia Lowry. He owned his wagon and hauled coal for a living. Julia was a member of the church before him and he joined in 1901. He was appointed a trustee at Saints Home COGIC in 1907. Part of his testimony was that he was "saved" and "sanctified" under the tent! On the other side of the Roberts' family at 625 Stephens were Arthur Washington and his family. He owned his wagon and was an express man for Gayoso Oil (cooking oil) Works Company. His twenty-three year old brother, John, lived with them. He worked for the railroad. He was also a member of Saints Home COGIC. Several houses down living on the same side of the street were the residence of Bishop and Lelia Mason at 609 Stephens Avenue. Indiana Washington, the mother of Lelia, was living with them, and they all moved to Lexington, Mississippi, in 1908.

In 1917, Bishop Mason answered another call that came from then evangelist Lillian Coffey of Chicago to send a preacher to teach and preach the Word. Elder William Roberts was sent by Bishop Mason. He moved from Memphis to Chicago and rented a house on East 36th Street with his wife and nine children. All of the children except the youngest two were born in Tennessee. Their son Robert Mason was the seventh child born and was named after Bishop Mason, which is significant because it shows the love, devotion, and respect they had for him. There were twelve children in all born to Elder William M. and Mamie R. Roberts. After the demise of Bishop William Roberts, his son Isaiah Roberts became pastor of the church.

When Elder Roberts arrived in Chicago in 1917, it took only two years to establish the first state convocation held in 1919. To celebrate their twentieth anniversary in 1939, they planned and expected a grand time because their state motto was "It Can Be Done." A notice was sent out informing and inviting the people to come to:

The 20th Annual Convocation of the Churches of God in Christ of the State of Illinois convening at 4021 South State Street, Chicago, Illinois, August 11-20, 1939.

Sanctify ye a fast, call a solemn assembly, gather the Elders and all the inhabitants of the land into the house of the Lord your God, and cry unto the Lord. Joel 1:14.

We are expecting a grand and glorious time. First two days fasting and praying. Senior Bishop Charles H. Mason and associate Bishops, Overseers, Superintendents, Elders, State Mothers, Missionaries, and Workers of neighboring states are expected to be with us. Bring the sick for healing. Let the sinners come. Jesus loves you.

All Pastors, Elders, and Workers of this State will help to make this meeting a great success by cooperating with our Bishop in attendance and finance, as well as the spiritual service. Good Music, Gospel Singers, Talented Speakers, and Singers will feature this meeting. [3]

Before approximately ten thousand communicants at the 26th Holy Convocation held in Memphis in 1933, Bishop Mason consecrated William M. Roberts to the office of Bishop by the laying on of hands and praying for him and four other state overseers as they sat before him and the convention. Overseers Isaac S. Stafford, Riley F. Williams, Ector Morey Page, and Ozro T. Jones, Sr., were also consecrated. We know that the legacy and memories of the Bishop William M. Roberts lives on today from the words of our late Presiding Bishop, Gilbert E. Patterson, when he recalled these precious memories at the 97th International Holy Convocation:

Yes, the editorial staff of The Whole Truth is standing in full support of Presiding Bishop G. E. Patterson and is embracing his theme for the year and the 97th International Holy Convocation as the publication's official salutation. After all, it would be an overt act of disrespect for COGIC's official news source not to endorse an official act of its publisher. At the 2004 Leadership Conference our Chief Apostle revealed that God had indeed given him the declaration of Let Peace Continue [Ephesians 4:3] as the Church's official theme for 2004 and the 97th Annual International Holy Convocation.

In making the announcement, the Presiding Bishop recalled how the late Bishop W. M. Roberts of Chicago would salute his members with the greeting: "Peace Be Unto The Saints." The congregation then would reply, "Peace Be Multiplied." The recollection of this moving event spurred his inspiration for the theme: Let Peace Continue. [4]

Eddie R. Driver, Sr.

He was born Edward Robert Driver to Robert and Amanda Driver of Nesbitts Station, Desoto County, Mississippi, in 1869; and he was the second child born of eleven children. His siblings in 1880 were William, nineteen years old; Martin was nine; Mary was seven; Ezekiel was five; Lizzie was three and Robert was one year old. After 1880, four more children were born. They were Georgia, Anna, Bruce, and Lorie. In 1900, Robert and Amanda had been married thirty-one years. He had farmed all his life and she had been a housewife.

Driver graduated from LeMoyne Normal School in Memphis, Tennessee, and returned to his hometown to teach school. He married Annie Smith in 1890 and returned to LeMoyne to study law. In 1892, he was permitted to practice general and corporation law in Memphis, Tennessee. In 1893, he accepted the call to preach. He was licensed and became a pastor in 1894. He pastured Salem Baptist Church of Memphis, Tennessee, until 1896. [5]

Edward and Annie moved to Memphis in December of 1891 and rented a house at 165 Kirk Avenue. Their first child, Foster, was born in 1896; the second son, Louie, was born in 1900; their third son, Mason Charles (named after C. H. Mason) was born in 1903; their fourth son, Russell, was born in 1908; and a fifth son, Edward Jr., was born in 1912. They lost their son Russell, sometime between 1911 and 1920. He wasn't enumerated with the family when the U. S. Federal Census was taken in 1920 after they moved to California.

It was June of 1901, when Elder Driver and his family joined Saints Home COGIC on Wellington Street in Memphis as he told it in his own words during the taking of a deposition in 1908. He was drawn to the "powerful" preaching and teaching ministry of Bishop Mason, which drew him out of the Baptist denomination. Already having been a pastor, it wasn't long before he was appointed a church under the Churches of God in Christ, headquartered in Jackson, Mississippi, where C. P. Jones was the chairman. His churches in 1908 were located in Hazlehurst, Copiah County, Mississippi, about forty miles south of Jackson, Mississippi and West Point, Clay County, Mississippi, over 200 miles from each other. He also had a small charge in St. Peters, Mississippi. Elder David J. Young later took over his church at West Point, Mississippi.

He was a strong confidant and supporter of Mason's doctrine even after they excommunicated Mason from the Churches of God in Christ Convention in 1906. The members that were part of the Jones faction during and after the trial of Mason were warned about the austere behavior of the "sharp-tongued" intellectual that could stand his ground spiritually on the doctrine of Jesus Christ. It was during this time of stress and pressures from the ministry that Elder Driver lost his mother, Amanda, or Mandy, as she was sometimes called. She was only about 54 years old and her youngest child, Lovie was only eleven years old when she died.

Elder Driver was asked my Mason in 1914 to answer a call coming out of California for a preacher to come and organize a group of praying women in an Apostolic Mission into a church body. He agreed to go; and just one year later in 1915, they had organized the first Church of God in Christ on the West Coast. The church was named after Bishop Mason's church in Memphis, Saints Home

COGIC. At the 1916 California Holy Convocation, Bishop Mason appointed him State Overseer and his wife Annie, as State Mother. Elder Driver was probably the first preacher in COGIC to receive such an assignment in a major metropolitan area like Los Angeles.

In 1920, the Driver family was renting at 1527 East 22nd Street in Los Angeles; and Foster, their oldest son, was twenty-three years old, owned his own grocery business, and was attending college. The other boys were still in school, and Louie, the second oldest, had just finished high school but was not yet publicly employed. Sometime between 1920 and 1930, Annie's eighty-year old widowed mother, Sarah Smith, came from Tennessee to live with them.

We knew that Elder Driver was of mixed ancestry, but it wasn't until the U. S. Federal Census in 1930 that he felt comfortable revealing that his father was from India. It probably was the southern climate of "prejudices" and "racism" that deterred him from revealing it earlier. His son Eddie, Jr., was twenty-two in 1930, and probably caused his father to be a little concerned with his choice of a career and employment as a musician in a nightclub. Foster, the oldest of the boys, had been attending a pharmacy college, and had graduated, and was now employed as a pharmacist in a drug store. Louie married Myrtle in 1922 when he was twenty-three and she was eighteen. He and his wife rented the upstairs apartment from his father for $25 a month. He was employed by the U. S. Postal Service as a mail carrier. In 1924, Louie, Jr., was born, making Elder Driver a grandfather. Mason Charles had married a good looking "chick" from Louisiana named Virginia. They also rented an upstairs apartment from his father for $25 a month. Mason was employed as a professional tailor at a tailor shop and his wife stayed home.

Louie Driver followed in his father's footsteps and was called to the ministry. He pastored his father's church in Los Angeles after his father died and was very active in COGIC long before his father's demise. He was very active during the general assembly meetings and on various committees in which the Board of Elders would appoint him.

Edward Driver, Jr., passed away March of 1973; Mason Charles passed November 15, 1983, and Louie Driver died October of 1975. Foster Driver's date of death couldn't be determined at this writing.

Lillian Brooks-Coffey and Family

Lillian was born to Jeremiah (Jerry) and Lula Brooks in Memphis, Shelby County, Tennessee in March of 1891. [6] Jerry was born in Fosters, Tuscaloosa, County, Alabama, August of 1859, to parents unknown at this time; but at ten years old, he was living and working as a farm hand in the household of Martha Adams and her two children in Fosters. Ten years later in 1880, Jerry some how made his way to Memphis and was working on a farm in the fifth district of Shelby County at age nineteen.

Lula was born in September of 1871, to Jack and Millie Miller of Concordia, Bolivar County, Mississippi. Jack and Millie owned their property which was valued at $1,000. Lula's siblings were Polly, Sallie, and John. Her father was born in Texas in 1835 and her mother was born in Virginia in 1845.

How and when Jerry and Lula met is unknown, but they married in 1888, and Lillian was born in 1891. They lived at 226 Pontotoc Street in Memphis in 1892; and at the time, Lula was "taking in laundry," and Jerry was training as a plumber with Edward McGowan Plumbing Company. This was about the same time the "Curve" murders occurred in Memphis that almost pushed the black community to the brink of rioting. It just so happened, during all this rivalry, living down the street from the Brooks' family at 94 Pontotoc Street was William Joseph Seymour, the twentieth century Azusa Street Revivalist. I will talk more about the "Curve" murders and Seymour in another chapter.

In 1895, Jerry and Lula may have experienced some marital problems since Lula and Lillian were listed as living at 352 Beal Street in 1896, and Jeremiah (Jerry) was listed as living on Monroe Street. Also, in June of 1895, Lula gave birth to Morris, their only son. Apparently by 1897, they had worked their problems out and found another place to live and were reunited. Moving to a new location brought a new change in their lives when they rented a house at 309 Wellington Street across the street from where Bishop Mason's church tent was erected on a lot in which the congregation would eventual purchase and build their church, Saints Home COGIC. Jerry switched jobs around this time and eventually started working for E. L. Rawlings and Tisdale Plumbing Company.

In March of 1900, Lula gave birth to Elise, their last child. From 1888 to 1900, Lula had six pregnancies, but only three children survived. Failed pregnancies were not uncommon during this period of time for women to experience due to so few or no doctor visits and the inability to pay for good medical care among other reasons.

Mother Coffey stated that she got saved under Bishop Mason's ministry in 1907 when she was sixteen. She and her mother could have joined the church anytime between 1897 and 1907; but according to Mother Coffey's accounts, it was likely around 1900. In 1963, Mother Coffey gave her personal account and history called, "This Is My Story," and this is what she wrote:

Greetings to the sainted family of God everywhere, especially to those of you who share with me many days of our beloved Bishop Mason's Ministry.

It is with great joy that again I bring to your attention a few facts that I observed of him from my early childhood and all through my life.

My first remembrance of Bishop Charles Harrison Mason was when I was a "wee little girl." He was invited (as I was told in later years) into our home by my Grandfather who was a Baptist Minister. He had previously met Brother Mason (as he was then called) in Arkansas.

Bishop Mason started his Church in Memphis and when they wanted a Sunday School in their Church Tent just across the street from where we were living at 329 South Wellington-I, along with other neighborhood children was carried to the services.

I liked the singing and soon learned to sing the songs in my childlike manner. I remember them singing "Jesus is a rock in a weary land," and I thought they were saying "Jesus is a rocking in the weary land." I did not know who Jesus was and did not understand anything about it. But Brother Mason (which was a popular name to be called at that time) would take up so much time with me and the other children in the home. I was always glad when he visited.

As time went on after the establishment of the Sunday School, Brother Mason came in one Sunday morning and taught us about Jesus in a childlike manner. He told us stories about Jesus as a little boy, how He would make little things like the other boys, but how Jesus' little things would move around and do differently from the things of other little boys making. He told us how Jesus loved His playmates. How He would pick them up and wipe their tears from their eyes when they got hurt. He talked on and on when he got to the part of the story where Jesus grew up and when He became a man His friends killed Him. I felt so sorry in my heart that friends would do good Jesus that way.

As he taught, my little heart was touched. I began crying and said to Brother Mason, "I won't do Him like that; I want Him to love me."

That morning the Lord touched my little tender heart and saved me. I have been in this Church under Bishop Mason ever since. As I grew, he carried me into Lexington every summer to help Sister Mason with the babies; Alice, Baby Sister as we called her; Mary, who passed and Tiny, who is now Mrs. Lelia Bias, manager of the Cafeteria in our National Dining Room (Diets).

I was happy to take my vacation in their home. As I grew older and he preached, as I grew in knowledge, I traveled on the road with Brother Mason and older Sisters. I sang and read the Bible as he preached, as we always did in those days. He influenced me and saw to it that I read through the Bible once every year. It was hard reading with all my school work to do but he had me do this eleven times (11 times). I had to continue this even after I was out of school. Yes, I was reading the Word of God which I loved so dearly. He exhorted me to live by the Word, he explained the Word to me never too busy to take time with me. He was loving and tender with me, and seldom scolded me because I always tried to please him in everything.

When my parents died he became my earthly Father. He inquired persistently and was interested to know how I was getting along, for they left some young children behind to be reared which I brought to the big city of Chicago.

I was blessed to sit for hours under his tutorship. I worked as a secretary in his office for twenty-one years (21 years). Part of the time I assisted Sister Jessie Strickland who then the Financial Secretary. I held that office until I was made National Mother.

He knew I was interested in his welfare and the welfare of his family. He would tell me about the Work and during those days he would not allow me to be too idle. He often had me reading the Bible even while he slept in the office. I would complain at times, for as other youngsters, I wanted to go down into the basement and laugh and talk with the folks. He would often say to me, "Watch yourself for your future … some day you will lead the Women of this Church, and anything you do now will count heavily against your leadership. Now I cannot say I was always too willing to obey, for I was young and full of life, but I put aside my will and heard what Bishop Mason had to say.

He forbade my remarrying and told me it would slap me in the face when I wanted to teach God's Pure Word. This I often wondered about, but he said do it and remain as I was, so I remained single until this day. I do not regret that I obeyed Bishop Mason in that I had the privilege of following him all the way through the Church. He was my Pastor long before he received the Baptism of the Holy Ghost. I believed every word he said! I believed in his Administration! I accepted all of it and it became a part of me.

I stood by in those hours when he was slowly leaving us and prayed out of my broken heart for God to leave this Great Man with us. One whom I had seen Prophesy and his Prophesies came to pass. Long before radio and television was known of, he told us that we would stand here and be heard and seen to the ends of the world. He took his odd roots and eggs and other things of nature and got great Revelations from them. Yes, and in addition to all this, he sang thousands of songs. Oh, if we had only had ears to hear and have written his songs. It seemed that we did not realize that he would leave us some day. He counseled as no other man I have ever heard. Few of his sons left the Church under his administration. I have seen him go in where there was Great Confusion, and pray for hours and hours. When he got up, the trouble was ALL OVER! HE LOVED HIS SONS AND DAUGHTERS! He always kept some of his Daughters near him and would let Women of God WORK in the Church and make use of our God given talents.

I have missed that Sweet Communion, and OH THESE YEARS HAVE BEEN YEARS OF YEARS FOR ME! IT WAS FROM HIS MOUTH THAT I GOT MY ORDER OF THE DAY!

As I consider his advice; his instructions; his great love; his humility; his peaceable disposition; his kindness to everyone; his loving smile; his readiness to help at any time of need regardless of race or creed; his ever reaching out for souls; his concern about the needy; I pray that his Spirit will be emulated in these he has left behind to lead us!

Now that we have another Senior Bishop, let's respect, love, obey, and follow him! We all know him. He is a God Man Worthy of the Promotion. Remember the Golden Rule. Lillian Brooks Coffey, International Supervisor [7]

There is no evidence that Lillian Coffey's father was ever a member of the church. A roster of all the members of the church was required in 1908 during the legal battle between the church and the C. P. Jones faction; however, Jerry Brooks name wasn't on the list. Lillian's mother, Lula Brooks, was on the list, but Lillian's wasn't; however, it wasn't uncommon for the children names to be missing from the list because they were minors.

Between 1903 and 1907, Jerry moved two or three times, possibly with or without Lula and the rest of the family. He lost or changed his job with the plumbing company around 1908 and went to work in a lumberyard. If there were problems and separations in the family, they always seemed to have worked them out.

In 1913, Lillian and Morris rented a room from Laura Burton down the street from the church at 375 S. Wellington, where church member Rebecca Carroll lived up stairs. This was about the same time their father's health rapidly deteriorated. In December of 1913, Jerry Brooks suffered an attack of paralysis agitans (similar to Parkinson disease). His condition began to deteriorate further; and on May 27, 1914, the doctor was called, but he died on May 30 at 4:00 pm. He was treated by Dr. James W. Hose, a black physician and a native son of Memphis, who was an instructor in Physical Diagnosis on the faculty at the University of West Tennessee Medical College. The predominately African-American medical college moved from Jackson, Tennessee, to Memphis in 1907. Dr. Hose was one of several that graduated in 1908 after the school relocated to Memphis. If Jerry was hospitalized it would likely have been in the Negro Baptist Hospital, Collins Chapel Hospital, University of West Tennessee Hospital, or the Hairston Hospital. These were all black-managed health facilities.

Jerry was fifty-four years old and had been married twenty-six years at the time of his demise. They were living at 403 South Howe Alley when he died, and Lula was the informant on the death certificate. He was buried in Zion Cemetery, May 31, 1914, with Barnett and Lewis Funeral Directors of Memphis in charge. [8] After the death of her husband, Lula moved to Water Valley, Yalobusha County, Mississippi, and lived there for about three or four years, returning to Memphis around 1920. Between 1920 and 1925, she continued to "take in laundry" and do private duty housework for wages.

On October 14, 1924, Lula was hospitalized at Memphis General Hospital for abdominal pain and was treated by Dr. J. C. Beard. Three months and eight days later on January 22, 1925, Lula passed away at 8:15 pm from complications due to her illness. According to her death certificate she apparently remained hospitalized throughout the sixty-eight day illness and her medical certificate of death stated that the cause of death was fibroma of the uterus. [9] Taking in consideration the time she spent in the hospital, she probably had surgery and died from complications of surgery and her disease.

Daniel Marker, a hospital employee was the informant on her death certificate, which suggests two things: Lula had shared some personal information about herself and family which only close family members would know; secondly, the information could have been requested and documented because she wasn't expected to live. There were no relatives available to give the information required on the death certificate. Lillian, Elise, and Morris were in Chicago; and possibly due to inclement weather conditions, or other reasons were not able to travel; and her husband was deceased. Her last given address was 414 S. Wellington where she lived with Gertrude Jones, possibly a relative or friend. This was just a few doors up from where she first lived when they moved on Wellington Street in 1897.

Lula's place of burial was Gunnison, Bolivar County, Mississippi, with Campbell-Wiggins Funeral Directors of Memphis in charge. This was the same county where she was born and she likely had family members still living there. When Lula returned to Memphis from Mississippi in 1920, she relocated in the same area (Wellington Street) where there had been so many wonderful memories of church under the tent and the day Lillian walked down the aisle to the alter giving her life to the Lord while Bishop Mason preached under the anointing. She departed this life in peace knowing that she made the right spiritual decisions for herself and her children.

All About Business

Between 1920 and 1930, Lillian Coffey was recognized as an evangelist in COGIC. Even before then, she was using her gift to preach and minister God's Word. Unfortunately, during this same period of time, she separated and later divorced her husband. They had two daughters, Cleotha and Laverne; both were born in Illinois. They were doing well and God had been good. Lillian was blessed and able to buy a large apartment building around 1925 on East 44th Street in Chicago that she purchased for around $13,500. Her sister Elise and her husband were living with them and helping out. Elise's husband, Lamar Fullilove, worked as a mechanic at a garage while Elise stayed home and took care of the house, her two children, and Lillian's children. Lillian's brother, Morris Brooks was living with them and painting houses for a living. It must have been a very large house or an accommodating size apartment to have had twenty-two boarders in all, five separate families and four individual boarders including her brother, Morris paying twenty dollars a month in rent. The total rent collected each month was $200, and there were several persons renting rooms that were from Tennessee and others, possibly church members. There is no doubt this provided Lillian with a good income and shows she was very "savvy" in the area of business and real estate.

Mother Lizzie Robinson was the National Supervisor of Women from 1911 to 1945; and after her death, Lillian Brooks-Coffey took over the position and served as National Supervisor of Women from 1945 to 1964. Mother Coffey has been given credit for transforming the National Women Convention into the International Women Convention of COGIC in 1950.

Indiana N. Washington

Indiana Washington, the mother of Lelia W. Mason and mother-in-law of Bishop Mason, was born Indiana Neal into slavery July of 1857 in Macon, Fayette County, Tennessee. Her parents were Burt and Leah (sometimes called Emerline) Neal. Burt and Leah were born in Tennessee, he in 1836 and her in 1835. Indiana was the oldest of six children. Her siblings in 1870 were Charles (4), Robert (3), Eveline (2), Marshall (born in 1871), and Elizabeth (born in 1873). The ages of the children given in the 1870 U.S. Federal Census were probably incorrect. Indiana and her mother were both pregnant at the same time, Indiana gave birth to Henry Fuller in 1873 and Leah gave birth to Elizabeth the same year.

Indiana Neal and John Washington were joined in Holy Matrimony by Abraham Coburn, a black farmer and minister of the gospel on Wednesday, March 21, 1880, in Macon, Fayette County, Tennessee. [10] She was twenty-three years old when they got their marriage license at the court house in Somerville, the county seat. John was accompanied by his friend and witness for the grand occasion, James Granberry. The marriage license clearly revealed that his first name was John; however, the 1880 U. S. Federal Census reported his name to be Jacob. Oftentimes mistakes were made in the census due to illegible handwriting; however, there is a possibility that his full name was John Jacob Washington. Since the marriage license is a legal document, we will abide by its information and use John. He was born in Virginia around 1851 and was probably sold and brought to Tennessee as a slave by his owner.

Indiana left her family in Macon in 1880 where her father was farming, while her mother, Leah kept the house. Leah was fortunate enough to be a housewife and not a field hand like many of the other wives. Charles was in school; Robert and Eveline were chopping cotton. Marshall and Elizabeth were too young to work in the cotton fields. Indiana's father was dead by 1900 and her mother went to live with her nephew, Pender Mebane and his wife, Fannie in Macon. Leah was still healthy and strong enough in 1900 to work as a field hand. She died between 1901 and 1909.

Between March and June of 1880, John and Indiana moved to Memphis from Macon in time to be enumerated for the U. S. Federal Census of 1880 taken on the 8th day of June. After relocating to Memphis, the family found a place to rent at 353 Sixth Street in the city. With them were their children: Lithania, four months old; Henry Fuller, seven years old and the step-son of John. Albert McNeal, a brother-in-law of John was also living with them. John's occupation was day laborer, and Indiana was a washerwoman. John's brother-in-law, Albert, was also a day laborer. Being a day laborer meant being hired out on a daily bases to do whatever job you agreed to do for a certain wage. Oftentimes you would just hang around in a particular area in the neighborhood and wait for an individual to come by looking for those who wanted to work. In modern times this practice can clearly be seen in Mexican communities across the country. Hiring out her services as a "washerwoman" afforded Indiana the privilege of being able to stay home if necessary with young children and be a housekeeper while "taking in laundry" and receiving merger wages for her labor working at home. Her most expensive investments would have been her washboards and boiling pots.

By 1900, they moved to Walker Alley from Stephens Street and Indiana now had four children at home. Arthur was born December of 1882; Lelia was born in April of 1885; John, December of 1886; and Alice, January of 1888. Alice and John were in school. Arthur and Lelia were working; he was eighteen and she was fifteen working as a cook. Arthur was a hostler, responsible for the care of horses when customers patronized his place of employment. In modern times, he would be referred to as a "valet." Also, in 1900, John's stepson Henry Fuller was now an adult, married, and living in Chicago with his wife, Laura. They lived at 5200 Lake Avenue. He worked as a waiter and she was a housewife. The couple married in 1895; however, she hadn't given birth to any children.

Indiana's husband died between 1888 and 1899, making life a little bit more difficult for Indiana and the children. Afterwards in 1904, Alice died adding to their sorrow. Indiana's husband likely died around 1892 and I base this on the fact that their residence was listed for the first time in the Memphis City Directory in 1893, which advertised her occupation as a washerwoman, and since she was the only adult "breadwinner," she would have needed the advertising to help her get work after the death of her husband. It's difficult to pinpoint exactly when Mother Washington joined Elder Mason's church; however, it was likely around 1901. She wasn't left without any family support after her husband died. There were other family members close by that she could depend on such as her brothers, Professor Charles J. Neal, a school teacher and later principal of Carnes Avenue School; and Robert Neal, a grocery store owner and skilled worker who lived next door to her.

Living on the other side of her in 1900 at their Walker Street Alley address were her brother-in-law, Robert W. Washington and his wife, Lola. He was from Virginia and likely came here as a slave or migrated to Tennessee after the slaves were freed. They had no children and she was a housewife. He owned his wagon and was an express man for Desoto Oil Company. Oil referred to here of course was not modern motor oil or any other kind of petroleum product, but rather oil used for cooking and made from butter.

Mother Washington was living with Bishop Mason when she became ill and suddenly died. Dr. Pendleton W. Bailey, a black physician, was called on January 5, 1928, but she died on the 6th at 10:25 am. Her certificate of death stated the cause of death was Aortic Insufficiency, which meant a malfunction of the valves in her heart. She was buried in New Park Cemetery, January 9, 1928, with S. W. Qualls & Company Funeral Directors of Memphis officiating.

One of her closest friends, Mrs. Elia V. Sparks, editor and manager of *The Whole Truth*, COGIC's newspaper, wrote this wonderful article about her dear friend after she passed:

Beloved Sister Indiana Washington, dear mother of Sister C. H. Mason; mother-in-law of Elder C. H. Mason, departed this life Jan., 6, 1928, aged about 68 years.

She was born in Macon, Tenn., was converted at an early age and joined the Baptist Church. She lived a clean and upright life from her youth, an unspotted character before the world.

After hearing the true gospel preached by Elder Mason and other God-sent ministers being an earnest Christian and a dear lover of God and his word, she soon realized her spiritual needs and shortcoming and accepted the more excellent way that God has provided for His people; a life saved completely from sin.

After walking with God in the beauty of holiness for many years, she later received the baptism of the Holy Ghost according to Acts 2:4.

She was a praying woman, giving much to her time in fasting and prayer and reading the Bible. She was faithful in attending the service until her health failed her a few years ago.

She also spent much of her time aiding Elder Mason's family in his absence, thus allowing him to go and serve others and spread the good tidings of great joy, even the true gospel to a lost world.

Besides Sister Mason, she leaves two sons, Arthur and John Washington, having lost a daughter in 1904 at the age of 16 years. She also leaves three brothers, Mr. Robert, Marshall, and Prof. C. J. Neal, and several grandchildren to mourn their loss.

She reared her children according to the advice of Solomon in Prov. 22:6, reading thus: "Train up a child in the way he should go; and when he is old he will not depart from it."

Some of her family lessons being as follows: Remember thy Creator in the days of thy youth; A good name is rather to be chosen than great riches; A virtuous woman [Prov. 3:10]; who can find a virtuous woman? Her price is far above rubies. She loved and esteemed a good character.

Sister Washington's last remarks were: "I have done all I could, I am ready and willing to go," and turned to her daughter, Sister Mason and said: "You and your children are dear to me." Sister Washington was loved by the Saints and all who came in touch with her. Her life was full of kind deeds.

She was well acquainted with the editor of this paper; often spoke encouraging words to her, as Titus in the second Chapter and third verse said for the aged woman to do. She is gone but not forgotten.

Blessed are the dead that dieth in the Lord. They shall henceforth rest from their labor and their works do follow them. [11]

In 1880, Mother Washington had a daughter born in January, named Lathania (if spelled correctly). I'm curious as to the reason why she wasn't mentioned in Mother Spark's article. Was it because she had been dead for several years and simply forgotten? I'm aware that Alice died in 1904, at sixteen, but I'm curious as to what happened to Lathania.

Around the time Mother Washington died, Bishop Mason lost all the money he had in a local bank after it financially collapsed. Some of the children were away in school and had to come home. Supervisor Lizzie Robinson through the pages of *The Whole Truth* asked the saints to send donations to help Bishop Mason and his family.

Leonard P. Adams

Born near Waverley, Humphreys County, Tennessee, July of 1866, Leonard's mother, Elizabeth raised four children by herself and ran the family farm. She managed to educate Leonard and he graduated from Normal school and went on to law school. He married Elizabeth Sarah Price, January 13, 1891, at Dickson, Tennessee. [12]

Attorney Adams walked away from his law practice around 1896 to preach the doctrine of sanctification and holiness. In his own words he said, "I walked straight from the law office to the pulpit." He first preached sanctification in Erin, Tennessee; then Houston, Texas, and later Canada. Before then he felt a call to the ministry around 1886 when he first heard holiness preached but felt he didn't have the power to do so.

He and his wife moved to Memphis in 1902, but they had been in and out of Memphis starting in about 1898. In 1900, he lived with his wife in Cordova, Walker County, Alabama, preaching holiness and spreading the word. They had adopted two children, Thomas Hawkins, sixteen years old and Sadie M. Adams, six years old. [13] When he first arrived in Memphis, he preached under his own tent at the corner of Looney and Manassas Streets. The crowds continued to grow until at times there were upwards of 150 people. He was never interested in organizing a church, only preaching sanctification and doing mission work.

Minister Adams was acquainted with Bishop Mason and went to hear him preach several times after locating in Memphis. He agreed with Bishop Mason's doctrine and was himself filled with the Holy Ghost. He was white; and when asked by an attorney during the taking of a deposition if his congregation was all white, he replied, "We don't restrict ourselves to the baptism, but the love of God and a pure heart." Minister Adams and Bishop Mason's relationship was probably strengthened after Minster Adams agreed to give a deposition in defense of Bishop Mason and the church in the legal battle with the C. P. Jones faction. The lawyer for COGIC at the time was probably informed by Bishop Mason or one of the trustees of the church of the value of Minister Adams's testimony in the case. An educated and prominent white minister that supported Mason's doctrine and was himself filled with the Holy Ghost and spoke in tongues was a very "favorable" witness for the defense team.

Rev. Adams accompanied G. B. Cashwell, Mack M. Pinson, and Glen Cook when they visited Mason's church on a Sunday night shortly after Glen Cook returned from Los Angeles, California, spreading the Pentecostal message and the experiences he had had at the Azusa Street Revival led by William J. Seymour, a one eyed, self-educated son of slaves. Mason was still in California the night they attended services at the church when a young man named F. C. Ford had a Holy Ghost, "tongue talking" and "lying out in the floor all night" experience. Rev. Adams is likely the same man referred to as Brother Adams in a popular photograph taken with the Azusa Street Revival leader, William J. Seymour, and Ministers F.F. Bosworth, Tom Hezmalhalch, and John G. Lake.

Rev. Adams probably received permission and support from C. H. Mason in 1908 to establish the Church of God Bible Institute and Training Home. He was the pastor and overseer of the school, which was probably the first school of its kind established for training COGIC preachers black and white. After the opening of the school in 1909, I noticed his title changed from Reverend to Elder Adams, which may indicate that he was given the right hand of fellowship as part of the Church of God in Christ denomination under C. H. Mason. If so, Elder Adams may have been the first white COGIC pastor with a congregation under Mason. It's difficult to know exactly how long the school was in operation; however, it was listed in the Memphis city directory from 1909-13, and Elder Adams was listed as a Church of God pastor. In many instances you will discover when searching city directories, that the name Church of God in Christ was only partially used and simply listed as Church of God.

Elder Adams may have operated and continued the Institute and Training School as an Auxiliary or Outreach Ministry of the Grace and Truth Church he organized and pastored in 1917. I believe Grace and Truth Church of Memphis was a Church of God in Christ white congregation and Elder Adams was later part of Bishop Mason's "urban strategy" to spread COGIC. In 1918, Elder Adams relocated or was sent by Mason to Birmingham, Alabama where he pastored a church and by 1930, he and his wife Elizabeth were living in Austin, Texas, spreading the gospel message and pastoring.

John E. Hightower

Elder Hightower was born to William and Mary Hightower of Sardis, Panola County, Mississippi, in June of 1865. He was the oldest of six children and took on a lot of responsible after his father died around 1890. John married his first wife around that time, but she later died before he moved to Memphis. In 1900, his mother, Mary, who was fifty-two years old and a widow, lived with him. Also, living with him were his two sisters, Mary, who was twenty-two years old and single; and Dora Abrams, who was twenty-six years old and a widow with two children, Thomas and Willie Mae. They were all living with him at 294 Broadway Street in Memphis where they were renting. He worked as a day laborer and his sister, Mary, was a school teacher. Dora was a cook for a private family. His mother was unemployed, so she was the housekeeper and took care of Dora's two children.

He was a member of Elder Mason's church, Saints Home COGIC on Wellington Street, but there were no signs that his mother or sisters were members. It was necessary for all the members of the church to sign a roster in 1908 for legal purposes; however, Elder Hightower's mother's and sisters' names were missing.

Elder Hightower was fairly active at the Holy Convocations which were held at the church on Wellington. At the 12th Holy Convocation in 1919, he was appointed to a board of elders that was to investigate applications for ordination. The following morning he led the board in prayer; afterwards, the Board of Elders, of which he was a member, approved six of the brethren for ordination.

By 1920, he was able to buy a house on the westside of Main Street near the L & N Railroad in Memphis. He and Lillie had married around 1913, and they were living alone. He was now a concrete finisher and was making more money, while she stayed home and took care of the house. John and Lillie were now in their late forties and had no children. Between 1920 and 1925, Bishop Mason sent Elder Hightower to pastor a church in Marianna, Lee County, Arkansas. They sold their house in Memphis and bought a house on Church Street in Marianna valued at $2,500, which was above average compared to other property in close proximity. Living with them and renting a room was Mildred People, a twenty-one year old single black female, who was a cook for a white family.

Elder Justus Bowe had been overseer of Arkansas since 1907; but in 1932, when he temporarily disassociated himself from COGIC, Bishop Mason appointed Elder Hightower as overseer in his place. Elder Hightower was already serving as Assistant State Overseer. In 1942, a case came up against Elder Hightower before Bishop Mason and the Board of Elders during the 35th Holy Convocation General Council Meeting. Bishop Mason spoke briefly on the matter and exonerated the action of the board, which didn't disclose the matter or the action taken.

Isaac S. Stafford

Isaac Jr., was one of thirteen children born to Isaac Sr., and Ann Stafford of Lower Fork, (later named Valdosta) Lowndes County, Georgia in 1863. His father and mother were both born in Georgia in 1839. In 1890, Isaac Jr., married Leah. Their first child, Paul Hezekiah, was born in April of 1890, and their daughter, Maude in 1892. It was probably in 1893 when Isaac Jr., enrolled in Meharry Medical College in Nashville, Tennessee, and graduated in 1897. His family likely stayed in Valdosta while he was in medical school.

I hesitated several times before I finally decided to research for more information about Dr. Stafford. I was reluctant to do so at first because I felt there wasn't enough information available for me to pursue a history. I finally decided to take a closer look and what I discovered was absolutely a total surprise! Looking through my Meharry graduation files because I had read that he was a medical doctor, I discovered that Dr. Stafford and my grandfather, Dr. Samuel H. Broome, were classmates at Meharry, both graduating in 1897 in a class of thirty-four students. After graduating my grandfather began practicing in Brownsville, Tennessee; and Dr. Stafford went back home to Valdosta, Georgia. Dr. Stafford was likely the first African-American to practice medicine in Valdosta.

Isaac Sr., and his family apparently joined the Colored Methodist Episcopal Church after it was founded in 1870. Before then they were likely members of a white Methodist Church or one of the local black congregations (possibly Bethel CME) in Valdosta. Dr. Stafford was busy engaged in building a medical practice and didn't indulge much in church work accept attending services on Sunday. He attended his first General Conference of the CME Church held in Memphis, Tennessee, May 2, 1906. His presence in Memphis could have provided the opportunity for him to meet C. H. Mason or some of the sanctified brethren and gain some interesting knowledge about the sanctified church. Exactly when or why Dr. Stafford crossed over from the CME Church to COGIC is a mystery; however, it was likely around 1910-15.

In 1920, Dr. Stafford was living in Valdosta, Georgia, at 114 Rogers Street, with his wife Leah and sister-in-law, Jessie Walker. He owned his home and it was the only house on his street that was mortgage free. If he sold his home prior to moving to Detroit, this would have given him a fair amount of money for a down payment on the luxurious home they purchased or he could have used the house for collateral.

Bishop Mason appointed Dr. Stafford as overseer of Michigan around 1920 although his residence as still in Georgia. Dr. Stafford was part of Bishop Mason "urban strategy" to spread holiness and sanctification through COGIC. Around 1922 Dr. Stafford moved to Detroit, Michigan, and took up residence at 5867 Begole Avenue, where he purchased a home that was valued at $16,000. This would have been almost a mansion size house and large enough to accommodate his family and entertain small groups from the church. Along with his wife Leah, living with them in 1930, were Cohen White, his son-in-law, who was a real estate agent, and his wife Maude, owner of a beauty shop, and their three children; Zenobia, Cohen Jr., and Harold. His sister-in-law, Jessie Walker was still living with them and was seventy years old. Maynard Marbley, a nineteen year old single black male from Georgia was their live-in servant and chauffer. The Stafford's had only two children; however, they raised a nephew and helped raise their grandchildren. I was pleasantly surprised again when I realized Dr. Stafford was sent to Detroit where my grandfather, Dr. Broome, had migrated to during the great "exodus" of blacks to the North in the 1920's. I will forever wonder if the old classmates crossed each others paths once again.

Elder Stafford was one of five overseers that were consecrated to the office of Bishop in 1933. This was a big change in COGIC and each bishop was given several states over which he was to preside.

7

EARLY LEADERS AND DEPARTMENT HEADS IN COGIC

Author's Note

In Carter G. Woodson's eloquent style he did an excellent job describing the challenges of Negro washerwomen in our history. I want to use his essay to introduce to some and present to others three Negro washerwomen of the Church of God in Christ that were a part of Bishop Mason's early ministry and certainly would have faced some of the challenges Dr. Woodson wrote about. In Chapter Five, I mentioned Lillian Brooks-Coffey's mother, Lula Brooks, who was a washerwoman (laundress) and a member of Bishop Mason's first congregation in Memphis, Saints Home COGIC.

Bishop Mason's mother-in-law, Mother Indiana Washington, served as one of the church mothers and was a washerwoman. One advantage of being a washerwoman was that one could stay home, keep the children, and get one's work done while making money, and allowing relatives to work and pursue other opportunities. Such was the case in Bishop Mason's household with the presence of Mother Washington.

This chapter gives special attention to Mother Lizzie Robinson, the first National Supervisor of Women in COGIC appointed by Bishop Mason in 1911 and a washerwoman for many years before joining COGIC. Her daughter, Ida Holt-Baker, worked for many years by her side as a washerwoman, and there were countless other women in COGIC that made their living and paid their tithes and offerings from money received by "taking in laundry." When information was collected for telephone directories and the U. S. Federal Census, you will find their occupation occasionally listed as "laundress" instead of "washer-woman," although they were the same. This chapter is dedicated to Sister Lula Brooks, Mother Lizzie Robinson, Mother Indiana Washington, and all the past washerwomen in COGIC that toiled, labored, and made sacrifices as wives, widows, and single black women in the area of domestic work to help bring their families through "extremely" difficult times.

The Negro Washerwoman: A Vanishing Figure by Carter G. Woodson

The Negroes of this country keenly resent any such thing as the mention of the Planta-tion Black Mammy, so dear to the hearts of those who believe in the traditions of the old South. Such a reminder of that low status of the race in the social order of the slave regime is considered a gross insult. There is in the life of the Negro, however, a vanish-ing figure whose name every one should mention with veneration. She was the all but beast of burden of the aristocratic slaveholder, and in freedom she continued at this hard labor as a bread winner of the family. This is the Negro washerwoman.

This towering personage in the life of the Negro cannot be appreciated today for the reason that her task is almost done. Because of the rise of the race from drudgery and the mechanization of the industrial world the washerwoman is rapidly passing out. Confusing those women employed in laundries with those washing at homes, the Bureau of the Census in 1890 reported 151,540 washerwomen, 218,227 in 1900, and 373,819 in 1910. In 1920, however, there were actually 283,557, but this number has comparatively declined. Through machinery and the division of labor the steam laundry has made the washing of clothes a well organized business with which the toiler over the wash tub cannot compete. The price required for this laundry ser-vice is not always lower than the charges of the washerwoman, but the modern laun-dry offers so many other conveniences and advantages that the people are turning away from her to the new agency. Only the most unfortunate and the most inefficient wash-erwoman who is unable to do anything else and must work for the lowest wages remains to underbid or obviate the necessity for introducing the steam laundry system. The Negro washerwoman of the antebellum and the reconstruction periods then has passed from the stage. For her, however, an ever grateful people will have a pleasant memory, and generations unborn may honor her in brass and stone.

And why should the Negro washerwoman be thus considered? Because she gave her life as a sacrifice for others. Whether as a slave or a free woman of color of the antebel-

lum period of as a worker in the ranks of an emancipated people, her life without exception was one of unrelenting toil for those whom she loved. In the history of no people has her example been paralleled, in no other figure in the Negro group can be found a type measuring up to the level of this philanthropic spirit in unselfish service.

The details of the story are interesting. When a slave she arose with the crowing of the fowl to sweat all but blood in the employ of a despotic mistress for whose household she had to toil often until late in the night. On return home she had to tax her body further to clean a neglected hut, to prepare the meals and wash the clothes of her abandoned children, while her husband, also worn out with the heavier burdens of the day, had time to rest. In addition to this, she often took in other work by which she saved sufficient money to purchase her freedom and sometimes that of her husband and children. Often she had compassion on a persecuted slave and used such savings to secure his liberation at a high cost only to let him go free for a nominal charge.

As a slave, too, the washerwoman was the head of the family. Her husband was sometimes an uncertain quantity in the equation. Not allowed to wed according to law, they soon experienced that marriage meant living with another with the consent of the owners concerned and often against the will of the slaves themselves. Masters ordered women to take up with men and vice versa to produce numerous slave offspring for sale. When the slave hesitated because of the absence of real love the master's will prevail. Just as such matches were made according to the will of the master they were like wise broken by the selling of the man or the woman thus attached, and in the final analysis the care of the children fell to the mother while the father went to the bed of another wife on some remote plantation. To provide for her home the comforts which the custom of slavery did not allow she had to plan wisely and work incessantly. If the mother had not developed sufficiently in domestic art to earn a little money at leisure she usually fell back on "taking in washing."

When free during the antebellum period the drudgery of the Negro washerwoman was not diminished. The earning power of her husband was not great since slave labor impoverished free labor, and the wife often had to do something to supplement the income of her unprofitable husband. Laboring, too, for those who were not fortunately enough circumstanced to have slaves to serve them, the free Negro women could earn only such wages as were paid to menial workers. In thus eking out an existence however, the washerwoman was an important factor. Without her valuable contribution the family under such conditions could not have been maintained.

In the North during these antebellum times, the Negro washerwoman had to bear still heavier burdens. In the South, her efforts were largely supplementary; but, in the North, she was often the sole wage earner of the family even when she had an able-bodied husband. The trouble was not due to his laziness but to the fact that Negro men in the North were often forced to a life of idleness. Travelers of a century ago often saw these black men sitting around loafing and noted this as an evidence of the shiftlessness of the Negro race, but they did not see the Negro washerwoman toiling in the homes and did not take time to find out why these Negro men were not gainfully employed. Negro men who had followed trades in the South were barred there from by trade unions in the North, and the more enlightened and efficiently trained Irish and Germans immigrating into the United Stases drove them out of menial positions.

In many of the Northern cities, then, Negro men and children were fed and clothed with the earnings of the wife or mother who held her own in competition with others. In most of these cases the man felt that his task was done when he drew the water cut the wood, built the fires, went after the clothes, and returned them. Fortunate was the Northern Negro man who could find acceptance in such a woman's home. Still more fortunate was the boy or girl who had a robust mother with that devotion which impelled her to give her life for the happiness of the less fortunate members of an indigent group. Without the washerwoman many antebellum Negroes would have either starved in that section or they would have been forced by indigent circumstances to return to slavery in the South, as some few had to do during the critical years of the decade just before the Civil War.

The Negro washerwoman, too, was not only a breadwinner but the important factor in the home. If the family owned the home her earnings figured in the purchase of it. When the taxes were paid she had to make her contribution, and the expenses for repairs often could not be met without recourse to her earnings. When the husband could not supply or showed indifference to the comforts of the home it was she who replaced worn out furniture and unattractive decorations and kept the home as nearly as possible according to the standards of modern times. She could be depended upon to clean the yard, to decorate the front with flowers, and to give things the aspect of a civilized life. In fact, this working woman was often the central figure of the family and the actual representative of the home. Friends and strangers calling on business usually asked for the mother inasmuch as the father was not always an important factor in the family.

This same washerwoman was no less significant in the life of the community. The uplift worker sought her at home to interest her in neglected humanity, the abolitionist found her a ready listener to the story of her oppressed brethren in chains, the colonizationist stopped to have her persuade the family to try life anew in Liberia, and the preacher paid his usual calls to connect her more vitally with the effort to relieve the church of pecuniary embarrassment. While burdened with the responsibility of maintaining a family she was not too busy to listen to these messages and did not consider herself too poor to contribute to the relief of those who with a tale of woe convinced her that they were less favorable circumstanced than she. Oftentimes she felt that she was being deceived, but she had rather assist the undeserving than to turn a deaf ear to one who was actually in need.

The emancipation of the Negro as a result of the Civil War did not immediately elevate the status of the Negro washerwomen nor did it bring them immediate relief from the many burdens which they had borne. In this new freedom certain favorably circumstanced Negroes were disposed to assume a haughty attitude toward these workers. After emancipation Negro men rapidly withdrew their wives and daughters from field work and restricted their efforts largely to the home; but the washerwomen who went out occasionally to do day work or had the clothes brought home, remained for several generations. There was yet so much more for them to do in the reconstruction of a landless and illiterate class that the importance of this role could not be underrated. For a number of years thereafter, then, certainly until 1900 or 1910 there was little change in the part which these women played in the economic life of the Negro.

Why should the Negro washerwoman have to continue her unrelenting toil even after emancipation? This makes an interesting story. In the first place, the Negro was nominally free only. The old relation of master and slave was merely modified to be that of landlord and tenant in the lower South. The wage system established itself in the upper South, but soon broke down in certain parts because there was no money with which to pay; and the tenant system which followed with most of the evils of slavery kept the Negro in poverty. With such a little earning power under this system it was a godsend to the Negro man to have a wife to supplement his earnings at some such labor as washing. She did not always receive money for her services, but food and cast-off clothing and shoes contributed equally as much to the comfort of her loved ones. White employers and black employees were all hard up to it while the South was trying to recover from its devastation and the whole country was undergoing a new development, but one class could help the other, and both managed in some way to live.

In the course of time, too, when the problem of eking out an existence had been solved there came to the ambitious program of the freedmen other demands which made the services of the Negro washerwoman indispensable. In the first place, the freedmen were urged to buy homes, and they could easily see the advantage of living under one's own vine and fig tree and of thus forming a permanent attachment to the community. Land was cheap, but money was scarce. To make such a purchase and at the same time carry the other burdens did not permit the withdrawal of the washerwoman from her arduous task. Often she was the one who took the initiative in the buying of the home, for the husband did not always willingly assume additional responsibilities.

Then when the home had been purchased the children had to be educated. Negroes were ambitious to see their children in possession of the culture long since observed among the whites; and they were urged by the missionary teachers from the North to seek education which, as a handmaiden of religion, would quickly solve their problems. This often meant the education of the whole family at once; for, since the indifference and the impoverished condition of the South rendered thorough education at public expense practically impossible, the washerwoman had to come to the front again to bear more than her share of the burden. The missionary schools established by teachers from the North required the payment of tuition as well as board and room rent. Many things now supplied to students free of charge, moreover, had to be purchased in those days by their parents.

Sometimes, too, when there were no children to educate, the husband was ambitious to become a teacher or minister, and he had to go to school to qualify for the new sphere. The wife usually took over the responsibility of the home which she often financed through the wash tub. The Negro teacher or minister who did not receive such support in obtaining his education was an exception to the rule. Without this particular sacrifice of the washerwoman the Negro professional groups would be far less undermanned than what they are today. Many of the prominent Negro teachers, ministers, business men, and professional workers refer today with pardonable pride to sisters, mothers, and wives who thus made their careers possible.

In not a few cases the earnings of the Negro washerwoman went to supplement that of her husband as capital in starting business enterprises. This effort today is not easily estimated because most of such enterprises never succeeded. For lack of experience and judgment these pioneers in a hitherto forbidden field soon ran upon the rocks, and the highly prized savings of their companions together with their own accumulations sank beneath the wave only to discourage a people who had to grope in the dark to find the way. As a rule however, the woman bore her losses like a heroine in a great crisis being the last to utter a word of censure or to despair of finding some solution of a difficult problem. Often when the man at his extremity was inclined to give up the fight it was his courageous companion who brought a word of cheer and urged the procession onward.

In cooperative business, this worker was a still larger factor. The Negro washer-woman, continuing just as she had been before the Civil War in social uplift and religious effort, served also in the capacity of a stockholder in the larger corporations of Negroes. Being already the main support of the school and church, she could easily become interested in business. At the same time the Negro teachers and professional classes, who in being taught solely the superiority of the other races had developed an inferiority complex, could not have confidence in the initiative and enterprise of the uneducated Negroes who launched these enterprises. The Negro working women who had not been misguided by such theories had no such misgivings. The only thing they wanted to know was whether it was something to give employment, prestige, and opportunity for leadership. They believed in the possibilities of their own group and willingly cooperated with any one who had a high sounding program. They were not the ignorant and the gullible, but the true and tried coworkers in the rehabilitation of the race along economic lines.

Some of the leading enterprises like the St. Lukes Bank in Richmond, the North Carolina Mutual Life Insurance Company of Durham, and the National Benefit Life Insurance Company of Washington still count among their stockholders noble women of this type. These businesses have developed, to the point that the well-to-do and edu-cated Negroes now regard them as assets and participate in their development, but the first dimes and nickels with which these enterprises were launched came largely from women of this working class. [1]

Mother Lizzie Robinson: First National Supervisor of the Department of Women in COGIC: 1911-1945

She was born April 5, 1860, in Phillips County, Arkansas, where she and her mother and siblings were freed from slavery with the millions emancipated after the Civil War. [2] Accounts of her early life are very sketchy until 1880 when on September 20, her only child, Ida Florence Holt was born. It has been reported and apparently it was true that she was married to William Holt when their daughter was born. However, I can't find the marriage certificate, which would give us her maiden name and solve the mystery surrounding her childhood and family.

After divorcing William, she met and later married twenty-one year old Henry Wood when she was thirty years old on February 15, 1890, in Marianna, Lee County, Arkansas. [3] Their marriage rites were preformed by H. N. Word, (white) a Justice of the Peace and Judge. Their license clearly stated that Lizzie Holt was to marry Henry Wood and not "*Woods*"; however, somewhere along the way, an *s* was added or left out from the beginning of the surname "*Wood.*" In the 1900, and 1910 U. S. Federal Census, she can be found listed as a *Woods.*

Unfortunately, she also divorced Henry around 1892, and she then moved from Helena to Pine Bluff, Arkansas. She and Ida lived in Pine Bluff for about three years before moving to Little Rock. Lizzie Woods was listed in the 1897-98 Little Rock city directory living at 311 W. 10th Street; and it listed her occupation as a laundress, which is consistent with her history before joining COGIC.

By 1900, Mother Robinson and Ida had moved back to Pine Bluff, Jefferson County, Arkansas, from Little Rock and were living at 802 West 7th Avenue. Both of them were listed in the 1900 U. S. Federal Census as a "laundress." While living in Pine Bluff, she joined a local Baptist church and continued to read *Hope* and communicate with Missionary Joanna P. Moore. Moore was able to persuade the Baptist Missionary Society to send Mother Robinson to the Baptist Academy in Dermott, Arkansas, and insisted that she stop "taking in laundry." Her relocating to Dermott, Arkansas, is consistent with her presence in the 1910 U. S. Federal Census living in Chicot County, Arkansas.

By 1910, Mother Robinson should have finished her courses at the academy. She was listed as head of household. She wasn't reported to be employed by the academy as a matron, but rather she was listed as a farmer and living with her as boarders were two females and two males. Three of the boarders worked at the academy (listed as a Denomination school), the two females were teachers and one of the males was a horseshoer at the school shop, and the other male was a school teacher at a public school.

One year later in 1911 during a revival at the academy conducted by Mason; Mother Robinson was saved and filled with the Holy Ghost. Bishop Mason was so impressed with her state of spiritual ecstasy that he believed she was the one led to him through prayer to lead the Department of Women in COGIC. She accepted and during the national convocation in 1911, Mother Lizzie Robinson was appointed and installed as the first National Supervisor of Women in COGIC.

Between 1912 and 1920, Lizzie Woods married E. D. Robinson, her third husband, a Tennessean and a COGIC preacher. Even while they were living there, was some confusion over the correct spelling of their last name. In a hand-written letter addressed to Bishop R. F. Williams, November 10, 1945, on her personal stationary, the letterhead was typed and read, "Mother Lizzie Robinson-General Supervisor of Woman's Work," and she signed her name at the end of the letter, "Your Mother L. Robinson." Still today her name is often misspelled in articles and memoriam expressions throughout COGIC.

As a husband and wife team, they were sent to Nebraska by Bishop Mason to spread the Word and open up the Midwest to a holy and sanctified gospel. They made their home in Omaha and were very successful in the ministry there, but not without many hard trials and attacks by the enemy. He left her to finish the work they started together in 1937 when he passed away. She served from 1911 until 1945 when she quietly passed away at the 38th International Holy Convocation in an atmosphere of "praise" and "worship."

A Passion for Black Women

More than likely during her residence in Little Rock, Mother Robinson continued to affiliate with Missionary Joanna P. Moore, who had settled there from Louisiana. A native of Pennsylvania, Moore had begun missionary work among freed black people in the South during the Civil War. The first woman appointed by the American Baptist Home Mission Society [ABHMS], Moore settled on an island in the Mississippi River near Memphis in 1863. There she worked with 1,100 black women and children who had fled to the union army for refuge from slavery. In 1864, she moved to Helena, Arkansas, and after the war, between 1868 and 1877, lived in the New Orleans area. [4]

In 1880, Moore was still in New Orleans operating a mission named Miss J. P. Moore's Home for the Aged and Destitute Women, located on Pitt Street. [5] When the 1880 census was taken, there were twenty-one patients in the home; and all of them were African-American females, ranging in ages from 7 to 125 years old. Moore's position was Acting Matron and working under her were four white missionaries and one black assistant matron, a forty-six year old mulatto named Elizabeth Bensen. All of Moore's patients had taken the "paupers" oath or was granted it automatically.

Moore moved on from New Orleans to other parts of Louisiana and after several years decided to return to Little Rock, Arkansas, around 1891. She had a passion for helping black women and was soon about her calling in the mission fields of Little Rock. Moore was listed in the 1893-94 Little Rock city directory as principal of the Wives and Mothers Training School, located at 1110 Pulaski Street.

Missionary Moore was the founder and editor of *Hope* a small booklet that was read across denominational lines. In 1885, Moore began publishing Hope in Plaquemine, Louisiana. It contained Sunday school lessons, guides for Bible bands, and instructions on child-rearing and family devotions. [6] What Mother Robinson received from reading *Hope* and taking advice from Moore plus being exposed to her ministry was a spirit of compassion for women that began to prepare her for the work of the ministry that God would be calling her to do in COGIC. However, first she needed to be trained and properly prepared to meet the challenge. Moore had about forty years experience as a missionary, organizer and caregiver of black women who helped motivate and encourage Mother Robinson.

Justus B. Bowe: Second Editor of *The Whole Truth*

Justus B. Bowe, Sr., was born January 1, 1873, in South Carolina. [7] He matriculated to the Mid-South at an undetermined point in time and got involved in ministry early as 1900. He was an affiliate minister in the Churches of God in Christ headquartered in Jackson, Mississippi, in which Charles P. Jones was the general overseer. However, he supported Elder Mason in his doctrinal views and left the fellowship when Mason was excommunicated. He was reported in the December 6, 1906, edition of the *Truth* periodical as pastor of two churches, one in Dumas, Desha County, Arkansas, and the other in Conway, Faulkner County,

Arkansas (C.H. Mason once pastored this church). Elder Bowe refused to accept sound legal advice in the litigations brought by the Jones faction against the churches in Arkansas. Because he refused to comply, the following action was taken:

> *As a result of that action, lawsuits followed for the control of church property in Memphis, Tenn., Lexington, Miss., and elsewhere.*
>
> *The brethren who were excluded were advised by* **Dr. R. E. Hart** *not to reorganize until all lawsuits were ended. Elder J. Bowe, of Arkansas refused to accept that advice and proceeded to reorganize the first convocation in the State of Arkansas in 1908. By doing so, all church property in the State of Arkansas at that time, was lost. However, those in Memphis, Tennessee and Lexington, Mississippi, who accepted* **Dr. Hart's** *advice, were successful in the courts in their claims of church property.*
>
> *In 1909 lawsuits were ended and advice was given by* **Dr. Hart** *to reorganize.* [8]

Elder Bowe responded to Elder Mason's call for all preachers that believed as he did to meet him at his church in Memphis, September 4, 1907, for a special meeting which actually was the first General Assembly meeting of COGIC, at which time Elder Bowe was appointed overseer of Arkansas.

The conception of *The Whole Truth* paper was likely Elder Mason's idea and was discussed at length in this meeting, at which time Elder David J. Young was chosen as the first editor. They also probably agreed that the press should be self supporting as soon as possible; for this was the most desirable method of operating a press. Without a doubt, *The Whole Truth* publication of COGIC was supposed to be a "deeper" witness of the truth that was expressed through the title and pages, which was meant to rival the Jones faction publication of the *Truth*. After the resignation of Elder David J. Young around 1910, Elder Bowe was chosen as editor. *The Whole Truth* was then switched from being published at Pine Bluff, to the new office located at 521 West 23rd Street in the town of Argenta (then, North Little Rock, unannexed), Arkansas. One street over was the resident of Elder Bowe at 513 West 24th Street. The earliest periodical of *The Whole Truth*, I have seen is Volume 4, Number 4, dated October 1911, with Justus B. Bowe as the editor and associate editors were Charles H. Mason, E. D. Smith, Robert E. Hart, Eddie R. Driver, C. W. Waddell, and David J. Young.

At the thirteenth annual session of the General Board Meeting in 1920, it was decided that Elder Burton D. Smith, replace Elder Bowe as editor of *The Whole*

Truth. It was agreed that he take the paper self-supporting. They agreed to pay the debt of $84.50 and helped him pay the $174 that he owed Elder Mason. In 1920, a yearbook was published by Sister Jessie R. Strickland using her own money with permission from the overseers and the general overseer Mason. It was agreed that Sister Strickland would be reimbursed and that she would work with Elder Smith for a year as the yearbook was going to be published by him the following year. After Elder Smith took over as editor, the press was moved from Argenta, to Little Rock, Arkansas. Based on Overseer Bowe's report to the Financial Board regarding future assessments they found out that they needed $700 to bring the press up to par. They decided to access the overseers and the twenty-two states that they were assigned to collect the money. The money was to be paid, July 1, 1921.

The 14th Annual Convocation began on December 6, 1921; and on the second day, the Board of Elders reassembled at 10:00 am. The first order of business was to hear the report of *The Whole Truth* paper. Nine members of the Board of Elders were appointed to further consider the challenges of the paper. The board of Elders that were appointed to consider the challenges of *The Whole Truth* assembled at 9:30 am on December 10, 1921, to share their decisions with the rest of the board. It was agreed since the state of Texas was publishing a paper known as the *Apostolic Bulletin*, that it be discontinued and *The Whole Truth* replace it.

After only one year Elder Burton D. Smith resigned as editor of *The Whole Truth* and the board decided to give the paper to Texas for one year. They voted to appoint Elder Houston Gallaway of Temple, Texas, as editor and gave him $100 to print the first issue with the stipulation that the paper should be self-supporting after one year. The name of the paper was temporarily changed to, *For The Whole Truth*. At some point later the name was changed back to *The Whole Truth*.

Elder Robert E. Hart: First President of the Department of Church Extension in COGIC

Under the leadership of Elder Robert Eber Hart, Overseer of Tennessee and the first President of the Church of God in Christ, Department of Church Extension, he was keenly aware of how a church extension department should function. Having spent twenty-plus years in the CME denomination and having a great deal of experience serving on committees, he had a broad knowledge of how committees and departments should be setup and what their functions should be.

It was likely in 1907 at the first general assembly board meeting, or shortly after that the discussion on developing a church extension department took place. The board would have had to vote and approve the Department of Church Extension and its function. After which, the motion would have been carried, and it would have been adopted by a vast majority that a church extension board be formed and a set of by-laws or a constitution governing the board should be drawn up and adopted so everybody would understand the function of the department. Also, officers would have been elected to govern the affairs of that board.

The Twelfth Annual Session of the General Board and Holy Convocation convened in Memphis, Tennessee, in November; and on December 12, 1919, at 10:00 am the board meeting was called to order. After the minutes were read, corrected, and adopted, the first order of business was on governing overseers. Next the church extension board was heard and reported about $1200 was on hand and everything was in good condition. The money was in the bank at Jackson, Tennessee. The secretary of church extension, Elder Stephen Rice, proposed to show a clear record of all receipts and disbursements by the next meeting. [9] I find it ironic that Elder Rice, like Elder Hart had matriculated into COGIC from the CME Church and was working beside Elder Hart in the church extension department.

After the death of Dr. Hart, the business of the Department of Church Extension was left up to the General Board to make the necessary changes. On Thursday, December 15, 1921, promptly at 12 pm the board reassembled for business to reconsider some matters in regard to the Church Extension Board. The General Board agreed that there should be a general financial board present when all monies were deposited in the bank and should be deposited in the name of the Church of God in Christ. Professor James C. Courts and Brother John Lee, both of Lexington, Mississippi, were appointed.

Ordinarily, a Department of Church Extension would assist in providing information, instructions, and money for erecting structures, repairing, and renovating church buildings from money rose through various methods within COGIC. It was like having money in a large "pool" and when it was needed, pending board approval, a withdrawal was made. The department would have the authority to supply money to congregations by lending and educating them on how to obtain loans for the purpose of expanding their ministry.

Mother Lizzie Robinson was sent to Jackson, Tennessee, in 1911 by Bishop Mason after she was appointed National Supervisor of Women to work under Elder Hart. I believe part of her tutoring was to learn from Elder Hart some valuable techniques of how to setup and oversee the new Women's Department. Elder Hart was the President of the Department of Church Extension and would want Mother Robinson to understand how important church extension was to the entire body. He knew how to help her organize the Women's Department, which was going to grow very rapidly. Her department was going to be an "incredible" spiritual and financial boost to the denomination. After all, literally all the funds for church extension were going to come from within COGIC and its auxiliaries. So it was vitally important to have the knowledge and have the understanding of the techniques of raising funds that were critical to the success of both departments. Funds for the Department of Church Extension could be raised all year in a variety of ways; however; the board early on probably realized that appropriating a small percentage to Church Extension out of the national budget would sufficiently fund the department temporarily.

Church Extension was so important to Elder Hart that he included it in his last Will and Testament. Elder Hart's Will was probated on May 28, 1921. In the sixth clause of his Will it states:

As to the Church extension money if there be any in my possession at the time of my death the church extension will show how much by Bank Book and I will that the said Bank Book be carefully preserved and turned over to the board of Directors. Elder Charles Mason, Memphis, Tenn. as Chairman of said Board. [10]

I found it surprising and a little insensitive of the General Assembly not to mention anything about the life and labor of Elder Robert E. Hart in COGIC at the 14th Annual Holy Convocation Board Meeting held in Memphis, Tennessee, December 6-15, 1921. There was no mention of Dr. Hart's contributions or death in the minutes; however, Elder Mason along with many others would have certainly attended the funeral, and Bishop Mason probably was the eulogist.

8

FRANK AVANT

vs.

C. H. MASON

Author's Note

Court papers were filed in this case to be heard in the Chancery Court of Shelby County, Tennessee, on the first Monday in October of 1907. A summons and an injunction were issued in the case and served on Bishop Mason and the officers of the Saints Home Church of God in Christ, January 9, 1908. This was the beginning of a legal battle between the Jones and Mason factions, which would last for several years over doctrinal differences and property damages between the two factions. The objectionable charges that were filed and the motives behind the charges weren't really over church property but rather over doctrine, faith, and the Holy Ghost with the evidence of speaking in tongues. Preposterous as it may sound, but the truth of the matter is the plaintiffs (Jones faction) contumaciously took the Holy Ghost to court and lost.

Some historians and researchers have written that the decision of the Chancery Court of Shelby County in 1908, which was in favor of the Complainants, but was later found in error and overturned by the Tennessee Supreme Court in Jackson, Tennessee, May 24, 1909, was all about Bishop Mason and his faction fighting with the C. P. Jones faction over who had the legal right to use the name "Church of God in Christ." However, that wasn't true, but rather it was a decision in favor of their right to reoccupy their church and property after having been barred from their church by an injunction in January of 1908, pending a trial. It was July of 1909, before they were able to reoccupy the church.

The basis of the complainants lawsuit and argument was that they, the defendants (C. H. Mason and congregation), had abandoned the original faith and order that the church was established and organized under and had introduced a heretical mode of speech or tongue, which no one could understand; therefore, the complainants claimed they wanted to prevent a diversion or division within the church by Bishop Mason and his adherents who had abandoned the faith and order of the original church. The lawsuits filed by the Jones faction in Tennessee, Arkansas, and Mississippi, were an attempt to take control of church property from all the preachers that followed the Mason faction.

The Injunction

The State of Tennessee to C. H. Mason, J. I. J. Prophet, Billy Frazier, Allie Frazier, Sam Jones, Eddie Rodgers, Charlie Wheeler, George Sparks, Willie Roberts, General Lowery, George King, S. T. Samuel, George Taylor and Noah Deberry. Whereas, Frank Avant, etal, hath lately exhibited their Bill of Complaint in the Chancery Court of Shelby County against you, the said C. H. Mason, etal, as Defendants therein, and obtained from the Honorable F. H. Heiskell, Judge, etc., an order that Writs of Injunction do issue according to the prayer of said Bill. We, therefore, in consideration of the premises, do strictly enjoin and command you, the said C. H. Mason, J. I. J. Prophet, Billy Frazier, Allie Frazier, Sam Jones, Eddie Rodgers, Charlie Wheeler, George Sparks, Willie Roberts, General Lowery, George King, S. T. Samuel, George Taylor and Noah Deberry, their agents, employees, etc., and all and every persons before mentioned, and each and every of you, that you and every of you, do absolutely desist and refrain from trespassing or going upon the church property known as the Church of God, and commonly known as the sanctified church, situated on Wellington Street in Memphis, Shelby County, Tennessee, and to turn over the keys of said church to complainants (Jones faction) until the further order of our said Court to the contrary. And this you shall in no wise omit, under the penalty prescribed by law. F. H. Heiskell, judge of Shelby County granted the injunction, October of 1907; however, it wasn't officially filed until, January 9, 1908, and it was read and served on the defendants, January 10, 1908. The injunction was the first piece of litigation carried out in this case.

The motion to dissolve the injunction was filed, February 11, 1908, by the attorney for the defendants, (Mason faction) Julius J. DuBose. The Clerk and Master of the Chancery Court responded with his answer:

This cause came on this day to be heard upon motion of defendants to dissolve the injunction herein granted upon bill and answer, and the court having fully heard and understood said motion, is of opinion that the answer does not satisfactorily meet the charges of diverting the church property from the purpose of which it was intended, and for which the church was organized.

It is therefore adjudged and decreed, that said motion to dissolve the injunction herein, be and the same is hereby overruled, and the injunction will stand until the cause is heard on its merits. [1]

This decision by the Clerk and Master to overrule the motion and dissolve the injunction was rejected; starting a sixteen month eviction for Bishop Mason and his congregation.

Lawsuit Filed in Chancery Court

The following article was published in the *Commercial Appeal* newspaper the day after the injunction was filed and served on C. H. Mason and his congregation:

"The Church of God, Sanctified," located on Wellington street, the negro religion organization which has caused much comment during the past several months by the unintelligible words uttered by its pastor, Rev. C. H. Mason and many of its members, is involved in a suit which was filed in the chancery court yesterday afternoon by B. F. Booth as solicitor.

The suit is styled Frank Avant and others against C. H. Mason and others, and the object of it is to oust Mason and his alleged heretic followers from the church and allow it once more to resume its normal functions as a religious organization. The complainants, of whom there are about twenty-five, assert that the defendants, an equally large number, have actually taken possession of the church and threatened to do violence to all who dare interfere with them in control of the edifice, despise the fact that they have all been excommunicated by the national association of the denomination, at a session held in Jackson, Miss., last summer.

The bill starts out with the allegation that the church was organized about eight years ago for the purpose of worshipping God along the lines laid down in the Old and New Testaments, the Ten Commandments, the Apostles' Creed and other well known and familiar Biblical chapters and portions.

It is then alleged that the "Rev." Mason was its pastor, but how or by what authority he got to be so the complaints know not, asserting that "he just sorter drifted in." It is then alleged that the church was prosperous until May, 1907, at which time Mason returned from a visit to Los Angeles, Cal., with a "heresy and a tongue wholly departed from the regular faith and order of the denomination."

It is next said that he has "adopted an heretical mode of speech, or tongue, not a language, but nonsensical, farcical, ridiculous and unheard of jabber, which nobody can understand, which has made the church a laughing stock, and a general place of amusement for the outside world and others.

It is next alleged that Mason and his strange and heretical actions and antics has diverted the church property from its regular faith and is now using it for the service of the devil instead of the worship of God, as it was intended, and that he is surrounded by a number of the former members of the organization, upon whose ignorance he has preyed, and that the entire lot of them are now nothing but a set of ignorant fanatics, who have defied the lawful and orthodox members of the church to take possession of it.

In the prayer of the bill it is asked that an injunction issue permanently restraining the defendants or any of them from holding such unintelligible, heretical, and farcical services within the church building, and a mandatory injunction calling upon them to give up the keys and surrender possession of the building to the orthodox and rightful members of the congregation, and further restraining the defendants named and all others who belong to the fanatical class from trespassing upon the property or in any way interfering with the complainants and their following in the peaceful possession of it as a house of worship.

Chancellor Heiskell issued a temporary injunction as prayed and the hearing of the application to make it permanent promises to prove interesting.

Mason claims that he had a vision from God out in California at which the tongue he now uses was revealed to him, together with the gift of imparting knowledge of it to others. **[2]**

In this article we can read for the first time some of the language that was used by the defendants' lawyer, Benjamin F. Booth in his opening brief to the Chancery Court. Charles P. Jones and his followers really believed that speaking in tongues by Mason and others after they had received the Holy Ghost weren't of God but rather of the devil. Why didn't they believe and why didn't they accept what they heard and saw with their own eyes? I believe it was a question of faith. They simply didn't allow their faith to receive or hope for the truth and believe that it was of God.

Subpoena To Answer

The subpoena to answer the charges filed by the Complainants was executed, January 15, 1908, on C. H. Mason, J. I. J. Prophet, Billy Frazier, Eddie Rodgers, Allie Frazier, Charles Wheeler, William Roberts, General Lowery and George King, by reading this writ to each of them and left a copy of the bill with J. J. DuBose, attorney for the defendants. Sam Jones, George Sparks, Saint T. Samuel, George Taylor, and Noah DeBerry were not found. J. J. DuBose accepted service for each of the parties not found. This subpoena was filed by Benjamin F. Booth, Attorney for the Complainants.

Julius J. DuBose: First Attorney To Represent C. H. Mason and COGIC

The honorable Julius J. DuBose, one-time judge of the criminal court of Shelby County was born near Millington, Tennessee about 1839. The son of a wealthy cotton planter, he was related by blood or marriage to many of the most aristocratic families of the South. He was married to Mary Polk, who was a member of the family of President James K. Polk. His early life was marked by a bright future, but not without serious deep dark activities which made him a man of dominant and aggressive behavior. He received his education in the country schools of Shelby County, and later enrolled in law school at Cumberland University, in Lebanon, Tennessee, and graduated having taken the full law course.

At the outbreak of the Civil War, he enlisted in the Ninth Arkansas regiment and saw considerable active service. Judge DuBose took part in the battle of Shiloh, and he served with distinction throughout the Civil War and was continually promoted until he reached the rank of lieutenant-colonel. He was one among a number of former Confederate solders who never surrendered. He often declared to his friends that he would have rather left the country than surrender.

Judge DuBose was one of the early members and head of the white celebrated KKK in Memphis, before and after the Civil War. At the close of the Civil War, he returned to Memphis and got involved in public service but retained his membership in the KKK. He was appointed City Court Clerk, December 15, 1870; however, he resigned from that position on September 28, 1871. In August of 1872, he was hired as a Deputy Sheriff by newly elected Chief Deputy W. J. P. Doyle; under his administration he served until, August of 1874. He was appointed to the bench as Criminal Court Judge of Shelby County, in 1887. Up until that time he was in private law practice.

DuBose behavior and character came under scrutiny in 1892 by a young and popular; aggressive black female name Ida B. Wells. At the time, she was an established newspaper owner/editor and community activist. Between 1890 and 1891, three close friends of Ida B. Wells, Thomas Moss, Calvin McDowell, and William Stewart opened the People's Grocery Company. The store was directly across the street from a white owned grocery store. Up until the time People's Grocery opened the white owned grocery store had all the neighborhood business. The stores were located at the corners of Walker Avenue and Mississippi Boulevard where the intersection curved sharply, giving the name of the murders that took place there the "Curve Murders" or "Lynching's at the Curve." Julius J. DuBose was the criminal court judge at the time the murders were committed and played a major role in the events that led up to the horrific crimes that were perpetrated.

It all started when a black youth by the name of Armour Harris supposedly assaulted the son of Cornelius Hurst, a white resident of the Curve. Hurst caught up with Armour and thrashed him. This infuriated Armour's father and some of the other blacks in the community when a fight broke out between the men with Hurst striking one of the black men with a club. One day later several black men congregated at the "Curve" when William R. Barrett (white), owner of the other grocery store tried to intervene and quiet matters when supposedly, he was physically assaulted and shot at by several blacks inside the People's Grocery Store. When the law enforcement officers arrived to make arrest and quiet matters, shots were fired on both sides, resulting in injuries and arrest.

Judge DuBose was appealed to and he issued a bench warrant for the youth name, Armour Harris and William Stewart, one of the owners of People's Grocery Store. DuBose also issued an order to disarm all the blacks in the area, including the Tennessee Rifles, a black paramilitary group of which Calvin McDowell was a member. DuBose was aware of the white posse of men patrolling the Curve but allowed them to carry their weapons. A few days later Calvin McDowell, Thomas Moss, and William Stewart, all in their twenties were brutally murdered by a white mob that stormed the jail and took them and the law into their own hands. [3]

What Bishop Mason did or didn't know about Mr. DuBose before he was retained as their attorney is a mystery; however, he didn't represent Bishop Mason and COGIC for long. There is no evidence that suggests because of Mr. DuBose's racist past, Bishop Mason had him replaced with a black attorney after a little over a month on the case. Bishop Mason probably wasn't aware of Mr. DuBose's judicial involvement several years earlier in the "Curve" murders and controversy. Although Bishop Mason probably wasn't in Memphis at the time, he certainly would have heard about the "mayhem" and murders that had taken place in his hometown. However, I can't totally discount his decision to change attorneys wasn't based on those events.

Henry R. Saddler: Second Attorney To Represent C. H. Mason and COGIC

Henry was born in Aberdeen, Monroe County, Mississippi, January 4, 1874, to Henry, Sr., and Melvina Saddler. He was the youngest of four boys. His father and mother had been slaves, and they both were born in Mississippi, his father around 1824, and his mother about 1830. In all, there were six children and their parents wanted an education for all of them.

He entered law school at Central Tennessee College, in Nashville, Tennessee, around 1893 and graduated in 1896 with a Bachelor of Laws. Central Tennessee College campus then and now was the same campuses where Meharry Medical College is located. Central Tennessee College changed its name to Walden University in 1900.

Henry and Lula Floyd were united in holy matrimony in 1899 three years after he began practicing law in Memphis. His first office was located at 164 Main Street on the second floor and his residence was 41 Polk Street. Between 1900 and 1910, he moved his office to 321 Beale Street and his private residence to 684 Phelan Avenue. Their only child, Henry R. Saddler, Jr., was born in 1902.

There were about fourteen black practicing attorneys in Memphis in 1907 that were available for Bishop Mason to choose from. Mr. Saddler wasn't considered to be the most popular or the busiest black attorney in the city; however, Bishop Mason obviously received some recommendations about Mr. Saddler from some source. About the same time, Bishop Mason needed to make a decision of who was going to be their next legal counsel, Green P. Hamilton, a local educator and principal, published in 1908 his book, *The Bright Side of Memphis*, which served as a biography and directory of the city's African-American professional, religious, and business establishments. Mr. Hamilton was indeed biased toward Bishop Mason and all holiness churches to have listed and recognized in his book Baptist, Congregational, Episcopal, African Methodist Episcopal, AME Zion, and CME preachers but ignored the Pentecostal-Holiness denominations and churches.

Whether Bishop Mason used this book as a reference cannot be confirmed, but the following biography was published in the book about Mr. Saddler:

The successful lawyer bearing the name of such an honorable occupation in life is a native of the State that seems to be the breeding place of distinguished men—the great State of Mississippi. His early education training was received in the schools of his native State and completed in the State of Tennessee, to which his parents had emigrated and brought him. He is an honored alumnus of one of our best local institutions of learning, and one to whose success it points with conscious pride.

Even when very young the distinguished subject of this sketch gave, in the literary society of his first Alma Mater, evidences of that distinction in address and forceful oratory that the opportunities of his profession have afforded him, and few occasions were considered complete without an exhibition of his oratorical graces. Endowed with such rich gifts and having such an auspicious and fruitful field for their display, it was only natural that he should have selected a profession that would not only furnish him unlimited opportunity for exercising his gifts, but would also bring him ample financial returns. Accordingly, after his graduation, he matriculated in the Law Department of Walden University, Nashville, Tenn., and earnestly pursued the study of the profession in which he has gained merited success. Having received the degree of L.L.B., from the same institution, he returned home and was admitted in 1896 to the practice of his profession. He was honored by the County Court of Shelby in 1896 with the appointment of notary public and executed the necessary bond for the faithful performance of his duties, which he has done up to this time.

He was the founder and Dean of the Law Department of Lane College, Jackson, Tenn., for a period extending from 1900 to 1903, and preformed the duties of his exalted trust with signal ability. He practices in all the courts but makes a specialty of chancery practice in which his success has been very gratifying to himself and friends.

He has gained distinction as counsel in the Supreme Court of the State of Tennessee, before which tribunal he appears yearly to plead the case of his clients. The number of his cases before this August tribunal is said to be nearly as great as those of any other counselor of color at the Memphis bar. He has a judicial trend of mind and weights every contention in the scales of impartial judicial analysis. He is a young man of bright legal promise and has merited in his profession a success that many an older lawyer has struggled to achieve in vain. [4]

The honorable Henry R. Saddler defended Bishop Mason and COGIC for about fifteen months until the case was appealed to the Tennessee Supreme Court; at which time, there was a disagreement between Mr. Saddler and Bishop Mason over the fee Mr. Saddler requested to continue prosecuting the case. The disagreement wasn't resolved, and Mr. Saddler's services were terminated.

Elder Robert E. Hart: Third Attorney To Represent C. H. Mason and COGIC

Elder Hart needs no introduction, only an explanation of how he got chosen as the attorney to represent Bishop Mason in the most "explosive" religious controversial trial of the century; as it relates and applies to the doctrines of two newly formed Black Pentecostal-Holiness denominations of the twentieth century.

In a previous chapter, we celebrated the graduation of Dr. Hart in 1901 from Lane College with a bachelor's degree in law. At that particular time, he had no interest in practicing law, only teaching law at the University of West Tennessee located in Jackson, Tennessee. Up until the time he was retained to represent Bishop Mason and COGIC (as far as I can tell from my research), this was his first case in the legal system and positively his first case before the Tennessee State Supreme Court. Elder Hart got indirectly involved in the case early as February of 1908 when the attorney for the complainants, Benjamin Booth, filed a petition against the rehearing of the order to dissolve the injunction in the case. An excerpt from the petition reads as follow:

*Complainants further, say, that C. H. Mason has accepted the judgment of the Court, and has abandoned the Church, and give up the fight and left the State, and moved with his family to the State of Mississippi, and this new move is made by one **Hart** who comes here from Jackson, Tennessee to interfere in this affair, with which he has absolutely nothing to do.* [5]

Attorney Booth implies in the petition that the case had already been decided because Bishop Mason had left the state with his family. This was simply not true, and the final decree in the case, which was decided against Bishop Mason and COGIC in the Chancery Court, was on July 28, 1908. However, immediately an appeal was filed by the defendant's lawyer, Elder Hart.

Hart Enrolled as an Attorney

Before Elder Hart could practice law in Tennessee, he had to be properly enrolled as an attorney before the court. This took place in Jackson, Tennessee, September 15, 1908, in the Circuit Court of Madison County. You may recall from a previous chapter that Dr. Hart had already been licensed in 1901; however, never enrolled. The following order was given by the judge:

*Order Enrolling **R. E. Hart** as a practicing attorney. Be it remembered that this day came **R. E. Hart** into open Court and exhibited his licenses to practice law issued to him on 16th day of February 1901, by Jno. M. Taylor, Circuit Judge and A. G. Hawkins, Chancellor of the State of Tennessee, and upon motion of M. V. Lynk, an attorney of this Court, it is ordered that he take the statutory oath required of practicing attorneys to wit:*

*To support the Constitution of the State and the United States and to truly and honestly demean himself in the practice of his profession to the best of his skill and ability; which oath the said **R. E. Hart** took in open Court and thereupon it is ordered by the Court that he be enrolled as a regular practicing attorney in this Court.*
[6]

It was surprising to see Elder Hart's friend and once parishioner, Dr. Miles V. Lynk, present and standing by his side; supporting Elder Hart when he needed him. These men were making history for Jackson in the area of law, Lynk being the first black attorney licensed to practice and Hart the second. Thirty-nine days after the appeal was filed in Chancery Court, in the case Avant vs. Mason, Elder Hart was enrolled as an attorney, making him eligible to practice law in Tennessee. There is no doubt at this point he was planning to get enrolled as an attorney for the specific purpose of representing Bishop Mason and COGIC. How Bishop Mason came to the conclusion to allow Elder Hart to be retained as their attorney, and how Elder Hart convinced Bishop Mason that he could effectively prosecute this case before the State Supreme Court having no experience practicing law before the courts is a mystery. Elder Hart had sixty-five days from the time, he was retained to prepare himself and the briefs (clients' statements and evidence) for the case, scheduled to be heard May 24, 1909, before the Tennessee Supreme Court in Jackson, Tennessee.

A notice of appointment of Robert E. Hart as attorney for the defendants, C. H. Mason and COGIC, was filed in the office of Lamar Heiskell, Clerk and Master of Chancery Court, which read:

*In the above cause, take notice that **R. E. Hart** having been authorized by the Pastor, Officers and members of the Saints Home Church of God in Christ to prosecute the appeal through the Supreme Court is now the authorized Solicitor in the above styled cause, therefore please serve all notices or processes upon him or W.M. Roberts trustee at 623 Stephens Avenue, Memphis, Tenn.* [7]

Even though the notice of appointment was filed after Elder Hart won the Tennessee Supreme Court decision, it was really filed, because of other litigation pertaining to the case (such as property damages that were prosecuted by Elder Hart) through the Chancery Court of Shelby County after the Tennessee Supreme Court decision. Evidently, everybody that should have heard that Attorney Hart was now representing Mason and COGIC and that H. R. Saddler had long been dismissed from the case, hadn't received the notice; therefore, a second legal notice was filed, August 25, 1909:

*Frank Avant vs. C. H. Mason—In the above cause, we the undersigned officers and pastor of the Saints Home Church, known as the sanctified church on Wellington Street, Memphis, Tenn., desire again to notify all concerned, that H. R. Saddler has long since been dismissed as an attorney from the above cause, and **R. E. Hart** given full power to act as attorney for us. Signed: C. H. Mason, pastor, J.I. J. Prophet, W. M. Roberts, and General Lowery; Deacons.* [8]

Benjamin F. Booth: Attorney Representing Frank Avant and the C. P. Jones Faction

Benjamin Franklin Booth was born in Baldwin, Prentiss County, Mississippi, October 17, 1858, and was raised on a farm. When the Civil War ended the family moved to Ripley, Tippah County, Mississippi, but his father was already dead. His mother was name Lucy and she was born in South Carolina in 1828. She and

Benjamin were living together in 1870. An older brother, Bill, was living next door with his wife Mary and their eight-month-old son, J. A. Booth.

In 1880 Benjamin entered school at the State Normal School for Colored in Holly Springs, Mississippi, on the campus of Rust College, where he showed impressive success in his studies. He graduated in 1884 and began teaching school in Mississippi; and for a couple of years, he taught school in Bolivar, Tennessee. He also taught school at Middleton, Tennessee, and while there, began reading law. He was aided in his reading and studying of law by Colonel Inge of Corinth, Mississippi, an outstanding white lawyer of that day. Booth was admitted to the bar and began practicing law while living in Bolivar, Tennessee, later moving to Memphis in 1888.

Fayette M. Hamilton, editor and manager of the *Christian Index*, mentioned in the local and personal column of the paper that Professor Booth of Bolivar, Tennessee was in the city of Jackson on business August 13, 1887. He noted that you couldn't get near him for the crowd of people. Professor Booth at the time was principal of Bolivar, Hardeman County, Colored Schools.

On March 21, 1901, Benjamin Booth along with his colleague Thaddeus W. Bradford, an African-American lawyer practicing in Memphis, entered the courthouse and obtained a license to marry Edith Martin. They were married the same day. Booth, a member of the CME denomination, was united in Holy Matrimony by his pastor, Dr. Nelson Caldwell Cleaves, at Collins Chapel CME Church.

Benjamin Booth represented and served the community in many different ways. He represented banks and served on boards and was involved in several other business and civic entities in the Memphis metropolitan area. For a few years, beginning in 1909, he was Professor of Medical Jurisprudence at the University of West Tennessee Medical College where Miles V. Lynk, M. D., was the president. In the dental department he served as professor of Forensic Dentistry.

B. F. Booth was loyal and sincere and he was tolerant; he was loyal to his family and always to his friends; he was loyal to his profession and loyal to his race; he was loyal to duty and loyal to the principles of life, which he recognized; but most of all, he was loyal to himself. Practically all of the lawyers at the Memphis Bar for the last quarter of a century had been friends of Booth. They were his friends because he did those things and maintained toward them the attitude that provoked their friendship. For more than fifty-four years Benjamin F. Booth was a familiar figure around the courtrooms of Shelby County. Now and then he showed up before the Supreme Court of Tennessee and several times in the highest court of the land at Washington, D. C. In the latter part of the nineteenth century and early twentieth century, he was by far the most prominent black attorney in the South and possibly in the United States.

He was proud of the fact that he was the oldest practicing attorney in Memphis, white or black. He kept right on practicing until he fell seriously ill. He died Saturday, May 31, 1941, at Collins Chapel Hospital, an African-American facility owned and managed by the CME denomination. He was survived by his widow, Edith Martin Booth; and by a daughter, Bennye Booth who lived in Memphis; and by a son, Arthur Booth, who lived in New York City. Services for the Honorable Benjamin Franklin Booth were held June 4, 1941, at 3:30 pm at T. H. Hayes & Sons Funeral Home. Burial was in Elmwood Cemetery.

Final Decree of the Chancery Court In 1908

This cause came on to be heard this day before the Honorable F. H. Heiskell, Chancellor, upon the whole recording the cause. Including the order of reference and the Master's report made in obedience thereto, which report is the final decision of the Chancery Court of Memphis, Shelby County, Tennessee, Frank Avant vs. C.H. Mason:

And the defendant having accepted to said report the same came on for argument. The exceptions taken by the defendant to the report of the Master made in this cause to the present term of the Court and the Court having heard read the report the proof referred to therein, and the exceptions and being of the opinion that all of said exceptions taken as aforesaid are not well taken and the same are hereby overruled and disallowed, and said report is by the Court on motion of the Complainant, in all things confirmed. It is therefore ordered adjudged and decreed, by the Court that the Complainants to this suit Frank Avant etal, as adherents to the original faith and order are entitled to the use, occupation and enjoyment of the Saints Home Church of God in Christ, called the Sanctified Church which is situated on the east side of Wellington Street near Vance Street in the City of Memphis, Tennessee together with the lands and improvements belonging or in any wise appertaining to the same and the defendants there agents, friends and sympathizers and each of them are hereby perpetually enjoined from in any matter trespassing on same, and the said C. H. Mason, his agents, friends and sympathizers are hereby perpetually enjoined from preaching or attempting to preach in said church or on said church property. The defendant C. H. Mason, J. I. J. Prophet, Billy Frazier, Allie Frazier, Sam Jones, Eddie Rodgers, S. T. Samuel, George Taylor, and Noah Deberry will pay the cost of this suit for which will issue as at law. To which said action of the Court the defendants then and there excepted, and now except, and have hereby prayed an appeal to next term of the Supreme Court to be held over for the Western District of Tennessee at Jackson on the Monday in April, 1909, which said appeal is granted by the Court upon the defendants giving an appeal bond as required by law. [9]

When C. H. Mason and his faction lost the Chancery Court decision in 1908, it was merely an opportunity for them to take the Jones faction to the "Red Sea." After seven months and approximately 328 pages of legal documents, the case went to the Tennessee State Supreme Court. It took only one day for the judges to decide in favor of C. H. Mason. Elder Hart apparently had a "masterfully" prepared brief with which he was able to demonstrate and validate his client's position. His opponent, the honorable Benjamin F. Booth, was an able and capable attorney; but this case was tried in the Supreme Court and the outcome orchestrated by the Supreme God.

Miracle of the Court Room in 1909

The previous biographical sketch of Benjamin F. Booth was only a partial synopsis of his life and accomplishments; however, it is fair to say that the opinions and facts reflect his character and ability as a good sound lawyer. Also, it gives one good ideas of the popularity Mr. Booth had before the courts and in the community, which will help one better understand and appreciate the "miracle" that took place in the courtroom between the factions. Avant was represented by Benjamin F. Booth, and Mason was represented by Henry R. Saddler and Robert E. Hart. The case was first decided in favor of the Charles P. Jones faction in the Chancery Court of Shelby County. I question whether the decision in that case was based upon the law or partially based on the notoriety of the Complainants' attorney, or whether the personal religious convictions of the Clerk and Master were a factor. The case was later decided in favor of Bishop Mason in 1909 before the Tennessee Supreme Court; however, it could have been decided in favor of Avant and the Jones faction given the ignorance, unbelief, and prejudices of the people against sanctification, holiness, and testifying of being filled with the Holy Ghost with the evidence of speaking in tongues.

The Tennessee Supreme Court judge(s) that heard the arguments from both sides in the case gave a memorandum opinion or decision, which meant a court decision that gives the ruling (what it decides and orders done) but no opinion (reason for the decision). "Can't you see God at work here?" What every member of COGIC ought to ask himself or herself today if Bishop Mason had lost this case, "What would the Church of God in Christ be like in the world today?" I hope every member sees and understands the significance of the miracle and how the Lord used an "inexperienced" lawyer; however, full of faith and the Holy Ghost, and how he went up against a "goliath" of a lawyer and a worldly court system and won! Glory to God!

The Tennessee Supreme Court Decision of 1909: Frank Avant
vs.
C. H. Mason

Be it remembered that this cause came on this day to be heard on the record from the Court below, assignments of error and arguments of Counsel, whereupon the Court is of opinion and doth accordingly adjudge and decree that there is error in the decree of the Chancery Court, and it is therefore reversed.

The Court is further of the opinion and doth accordingly adjudge and decree that the defendants, C. H. Mason and those adhering to him, are entitled to the use, occupation and enjoyment of the Saints Home Church of God in Christ, called the Sanctified Church, which is situated on the east side of Wellington Street near Vance Street, in the City of Memphis, Tennessee, together with the land and improvements belonging, or in any wise appertaining to the same, and the Complainants, their agents, friends and sympathizers and each of them, are hereby perpetually enjoyed from in any manner, trespassing on the same.

It is further adjudged and decreed that the defendants recover of the complainants, and of I. L. Jordan, their surety on the prosecution bond, all of the costs of this Court and of the Court below.

On motion of the complainants, the cause is remanded to the Court below for a reference for damages on the injunction bond. **[10]**

Assignments of Error and Briefs in the case were filed by Robert E. Hart on April 2, 1909; and the Reply Brief was filed by Benjamin F. Booth, April 27, 1909. On May 26, 1909, two days after the decision, B. F. Booth filed a petition to rehear the case; and on May 28, 1909, Henry R. Saddler filed a petition to rehear the case. Saddler was still disgruntled over the disagreement he and Bishop Mason had had over the fees charged in the case. The petitions filed by lawyers B. F. Booth and H. R. Saddler was denied.

Hart Prosecuted the Complainants For Damages to Saints Home COGIC

After the Supreme Court decision in favor of C. H. Mason and COGIC in 1909, Elder Hart began to prosecute for the damages done to the church while the injunction bond was in force through the Shelby County, Chancery Court. The complainants reoccupied Saints Home after Mason and his congregation was read out by the injunction. During their occupation, they damaged or by neglect caused disrepair to the church. The claims of the defendants, C. H. Mason, Jackson L. I. Prophet, Allie Frazier, Sam Jones, Eddie Rodgers, Charlie Wheeler, George Sparks, William Roberts, General Lowery, Saint T. Samuel, and George Taylor, amounted to about $1989; and they were also asking to be allowed statutory interest on the whole amount. On the list of damaged items to the church and what the defendants wanted to recover included sixteen months rent at $30 per month. One large tent under which the defendants were forced to worship. The cost to the defendants to replace the roof, ceiling, and floor that was allowed to ruin over a period of sixteen months. Attorney Hart prosecuted the case for about seventeen months; and in the end, he was only able to recover $400 of the approximately $1989 plus interest they claimed in the suit. The legal dispute between the Jones and Mason factions officially ended January 19, 1911, three years after it started. It is ironic, Charles P. Jones died on January 19, 1949.

9

ENEMIES OF MASON AND THE CHURCH

Author's Note

All of the statements made by the following individuals came from their depositions taken under oath before the Clerk and Master of the Chancery Court April 18-28, 1908, at his office in the presence of counsel for the complainants and defendants. A stenographer was present to record the proceeding of the meetings. The depositions were officially filed June 2, 1908, in the Chancery Court of Shelby County, Tennessee. All total there were nine individuals that gave depositions for the complainants in this case that I refer to as enemies of Bishop Mason and the church. They were John A. Jeter, Thomas J. Searcy, William W. Thomas, Robert Davis, Frank Avant, Charles P. Jones, William J. McMichael, I. L. Jordan, and Henry Scott. Searcy, McMichael, and Thomas were Baptist preachers who were told by I. L. Jordan to go and volunteer their testimonies against Bishop Mason and his church. Baptist denomination preachers were the only preachers that testified against Bishop Mason and the Sanctified Church. Davis, Avant, Jordan, and Scott were members of Bishop Mason's church before he was excommunicated from the convention by Charles P. Jones and his supporters. Afterwards, they defected from Mason's church over speaking in tongues and started their own church.

The deposition of Charles P. Jones is very important because it provided some facts about several uncertain historical points of interest, such as organizers and founders, organization name and disciplinary action taken on part of the Ministerial Council. All the depositions were later used to help the lawyers prepare briefs and try the case in an actual trial setting.

C. H. Mason and C. P. Jones were at odds only in their doctrinal and legal confrontations. I haven't seen any evidence that suggests there were ever any harsh words or physical contact between the two. Both men were of outstanding character and wouldn't have stooped to such a level. They would have done all within their power to make sure both factions acted in a fair and respectful manner.

Charles Price Jones

One of the first statements Elder Charles P. Jones made in his deposition when asked, "Are you connected with the Church of God?" He replied, "Yes sir, the name which we adopted at our convention was Churches of God in Christ in 1906." In the beginning they referred to the gatherings as Holiness Meetings; however, later they were called conventions or convocations, which lasted eight to ten days. When asked who founded the church he explained, "That the church is founded by Christ himself; of course, from a human point of view, the first men who preached the doctrine upon which this established set of churches were gathered together were myself and Brother John A. Jeter, Brother Charles H. Mason, and Brother William S. Pleasant; we four were first associated together as Baptist preachers and this church grew out of our reports as Baptist preachers. Jeter was over Arkansas; Mason over Tennessee; Jones and Pleasant over Mississippi." Jones also confirmed that the Ministerial Council had two meeting with Mason, Hart, Driver, and others trying to get them to "retract" their false doctrine (tongues) which Mason was teaching. They refused, that is when Jones and the council withdrew from Mason and all who associated and affiliated with him. Jones was later asked if Mason, Jeter, Pleasant, or he preached the doctrine in the beginning that Mason was excommunicated for. He replied, "He didn't; none of us did." None of us knew anything about it never had heard of it." I seriously doubt if the latter part of Elder Jones's statement was entirely true. What an oxymoron; Jones who had been the closest confidant of Mason for several years and performed the marriage rites between Elder Mason and Lelia was now "divorcing" himself physically and spiritually from his closest friend of several years over contradictory opinions of the scriptures.

Charles Price Jones was the publisher and editor of *Truth*, a religious periodical published weekly in Jackson, Mississippi, mainly in the interest of the Church of God in Christ. The purpose of the paper was to teach "high" and "holy" living. On December 6, 1906, on page four of the paper, Elder William S. Pleasant submitted an article titled, "Do Your Best, Brethren." According to the article, a school had been opened in the interest of the Churches at Jackson; however, the founding date for the school couldn't exactly be determined, although it probably was founded in 1897. The college was likely the sole vision of Charles P. Jones and was strongly supported by Mason, Pleasant, Jeter, and others. In the article, Elder Pleasant was asking for donations from all who were interested in the welfare of the Lord's school; Christ's Missionary and Industrial College (CM&I). The saints were asked to be liberal in their donations to help lift the $1600 note owed by the school. All monies were asked to be sent to Elder James L. I. Conic. Elder Jones and the Church of Christ (Holiness) U.S.A. were able to keep the doors of this college open into the 1930's and possibly beyond. The college was located in Hinds County, Mississippi, and possibly inside the Jackson city limits. In 1930, the college employed six people. James M. Edwards was the president; James L. I. Conic was a minister on staff, and Eudora (Emma) R. Conic, his wife, was matron. His son, Major R. Conic (named Senior Bishop of COCHUSA in 1949 after the death of Charles P. Jones), was a teacher and was only twenty-years old. Hattie McCarty and Hattie Holloway were both teachers at the college. Elder Conic and his wife were originally members of the Church of God in Christ when it was founded and pastored by C. H. Mason in 1897, located in an old gin house in Lexington, Mississippi. He followed and supported Mason in the early years; however, like so many others, he later separated from Mason over speaking in tongues and followed the Jones faction.

About eight months after Mason was excommunicated, Charles P. Jones revealed in his deposition what probably was the real reason for rejecting Mason's doctrine on speaking in tongues. When asked by the attorney if he and Mason preached the same doctrine on the diversity of tongues and the speaking of new tongues, he replied, "Now as far as the preaching of the tongue doctrine, we didn't object to it or contend or bother with it in our sermons." It was a doctrine, which was a mere "historical" doctrine, just as we would refer to raising the dead." Unfortunately, even today in the body of Christ, this is the attitude toward this doctrine with many Christians.

It is ironic how the lives of Jones and Mason collide at certain points. In 1917 Bishop Jones moved from Little Rock, Arkansas, after the death of his first wife, to Los Angeles, California, and Bishop Mason moved from Lexington, Mississippi, to Memphis, Tennessee. Los Angeles, the city where the Azusa Street Revival was birthed and the outpouring of the Holy Ghost was given with the evidence of speaking in tongues. Elder Jones destiny seemed to have been connected to the very place where he had rejected what God had birthed, ordained, and anointed in the first decade of the twentieth century. He died in Los Angeles on January 19, 1949.

Frank Avant

Frank Avant was about fifty-two years old when he gave his deposition in the case, Frank Avant vs. C. H. Mason, April 18, 1908. He was not only a lead witness for the complainants but also the leading "archenemy" of Bishop Mason and a longtime member of the church. At the time he gave his deposition, he lived at 672 Lerose Street in Memphis and was an express wagon driver for a company. He stated in his deposition that he had been in and out of Memphis since 1861, but this had to be a typographical error made by the stenographer. However, he stated that he had been a member of the church since about 1890. Mr. Avant couldn't have been talking about the council at Jackson, Mississippi; for it hadn't been organized. Bishop Mason and his congregation didn't purchase the property in Memphis until 1900 and didn't build on the property until about 1901. Exactly what church Mr. Avant was referring to deserves a closer look. I refer you to Chapter Four and the comments made in the deposition of D. J. Smith who stated twice he had been connected with the church since 1889, and C. H. Mason was the pastor. D. J. Smith was one of the names on the deed when they purchased the property on Wellington Street.

Both men gave their testimonies under oath, which clearly show Bishop Mason had some form of organized church underway in Memphis as early as 1889, and it likely was street preaching and house to house worshipping. At this point, historians and researchers hadn't placed Mason back in Memphis this early. We know he got married in Arkansas, January 15, 1890; however, according to the testimonies, he had been in Memphis prior to traveling to Arkansas to get married. Exactly when he first arrived in Memphis, we don't know and how long he was gone or when he returned, we don't exactly know. To say the very least, he had a consanguineous relationship with his followers and whomever he left in charge of his followers. Avant also stated in his deposition that he was there from the beginning and helped build the church (Saints Home COGIC). He was likely the most vocal of the complainants and this was probably the reasons his name was used as the leading complainant in the case. He was one of several members that disagreed with Bishop Mason when he returned from California with the baptism of the Holy Ghost and speaking in tongues.

Before joining Bishop Mason's church, Avant was once a member of the Baptist denomination, having left to join Elder William M. Christian, pastor of the Church of the Living God, Christian Workers for Fellowship, a local holiness denomination known as the "Do Rights." Before and after Mason returned from California, Brother Avant refused to take the Lord's Supper; giving no reason as to why. When other members of the church began to be filled with the Holy Ghost, with the evidence of speaking in tongues, those that didn't believe were led away by Avant and Minister I. L. Jordan who was elected pastor of the group, and Avant was made a trustee. They started another church, which was loyal to the Jones faction on Wicks Avenue. It was after this division that the lawsuit was filed by the Jones faction.

Isaac L. Jordan

When Elder I. L. Jordan gave his deposition, he was living in Hollywood, Mississippi. He stated that he had been a member of the Saints Home COGIC almost from the very beginning, before the church was built. He said, "They first began their work holding tent meetings on the ground where the church is now located and C. H. Mason was the pastor." Mason from time to time would allow Minister Jordan to preach. Minister Jordan was against Mason and what he called the "tongue language" and complained that Mason preached in some kind of a "jabber" that they couldn't understand. Jordan claimed that he couldn't understand it; and then Mason would sing and go off into some kind of a muttering, a kind of a chant, that he called songs. He claimed that he got them direct from heaven, or some spirit brought it to him. Jordan said, Mason had abandoned the song books and carried on his song service in a way which no one could understand.

Frank Avant and Henry Scott were the elected deacons and trustees, and Robert Davis was the clerk of this newly formed church group that broke away from Mason. However, none of them were ever officers in Bishop Mason's church. I. L. Jordan was their elected pastor, having served as an evangelist for most of the thirteen years he had been in ministry. He once served as a pastor in Oak Grove, Mississippi. William S. Pleasant also once served as pastor of the church at Oak Grove.

Jordan was responsible for sending Searcy, McMichael, and Thomas, all Baptist preachers, to testify against Mason in the depositions. Searcy stated in his deposition that they were told by Jordan to go and volunteer their statements.

Thomas Jefferson Searcy

Thomas Jefferson Searcy, one of Memphis' outstanding religious leaders of color, was born a slave on November 4, 1852 on a farm in Rutherford County, Tennessee. There was no opportunity for a slave child who grew up in a rural area prior to the Civil War to obtain an education, but Thomas had an intense desire to learn and took advantage of every opportunity to acquire knowledge.

While attending Roger Williams, he accepted the invitation to become pastor of the First Baptist Church in Brownsville, Tennessee, and remained there for several years. Later, Dr. Searcy became pastor of Metropolitan Baptist Church, one of Memphis' largest churches. During his tenure the membership increased to approximately seven hundred persons. A good mixer with a flair for oratory, he was a popular and respected leader in the religious community in Memphis and elsewhere, and was in great demand as a speaker and lecturer. [1]

Reverend Searcy had invited Bishop Mason to his church several times to preach before and after Bishop Mason erected a building, and Mason had invited Rev. Searcy over to preach for him. Rev. Searcy's church was located around the corner from Mason's church on Vance Street; and he stated in an affidavit January 27, 1908, that he had to pass by the door of Saints Home COGIC almost daily and therefore, knew first-hand that they had changed the form of worship. He and Mason spent time together beyond the pulpit talking about the gospel and their differences of opinions. Rev. Searcy made several statements in his deposition opposing Bishop Mason and the way his congregation worshipped. Here are a few of those statements:

"The services held then was just a kind of a jabber; they wasn't language, they wasn't anything but confusion. He would speak a while in English and would then go into something like this. [Here witness gives an illustration] I heard all of that."

"There is none of us-not to say anything about religion-we wouldn't tolerate the disgraceful things that happen in that church. Your wife is to be stretched out on the floor with her tongue out, and anytime you go there is a crowd there laid out and they

are stretched out there, both male and female, to get that tongue. Now our churches did oppose it. The men that went over have been the most ignorant we had."

"I can tell you that—now when Mason preached for me Mason behaved himself, he preached nicely, and I told him when I had him there: "Don't you use it in my pulpit. You are vulgar." And he made this change since, and I didn't go to preach for him but once after he made this change, and I wasn't invited then." [2]

During the taking of Rev. Searcy's deposition he was cross examined by Attorney Henry R. Saddler. The questions and answers reflect the ideology, classism and prejudices people of other denominations had against Bishop Mason and the Sanctified Church. Here are a few of those questions and answers:

Q. Rev. Searcy, I will ask you if shouting is not frequently practiced and manifested on account of religious enthusiasm. Is not it practiced in all the churches of colored people?

A. Everybody rejoices; it depends on the intelligence of the people the extent they go.

Q. Will ask you if in Methodist and Baptist churches the women people don't manifest enthusiasm and fall over on the floor?

A. Certain classes-not falling over on the floor. The most illiterate sometimes go to an extreme.

Q. Take for instance where revivals are held, will ask if it is not your experience as a minister and exhorter in the church, if you have not seen cases where colored women and men coming through, as they call it, getting religion—haven't they shown manifestations which cause them to fall out on the benches and take some time to bring them really to their senses?

A. Oh, I have in a very decent way, and that is the most illiterate class. Now as to this shouting and falling under conviction, now in some of our churches,—in fact, in most of them, we have seen the time that not only some of our girls and women, but some of our men-but not in the way I have described this way. But when they have attempted to do that there is always someone that takes hold of them, and I say that is only those of the most illiterate and excitable nature.

Q. My last question is, is not it a fact that a church like other organizations of the colored people, ignorant people predominate?

A. In some churches they do and some they don't, and the one I am pastoring now, at least, seventy-five percent can read and write, and there is at least as intelligent worship as you see in the city.

Q. My question was, in most congregations of colored people whether or not the ignorant people predominate?

A. Well I don't know about it; it is owing to what you mean by the word "ignorant"? If you mean illiterate or something of that kind they don't predominate; as a general thing, they are led and controlled by the more intelligent. If you mean a majority, I may answer that the churches now as a general thing, are controlled by the more literate class. [3]

Reverend Searcy referred to Mason's speaking in tongues in the pulpit as vulgar. He wasn't interested in the Word of God being preached, but rather he was preoccupied with how many people were lying in the floor, and if Mason was preaching in English or in tongues. Rev. Searcy doubted Bishop Mason's academic abilities, although complimented his singing gift.

Unfortunately, even today classism plays a major role in how people praise and worship the Lord. My son may have gone to a historically black college, and your son may have gone to prison; I drive a Mercedes, and you're catching the city bus; my daughter went to medical school, and your daughter dances provocatively for a rapper; however, I'm thanking God we didn't have to go through some of the challenges you went through, and you should be asking God to bless your family with some of the opportunities I had. Sitting beside each other in a church service, you shouldn't be able to tell any difference in our praise and worship.

William J. McMichael

Rev. McMichael was serving as pastor of St. John Baptist Church in Memphis, located at 59 N. Lauderdale Street, when he gave his deposition. He had been pastor there for twenty years. Someone probably thought because he had a membership of about 800 parishioners and was well known throughout the city, his deposition would really matter. Pastor McMichael was well acquitted with Bishop Mason and had in the past invited Mason over to his church to preach. Pastor McMichael was asked by attorney Ben Booth, upon his visit to Mason's church, if he thought there had been a departure from the original faith and order. He answered, "Since that time there has been quite a departure, I have seen them put on a lot of stuff like they was trembling and hallooing and all talking like this, (illustration) they call it tongues, I believe."

The way Pastor McMichael answered other questions gives a good perspective of the mind-set of the people at the time, and how the community and many Baptist pastors felt about the Sanctified Church. Here are a few more of the questions asked first by Attorney Booth and then Attorney Saddler:

Q. I will ask you if you ever knew members who professed or claimed to have professed religion and been members of the church for years, to lie down on the floor in the church, unconscious, and lie there for hours at a time.

A. I have never known a person who was a Christian, who had been a Christian for any length of time, to lie down on the floor to serve God. I have never known it in all my ministry.

When cross examined by the attorney for the defendants Henry R. Saddler, he asked Rev. McMichael several questions:

Q. Rev. McMichael, as I understand you, the main objection you had to this doctrine Rev. Mason was preaching the last time you went there was that some persons lay on the floor?

A. The last time I was there there was, to my memory, at least three lying on the floor.

Q. Well there was nothing immoral about their lying on the floor?

A. I don't know what they was doing.

Q. I am asking you if you saw anything immoral in the church.

A. No, sir, but that looked wrong to me. **[4]**

John A. Jeter

Elder Jeter was born November of 1855 in Virginia as a slave. He and his parents were likely sold to a slave buyer and brought to Arkansas. He married Lena Evans, October 29, 1885, in Big Rock, Pulaski County, Arkansas, where they made their home. Lena had two children; however, only one survived. John A. Jeter, Jr., was born July of 1887 and later moved to Chicago and worked as a mail carrier.

John A. Jeter along with David J. Young accompanied Bishop Mason to the Azusa Street Revival in Los Angeles, held in the spring of 1907, to see for themselves if what was being broadcast around the world was truly sent from God or something else. All three were said to have received the baptism of the Holy Ghost. Eddie R. Driver stated in his deposition when asked if he had ever heard Elder Jeter speak in tongues. He replied, "When I was last with him he didn't, but at one time he did."

Elder Jeter was asked by attorney Booth, during the taking of his deposition, to state whether or not he had ever been present and heard C. H. Mason conduct services in the church? He replied, "I have, and he conducts his service at times with an unknown jabber that is claimed to be speaking in tongues, one hundred and five and sometimes four hundred and forty." He afterwards said the Lord had added to the one hundred and five, and he says that he speaks Sanskrit (an ancient Indo-Aryan language that is the classical language of India and of Hinduism) and all the others in the book are man made tongues and he sometimes preaches through in the tongue and gives his own interpretation and says all who don't accept his doctrine are false."

Elder Jeter was an eyewitness to what God did in Los Angeles and, according to a few other witnesses, received the Holy Ghost and all that the Lord poured out at the Azusa Street Revival. How or why he backslid is a mystery, but I have a theory that he allowed the enemy to deceive him into believing that God wouldn't pour out of his Spirit again like on the day of Pentecost. Elder Jeter's own explanation, taken from his deposition, was, "I believe that the tongues spoken in the Scriptures were by people to those who spoke them." In other words, he is saying, there were specific people that spoke in tongues then, and no one else could, but they and no one else has since. Although he said that he believed in tongues and preached about it, he referred to Bishop Mason and his followers as false hypocrites that pretended they were speaking in tongues. Judging from the statements made by Elder Jeter about speaking in tongues, it sounds as if he had been indoctrinated by Charles P. Jones and William S. Pleasant, after returning from California. Elder Jones stated in his deposition that speaking in tongues and raising the dead was merely a "historical" doctrine.

In 1906, Elder Jeter was pastor of the churches in Little Rock, Pine Bluff, Searcy and Hot Springs, Arkansas. Elder David J. Young was under his ministry in Pine Bluff, and Elder Daniel G. Spearman was under his ministry in Little Rock. Elder Jeter was head of the department of missions and treasurer of the missions' department for the Church of God in Christ headquartered in Jackson, Mississippi.

Robert Davis

Elder Davis, a former member of the Saints Home COGIC, defected from the church just before the lawsuit was filed by the Jones faction. His home for twenty-seven years had been in Whitehaven, Tennessee. Elder C. P. Jones stated in his deposition that it was Elder Davis who informed him through a letter to come and give his deposition against Mason. Elder Davis, Henry Scott and Frank Avant were elected officers of a small church group started by the few members that defected with them from Saints Home COGIC. Davis was elected church clerk, and Elder I. L. Jordan was elected pastor. Henry Scott, Frank Avant, and Brother Reaveley were elected deacons and trustees. They represented the faction of the Saints Home COGIC that was opposed to speaking in tongues. Davis was present at the winter convention in Jackson, Mississippi, January of 1906, when Mason was appointed Overseer of Tennessee; however, he was absent during the summer convention of 1907, when Mason was excommunicated.

Jordan, Davis, Scott, and Avant split away from Mason over speaking in tongues and began holding services in a small house on Wicks Avenue in Memphis. Immediately after Bishop Mason and his congregation were read out of Saints Home by an injunction in October of 1907, Jordan and his congregation moved back and reoccupied Saints Home, much to the disappointment of Mason and his congregation. They remained there until the court case was finally decided by the Tennessee State Supreme Court in 1909. Most of the questions asked by the attorneys during the taking of Davis's deposition were centered on doctrinal issues such as foot washing, faith, the Lord's Supper, speaking in tongues and baptizing with water. Davis's testimony didn't offer one shred of creditable evidence to justify the division and confusion he and the other brethren brought into the church.

Henry Scott

Elder Scott was once assistant pastor of Saints Home COGIC under Mason. He had been a member of the church from the beginning. In 1908, he was forty-two years old and living at 464 Wicks Avenue. He worked for the Stewart Brothers Company, which sold hardware and dry goods. It was Scott's house in which services were held after, he and several others left Mason's church.

Elder Scott didn't attend the convention in Jackson, Mississippi, in 1907 when Mason was excommunicated, but he was present at the meeting called by Mason, September 4, 1907, in Memphis at Saints Home COGIC. In his deposition, Scott explained, "They (the church) had an election and Mason told them all that wanted him to preach for them as he had been preaching to stand on their feet, and all that didn't want him to preach to stand on their feet, too, but they didn't need to assign a reason why they stood." Scott claimed that the members who couldn't speak in tongues didn't enjoy the services and weren't allowed to participate in the services. He also stated that they weren't allowed to sing and pray. These were no doubt false statements made by Scott under oath for retaliation purposes stemming from charges brought against him by Mason and the officers of the church.

Elder Scott was fired (he says resigned) from his Assistant Pastor's position of three years under fire over charges of immoral conduct with a woman in the congregation. He was a married man and his wife was a member of the church. Scott was a member of the Baptist church before joining the sanctified church. In his deposition, he associated Mason with preaching the so-called message of "come-outism." This was a message preached by some sanctified preachers (Mason may have been the first) calling the people out from under the Baptist denomination.

William M. Thomas

Minister Thomas was pastor of the Salem Baptist Church in Memphis, when he gave his deposition in the lawsuit. Salem was located at 23 W. Carolina Street. Minister Thomas resided at 1351 Kentucky Street. He became pastor of Salem in

1905 and had previously pastored Rock of Ages Baptist Church in Fort Pickering. Fort Pickering was a medium size community about two miles up the Mississippi River on a bluff. When Mason and his congregation were read out of the church by the injunction; Fort Pickering was where they worshipped most of the time. Salem Baptist Church had a membership of about 300 members, and Pastor Thomas was credited with increasing the membership from 100 to 300. Born in Mississippi, he began his ministry in 1895; and after settling in Memphis he pursued Bible studies at Howe Institute under Dr. O. T. Fuller.

Pastor Thomas stated that he only visited Mason's church once and observed that Mason had departed in his opinion from the original faith because at one time, he could understand the service; however, after he started speaking in tongues, he could no longer understand them. When he was asked by Attorney Saddler in his deposition, "How is it that you and Rev. McMichael and Rev. Searcy have all come up here to testify against the sanctified church?" He replied, "They asked me to." For what ever reason many Baptist preachers were adamantly against the Sanctified Church and they took it a step further when they deliberately lied and brought false accusations.

This is the same Baptist church in which Elder Eddie R. Driver became pastor in 1894 after he accepted his call into the ministry. He remained pastor only two years; and in 1901, he joined Bishop Mason's church, Saints Home COGIC.

10

FRIENDS OF MASON: MEMBERS OF COGIC AND THE COMMUNITY

William Joseph Seymour

What I found to be extremely fascinating and surreal was that William Joseph Seymour, (1870-1922) the prominent charismatic prophet, preacher, pastor and leading figure of the Azusa Street Revival in Los Angeles, California, from 1906-11, was in Memphis when the "Curve" murders and "mayhem" were committed. Immediately, I thought, "What effect if any did this experience have on him then and later after he arrived in California?" Judging from the time he departed Memphis, he probably left because of the brutal and riotous atmosphere created by the "Curve" murders. Black people were encouraged by other black activist to leave Memphis and seek safe haven in other cities, and as many as 5,000 to 6,000 did. Seymour was likely one of those that decided it was a good time to get out of Memphis.

Seymour probably arrived in Memphis around 1890 and was living with his relatives, Henry and Lydia Seymour, at 94 Pontotoc Street. He was employed in 1891 as a porter in a barbershop owned by Joseph Celle, a local businessman that also owned a grocery store on Poplar Street. By 1892, he changed jobs and was employed with the Tennessee Paper Company as a wagon driver. Henry, a brick mason, suddenly died, July 19, 1891, and his date of death was listed in the 1891 Memphis city directory. Living up the street from the Seymour family at 226 Pontotoc at the time Elder Seymour was in town were Jerry and Lula Brooks, the parents of Lillian Brooks-Coffey, who later became the supervisor of the Department of Women in COGIC. Mother Coffey wouldn't have had any memory of this because she was only one year old at the time, and it's only a possibility that the Seymour and Brooks' families would have been introduced to each other. Judging from the city directory listings, Seymour probably departed Memphis around the end of 1892 or early 1893.

Seymour frequently visited Memphis on occasions to attend the Church of God in Christ, Holy Convocations. One of the last, if not the last COGIC convocation he attended before his demise in 1922, was in 1919. The minutes of the 12th General Convocation held Thursday, December 11, 1919, recorded his arrival:

Elder W. J. Seymour of Chicago, who also was one of the founders of this great movement, came to us at this hour. How glad our hearts were made to meet him. Order of business was suspended for a few minutes to greet him. Elder Seymour then spoke of his long and wearisome trip and how glad he was to get here. He said he looked upon the Church of God in Christ to be the greatest movement on earth. Therefore he rejoiced to stand among the greatest people on earth. He asked us to contend for the doctrine. He also repudiated even the thought of fornication in the ministry. In his conclusion he urged that the ministry not only be fruitful but to show their fruits.

*Chief Apostle Mason made some very timely remarks by way of responding in the noble sayings of Elder Seymour. He concluded by singing in the spirit a song of welcome. Burton D. Smith and **Dr. R. E. Hart** both made some remarks in which they expressed our gratitude for Bro. Seymour.* [1]

Bishop Mason lost two of his best friends and two of the greatest voices of his time that preached holiness and sanctification when Elder Hart died in 1921 and Apostle Seymour in 1922.

Thomas A. Moore

Thomas A. Moore, a contractor and carpenter living in Memphis, was likely the man that built Saints Home COGIC on Wellington Street. He put up a $1,500 surety on the Appeal Bond that was necessary before the case Avant vs. Mason could be appealed before the Tennessee State Supreme Court. Moore wasn't a member of the church, so his faithfulness to Bishop Mason and the church must have come from a friendship formed under other circumstances. This would explain the kindness extended to Bishop Mason and the congregation by Mr. Moore before the trial. To secure the bond, Moore used his personal residence and lot on Farrington Avenue, which was worth $1,200 and three lots on Vollen-tine Avenue worth $100 each. Elder Eddie R. Driver's name was also on the bond with Moore, but there was no direct mention of property or monetary contribution on the bond by him; however, there was an addition $250 cash contribution that was documented as part of the surety, which was probably paid by Elder Driver. The appeal bond was filed August 7, 1908.

Dee J. Smith, Sr.

Relocating from Memphis to California with Elder Driver was D. J. Smith and his family. Dee J. and his wife, Mary, were the first couple C. H. Mason united in Holy Matrimony in Tennessee. [2] They were married on Wednesday, October 16, 1901, and were probably the first couple to be married in Saints Home COGIC, which was completed in 1901. Brother Smith was one of the trustees at Saints Home COGIC, and he was one of four brethren that made a contract on the Wellington Street property for the church. His name was on the property deed. When living in Memphis, Elder Smith lived between Kerr Avenue and the railroad with his wife, Mary, and their children, Dee J., Jr.; Virginia; and daughter, Elan. Brother Smith and his wife were in business for themselves, peddling dry goods from their wagon.

He and his family likely traveled with the Driver family to California, and both families settled in the seventy-third district of Los Angeles around 1915. They bought a house at 1121 (Mason's house numbers on Mississippi Boulevard in Memphis) East Washington Street in Los Angeles. Although Brother Smith turned sixty-five years old in 1920, he found a job in one of the foundries and his son, Dee J., Jr., was now eighteen and working at the foundry, also. Mary was employed as a maid for a private family, and the other children were in school. In 1930, Brother Smith was seventy-five years old and retired from the foundry. His wife was also retired. Their son, Dee J., Jr., was employed with the City Engineering Department and their daughter, Virginia, had taken over her mother's job as a private maid. Elan was training as a nurse at one of the local hospitals. All of them were members of Saints Home COGIC (west coast) pastored by Elder Driver, who named the church in honor of Bishop Mason's church back in Tennessee.

David J. Young

David J. Young was a few years older than C. H. Mason and was possibly born a slave in Dials Township, South Carolina, September of 1859, and was living and working as a farm hand on the property of Crane J. Knight, a white land owner. He managed to escape the hard labor of the farm and enrolled in Benedict Institute, now Benedict College, founded in 1870 on a former plantation in Columbia, South Carolina. From there he matriculated into Morehouse College in Atlanta and later graduated. Young's second marriage was to Priscilla in 1897, and their first child, Harold, was born in 1899 in Indiana. One year later, Melvin was born in Kentucky; two years later, Valleda was born in Illinois; and three years later, Peter was born in Arkansas. Elder Young's reason for moving from place to place was probably because he was accepting teaching positions in the various places before becoming a minister. Rosetta, Willie, and Celoya, the youngest of the children, were all born in Arkansas. Priscilla had eleven pregnancies; however, only seven children survived.

His sons, Harold and Melvin, would often travel with their father when he held meetings in churches and on the streets. These two children sang, testified and carried on other devotional services which afforded quite an adjunct to their father's efforts in his struggle for the progress of the Church of God in Christ. [3]

Elder Young moved to Arkansas around 1905 and settled in Pine Bluff, Jefferson County. This is when he met Elder Jeter and joined the Church of God in Christ at Pine Bluff under Elder Jeter. Elder Young was involved in all the affairs of the church from the Azusa Street Revival to the Charter of Incorporation in 1922 and beyond. He was the first editor of *The Whole Truth* newsletter, the official organ of COGIC, which was started in 1908.

There is a slight possibility that he and Elder Jeter may have known each other because both of them were from South Carolina. Between 1910 and 1920, Bishop Mason appointed Elder Young Overseer of Kansas and in 1920, he and his family were living in Kansas City, Wyandotte County, Kansas, at 1958 North 6th Street. The two oldest children, Harold and Melvin, were working in the wholesale meat business. Between 1920 and 1925, Elder Young grew increasing ill and in March of 1927, he passed away. Priscilla remained in Kansas after the death of her husband and continued to live in the house on 6th Street. In 1930, five of the children lived with her; and Rosette was the only one out of three grown children listed as being employed.

After the death of his father, Harold, Jr., took over as pastor of his father's church when he was twenty-eight years old. He and his wife Elizabeth had four children by 1930, and they were living at 654 Garfield Avenue in Kansa City, Kansas. Harold, Jr., passed away January 1964 with his last residence in Wichita, Kansas. Harold Young III was born February 8, 1924, and served as a private in the U. S. Army in World War II and died March 23, 1976. He was interred, March 29, 1976, in the Leavenworth National Cemetery in Leavenworth, Kansas.

Melvin J. Young was born September 5, 1899, and was the second oldest child of D. J. Young, Sr. In 1925, he married Odessa; and together they started their family. In 1930, there were two children; Melvin, Jr., and Blaine. Their father was working as a janitor for a music company. He and Odessa likely had more children after 1930. Melvin, Sr., passed away May 22, 1991, in Kansas City.

Richard H. Isaac Clark

Richard was born November 1869 in Mississippi to Anna Dawson who was the mother of eighteen children. She was born in Georgia in 1830; and after her husband died, she went to live with Elder Clark between 1900 and 1910. In 1900, Elder Clark lived at 225 Mulberry Street in Lexington, Holmes County, Mississippi, with his wife Mary Jane (Kitty) and his sons Richard and William. Living with them were his brother and sister, John and Valley Kelsey. In 1902, Valley married a man surnamed Pleas; however, I don't know if he was related to Bishop Charles H. Pleas. Elder Clark and Mary Ann married in 1887 when he was eighteen and she was fifteen years old. Everyone in the household in 1900 was reported to be able to read and write except William, who was nine years old.

Elder Clark and his wife were original members of the Church of God in Christ founded by C. H. Mason in a gin house in Lexington, Mississippi, February of 1897. He was one of Mason's faithful brothers and lifelong friends in the ministry. By 1910, they were able to purchase a house and several of their relatives were living with them. His eighty year old widowed mother came to live with them and his sister, two nephews, and a brother-in-law. In 1921, after Elder Hart's death, Elder Clark was asked by Bishop Mason to temporarily help oversee

Tennessee along with Elder A. B. McEwen. While Elder Clark was helping oversee Tennessee, he sent his family to Chicago; and they were living at 2348 South
State Street. Bishop William Roberts's church was located at 4021 State Street,
which probably meant they were worshipping and laboring in the ministry at his
church.

About the same time, Elder Mason moved back to Memphis (1917) from
Lexington, Mississippi, Elder Clark moved with his relatives from Lexington,
also. With him came his ninety year old mother; his sister, Louise Kelsey; and
nephew, Thomas Pleas. They found a small cottage to rent in the rear of a house
at 393 Wellington Street across the street from Saints Home COGIC. Elder
Clark found a job working as a porter at a dry goods store.

The Charter of Incorporation of the Church of God in Christ was adopted in
accordance with the resolution passed and adopted by the General Assembly of
COGIC held in Memphis, November 25, 1922, through December 15, 1922.
Elder Clark was the subscribing witness (his signature only on the charter) representing the twelve board members of COGIC when they applied to the State of
Tennessee for a charter incorporating themselves into a body. He and C. H.
Mason, E. R. Driver, C. C. Fredrick, Justus Bowe, William Curtis, Mack Jonas,
E. M. Page, D. Bostick, V. M. Barker, R. R. Booker, and D. J. Young, Sr., represented the board at that time. Bishop Mason probably requested that Elder Clark
act as subscribing witness, because out of all the board members present, he was
the only one that had been with him from the beginning when the church was
started in the old gin house in Lexington, Mississippi in 1897.

Justus Bowe, Sr.

Justus Bowe, Sr., was born on New Year's Day in 1873 somewhere in South
Carolina, according to the information on his World War 1 registration card. I
haven't been able to locate Elder Bowe in the 1880, 1900, or the 1910 U. S. Census. This is very unusual for an individual to be absent from three consecutive U.
S. Federal Census.

Elder Bowe was twice married. His first wife was Ludie and they had at least
one child who was born July 9, 1900, and his name was Justus J. Bowe. Oddly,
he named one of his sons Justus in his second marriage. Ironically, Elder Bowe
and his son, Justus J. Bowe, both registered for World War 1, September 12,

1918, in Little Rock, Pulaski County, on the same day; however, in different locations. Justus the first son died from unknown causes, January 12, 1929, in Little Rock, Arkansas.

In 1916, when Elder Bowe and Rizlee married, they made their home in Argenta, Pulaski County, Arkansas. Samuel, the first of at least six children was born December 12, 1916, and Justus, Jr., was born October 6, 1919. Elder Bowe bought a house and moved to Isbell, Lonoke County, Arkansas, in 1919 where he worked as a retail merchant selling his own farm produce. By 1930, Sedric, Osie, Alfonso, and Roberta were born. Justus, Jr., enlisted in World War II on June 25, 1943, in Little Rock and died in Michigan, October 17, 1988.

Elder Bowe founded Geridge Industrial School, which was probably located in Lonoke County, Arkansas. The school was one of three started by COGIC in the embryonic years. Elder Bowe passed away in 1951 at the age of seventy-eight.

Charles H. Pleas

Pleas was born September 15, 1879, in Holmes County, Mississippi, to parents he never knew. He was likely given up by his mother for adoption because of her inability to care for her child. Charles was named by his adopted sixty-one year old grandmother, Martha Pleas, in 1880. He was named after her son Charles who later helped raise him. In 1880, Martha stayed home and raised little Charles and Ella Pleas, who were both only one year old. Ella was likely the twin sister of little Charles. His uncle Charlie was born November 1858 and married Nancy Redman in 1887. Little Charles's adopted grandmother, Martha, was born December of 1826 and was the mother of sixteen children. In 1880, Martha and her three children that were still living at home were all farmers.

Charles Pleas and R. H. I. Clark were original members of the first Church of God in Christ that was pastored by C. H. Mason in the old gin house in Lexington, Mississippi. Elder Pleas was saved in 1896 when he was seventeen years old through the preaching of C. H. Mason. Shortly after he was saved, Bishop Mason appointed him to the deacon board of the first Church of God in Christ, Saint Paul COGIC in Lexington, Mississippi.

In 1900, twenty-year-old Charles Pleas was still living with his adopted uncle and his uncle's wife, Nancy. Their children, Johnnie and Sarah, were much younger than Charles. By 1910, Charles had moved out on his own and was renting a room from his friend J. H. Amans and his wife, Virginia. He was now an Elder at the church and had been trained as a skilled bricklayer. Around 1915, he received his first appointment from Bishop Mason. He was sent by Mason to pastor the church in West Point, Clay County, Mississippi. While pastoring in West Point, World War 1 broke out, and he was required to register for the war on September 12, 1918. After about three years pastoring at West Point, Bishop Mason asked him in 1919 to go to Parsons, Labette County, Kansas, and pastor a church there. While in Parsons, they resided at 2227 Appleton Avenue. Sometime before 1930, he was transferred again and sent to pastor the church at Independence, Montgomery County, Kansas, which was only about twenty-five miles away.

Elder Pleas married his wife, Cornelia, in 1914; and sixteen years later, there were no children born to the couple. In those days life was inexpensive, and they were able to rent a house for $10 a month when they moved to Independence. He was later elevated to Bishop and served the church many years.

In 1957, Bishop Pleas was seventy-eight years old and had been in COGIC sixty-one years when he authored the book, *Fifty Years of Achievements, 1906-1956: A Period in the History of the Church of God in Christ.* Bishop Pleas lived one more decade after publishing the book. He died July 15, 1967, having served God and COGIC seventy-one years.

Robert Eber Hart: Last Will and Testament

"KNOW ALL MEN BY THESE PRESENTS"

Being that I Robert Eber Hart of Jackson, Tennessee, Madison County, aged 58 years being of sound memory and discretion and realizing the uncertainty of life and the certainty of death do hereby make and publish, and declare this to be my last will and testament, hereby revoking any will formally made by me.

FIRST

I will that my just debt for I have no debts, as the City Lumber Co., is paid up to date. I will that my funeral expenses be paid.

SECOND

I will that my two (2) children, Phillis Elizabeth Hart, age 9 years, and Robert Mason Hart age (16) years last birthday shall at my decease share and share alike in all of my property real and personal. I will that my sister Nicy McDonnall have a life time estate in the house on Church Street. But as to Robert Mason Hart and Phillis Elizabeth Hart they shall hold in fee simple as to the house and lot on Church Street its meets and bounds are as follows. Being lot no. 30 of the Hopkins Dwight Co., subdivision of their Lancaster property on the Westside of Church Street beginning on the northeast corner of lot no. 31 of said Division heretofore sold to the trustees of the Colored School of the Fifteenth Civil District of Madison County, Tennessee and runs thence West 122 ½ feet with said lot no. 31 to the northwest corner of lot no. 29 now owned by Henry Saunders, runs thence east with said lot no. 29, 122 ½ feet to Church Street. Thence south to the beginning. The above described was purchased by me. On this same lot has been built a two room cement block house known as the storeroom and office. It was leased to the State Press for two years, at eight dollars a month beginning October 1, 1919, the press having paid in advance $192.00. And also as to the home on Tanyard whose meet and bounds are as follows: Beginning in the south margin of Tanyard Street at the northeast corner of a lot deeded by Robert B. Hurt to Henry Wilkins, run thence east with the south margin of said Tanyard Street fifty-one feet to a stake thence south ninety-nine feet to a stake. Said Wilkins southeast corner thence north ninety-nine feet to beginning. The above described lot was purchased by me.

Now as the two room cement block house now used as a printing office and store room is not a separate lot but belongs to the lot on Church Street upon which it is built. It is situated in the rear of the house on Church Street and is included in this will as well as all other buildings used as out houses. None of the reality mentioned in this will is to be sold. In case the children should die before grown and marry and have unto them heirs, this property shall fall to my sisters Nicy McDonnall and Ella.

THREE

I will that my insurance policy No. 666 in the Life Insurance Company of Virginia amounting to _____ be drawn and placed in the Bank of Commerce for Phillis and Robert Hart to be drawn out as hereinafter provided.

FOUR

I will that my monies in the Bank of Commerce be used in educating Phillis and Robert Hart. In the case it does not take the whole amount to educate them the remainder shall be divided between them when they become of age as Robert is the elder and will graduate first he must not be allowed to use but his half of the monies so deposited.

FIVE

It is provided that in drawing checks, every check to be drawn on my bank account for school purposes or any other must be discussed and agreed upon and signed by Robert and Phillis Hart and the Executer, each in his own handwrite before the Banker is allowed to cash it. The monies referred to in the bank includes the settlement derived from the administration from their mother's estate from the sale of the property in Atlanta Georgia.

SIXTH

As to the church extension money if there be any in my possession at the time of my death the church extension will show how much by bank book and I will that the said bank book be carefully preserved and turned over to the Board of Directors. Elder Charles Mason, Memphis, Tennessee as Chairman of said Board.

SEVEN

I will that the furniture, books and library remain in the house for the use of both Robert and Phillis Hart. I will that my sister that is already administrator shall keep the home as housewife and have special supervision over Robert and Phillis during their school life. They must dwell with her and share with her all the necessary provisions. I hereby appoint without bond Nicy McDonnall (my sister) as the Administrator and Executer of this will. Witnesses: Robert E. Hart, Mrs. Hattie Flake, and Mrs. Hattie Moore

Following in Her Father's Footsteps

Phyllis E. Hart-Bedford, the daughter of Elder Robert and Cornelia Hart, was born September 22, 1910, in Jackson, Tennessee. [5] After the death of her mother in 1918 and her father in 1921, Nicy McDonnall (McDonald), her father's sister, was given legal custody through his last will and testament. Nicy at the time was living in Detroit and working as a laundress. When her brother died, she moved to Jackson and took control of his estate. After all of the estate business was taken care of she went back to Detroit with Phyllis; and around 1926, they moved to Youngstown, Mahoning County, Ohio.

In 1930, Phyllis was nineteen; and her aunt Nicy was fifty years old. They were living at 919 Star Street in Youngstown and living with them were two boarders, Leonia Morrisette and twenty-eight year old, Nathaniel Bedford from Illinois. Nathaniel was born November 4, 1899, and came to Youngstown looking for work which he found in a tile factory as a car loader. Phyllis later married Nathaniel, and they lived all of their lives in Youngstown. Phyllis was trained professionally as a journalist. They joined a local CME church where she became heavily involved in the work of the ministry, particularly in the Women's Connectional Council during the 1950's. From 1963-71 she was president of the Women's Connectional (Missionary) Council of the CME Church, which promoted some of the particular needs of the church and its women. She also served as President of the Ohio Annual Conference Missionary Society. Phyllis was aware of her father's former membership in the CME Church and like her father was an ecumenist at heart. She was deeply involved in the Ecumenical movement within the CME Church. According to ninety-two year old, Mother Hazelle Trotter Simmons a resident of Jackson, Tennessee, who knew of Phyllis Hart through her mother and a mutual friend, described to me how Phyllis from time to time would visit friends in Jackson during the 50's and 60's. She also remembered her mother telling her about Dr. Hart and the conflict he had while transiting from the CME Church to COGIC. How much Phyllis knew about her father's involvement and accomplishments in the Church of God in Christ we simply don't know? Nathaniel Bedford passed away in July of 1985 and Phyllis died in February of 1986.

Robert Mason Hart

Robert Mason Hart, the son of Elder Robert and Cornelia Hart, was raised by his aunt; Anna Walton, his mother's sister. He was born September 18, 1904, in Jackson, Tennessee, right in the midst of his father's conflict with the CME Church. [6] After the death of his mother and father, Anna came to Jackson in 1921 and carried him back to Vicksburg, Warren County, Mississippi where she was living. He was only sixteen years old at the time and had just graduated from high school in 1920.

In 1930, Anna was a sixty-year-old widow who owned her own home at 306 Chestnut Street in Vicksburg and made a living as a laundress working out of her home. Robert was working as a chauffeur for a private family and he was married, although his wife wasn't enumerated within the household with them. Robert was given his middle name after C. H. Mason, showing the loyalty and respect Dr. Hart had for Bishop Mason. Ironically, Robert Mason passed away in October of 1961; and C. H. Mason passed away in November of 1961. It is also ironic that Robert Mason was fifty-eight years old when he died, the same age as his father, Elder Hart when he died.

CONCLUSION: LIVING OUT THE LAST DAYS IN THE CHURCH OF GOD IN CHRIST

There is no doubt, Charles Harrison Mason heard God and obeyed. Since those days, COGIC has been growing and expanding its territory for the Kingdom of God. Every step of the way and whatever the cost, they have been rebuking and destroying the works of the devil. This year represents the 100th Anniversary of the denomination's Holy Convocation and the 110th year of the church not only just existing but also spreading the gospel and saving souls in the name of Jesus all over the world. The outpouring of the spirit that gave birth to COGIC through Bishop Mason spread from a former stable used as a church in Los Angeles, California, were he received the baptism in the Holy Ghost with the evidence of speaking in tongues and returned to Memphis, Tennessee, empowered to preach the gospel.

Revered as one of the most significant religious movements in world history, the Azusa Street Revival and the Pentecostal-Holiness Movement spread by the Sanctified Church and others demanded and provoked moral change in a world that desperately needed it. The world "fiercely" fought against it; however, the anointing behind the outpouring wouldn't and couldn't be extinguished or contained by man. It literally spread around the world. Memphis became known as the "Mecca" of the Sanctified Church, and today it is the headquarters of the Church of God in Christ, and was home to the late Presiding Bishop, Gilbert Earl Patterson. Memphis is also the final resting place of Charles Harrison Mason, founder of COGIC, and he is entombed inside historic Mason Temple. The spirit of Bishop Mason lives on in the hearts and minds of many, but not enough. Bishop Mason's legacy deserves more emulation if we are going to have a people prepared to meet the Lord. Not enough of our members and the world are aware of Bishop Mason's legacy and the sacrifices the early pioneers made, because we haven't invested enough money, effort, and resources into providing a facility where the saints can come and be educated about our history. If Jesus tarries in the coming months and years; prayerfully we will see a COGIC Heritage Center or possibly a C. H. Mason Library based in Memphis and dedicated in honor of Charles Harrison Mason and the Pentecostal-Holiness Movement, which birthed the Church of God in Christ.

I believe we are truly living in the last days. Pastor John Hagee known for his end time prophetic ministry warns us that there is literally nothing else left in the Bible to be fulfilled before the coming of Jesus. He said, "Jesus could come at any second, minute, or hour." Whether we are caught up to meet him in the air or we pass away from this life before he comes, either way, it won't be long. I'm prepared, and I'm thankful God ordered my steps toward COGIC where I have begun maturing to a deeper level in Christ. The Holy Ghost has shown me how as a deacon, although chosen to oversee benevolence and business, I can "overleap" those limitations and allow the Lord to use me as He wills. He gave me gifts and abilities; therefore, He expects me to use them to "illuminate" His kingdom. The most significant way I can illuminate His kingdom is to "seek ye first the kingdom of God."

My first visit to Mason Temple was in November of 2006 at the opening of the 99th International Holy Convocation. I was excited and filled with anticipation of the service that was planned for the day. As I sat patiently awaiting the start of the service, I began to imagine what it would have been like to see and hear Bishop Mason. Then my thoughts were translated to the night Martin Luther King, Jr., stood in the pulpit and delivered his last sermon, "I Have Been to the Mountain Top," and what it would have been like to hear his "exodus" sermon. King's 1968, sermon wasn't his first speech and visit to Mason Temple. He was the invited speaker for a "Freedom Rally" held on Friday night, July 31, 1959. The Civil Rights rally was held in support of four black candidates running for public office. Mahalia Jackson was the guest soloist, and the doors opened at 6 pm with a $1.00 contribution. What was it like to sit in the presence of these great and anointed men and women of God? Would I have taken them and life more seriously? Would I have recognized and accepted what God was sharing with us through them? We cannot see the future, and we can only study the past, therefore, we must act upon events in our lives when they are happening if we are going to make the greatest impact upon our generation. More than anything else in these last days, we need to have eyes to see and ears to hear what the Spirit is saying to us and the church. The days should be gone when men and women of God boast about cars, clothes, money, and houses, but they should rather tell us what the Lord is saying. Teach me how to live right and develop my relationship with the Lord. Last, but certainly not the least, tell men and women that they need to be saved and filled with the Holy Ghost with the evidence of speaking in tongues. Also, tell them that the same lying demonic spirit that said one hundred years ago Bishop Mason and all who believed in his so-called doctrine of "jabber" were fanatics is still spreading that same lie today.

I'm thankful for COGIC and excited about what is on the way for 2007 and the coming years. We have some of the greatest preachers in the world helping to "galvanize" the Kingdom of God in these last days. The Church of God in Christ has made tremendous progress over the years in all sectors of the church and has made an enormous impact all over the world in winning souls for Christ. This has mainly been accomplished due to the exceptional ecclesial leadership the church had chosen down through the years, and the church continues to train and produce well-prepared men and women for the ministry. Also, there is discipline, order, and protocol practiced among the saints which are the main characteristics necessary to govern and develop a befitting denomination.

Some of the greatest challenges of COGIC in the last days will be to equip the saints as much as possible to handle natural as well as spiritual crises. It has become increasingly difficult over the years to stay physically healthy, and at times, a real struggle to stay alive. From the food we eat; the air we breathe; the natural and physical violence in the world; genetics, and the attacks of the enemy, we are troubled on every side. However, fear not; for God is with us. He promised us He would be with us until the end of the world. Spiritually, too many people in the church are weak. Many in the church are living like there is no heaven or hell, and many believe they will just go somewhere when they die. I recently spoke with a man that said, "I don't believe in a heaven and hell but in a positive and a negative," and his father; now deceased was a COGIC preacher. Some have backslid, and the enemy has tricked many in the church, and they are blind and lost. I'm grateful God has brought me thus far, and I'm thankful to be here. I personally don't have any problems living out my last days a member of COGIC. It does matter how I live my last days and the quality of life I aspire to live. Servants like the late, Presiding Bishop Gilbert E. Patterson, and Elder

Alfred Z. Hall, Jr., make me proud to be a member of COGIC and apart of Christian believers worldwide. I can learn from the exemplarary lives they lived and improve my life, which will bring forth fruit in the body of Christ just as their lives did, and now death will bring forth fruit through those they influenced. We honor Bishop Patterson's and Elder Hall's life and the legacy they left in the Church of God in Christ. Amen.

CSM

ENDNOTES

CHAPTER ONE: THE MAKING OF A PREACHER: ROBERT EBER HART

1. Meeks, Ph.D., Catherine. Macon's Black Heritage: The Untold Story. Macon: Tubman African American Museum, 1997.

2. 1870 United States Federal Census.

3. Tennessee Death Certificate of Robert E. Hart, May 22, 1921.

4. Article in the Christian Index, October 6, 1888.

5. Ibid., December 1, 1888.

6. Ibid, December 1, 1888.

7. Ibid, January 11, 1890.

8. Ibid, January 18, 1890.

9. Ibid, September 26, 1891.

10. 1880 United States Federal Census.

11. Article in the Christian Index, December 16, 1893.

12. Ibid, September 5, 1896.

13. Ibid, February 13, 1897.

14. Ibid, October 9, 1897.

15. Ibid, July 4, 1897.

16. Ibid, July 8, 1899.

17. The Washington D.C., Daily Record, reprinted in the Christian Index, October 4, 1899.

18. Article in the Christian Index, October 7, 1899.

CHAPTER TWO: COMING TO TENNESSEE IN THE TWENTIETH CENTURY

1. Lakey, D.D., Othal Hawthorne. The History of the CME Church (Revised): The CME Publishing House, 1996.

2. Ibid, pp.39.

3. Ibid, pp. 246.

4. Ibid, pp.

5. Article in the Christian Index, December 23, 1899.

6. Ibid, January 20, 1900.

7. Lane College Reporter, reprinted in the Christian Index, April 14, 1900.

8. Article in the Christian Index, August 8, 1903.

9. Ibid, August 15, 1903.

10. Ibid, May 5, 1900.

11. Ibid, July 21, 1900.

12. Ibid, October 20, 1900.

13. Lynk, M.D., Miles Vanderhurst. Sixty Years of Medicine or the Life and Times of Dr. Miles V. Lynk, self published, 1956.

14. Charter of Incorporation, University of West Tennessee, filed December 18, 1900, in Record Book O2, Nashville, Davidson County, Tennessee, State Archives.

15. Lynk, M.D., Miles Vanderhurst. Sixty Years of Medicine or the Life and Times of Miles V. Lynk, self published, 1956.

16. Minutes of the Circuit Court of Jackson, Madison County, Tennessee, February 13, 1901.

17. Article in the Christian Index, June 15, 1901.

18. Minutes of the Circuit Court of Jackson, Madison County, Tennessee, May 23, 1901.

19. Excerpt from the article, University of West Tennessee Medical College, The Indianapolis Freeman newspaper, August 15, 1903.

20. University of West Tennessee Medical College catalogue for the 1909-10 sessions.

CHAPTER THREE: THE HART CONTROVERSY BEGINS

1. Doctrines and Disciplines of the CME Church, revised edition 1910, Publishing House of the CME Church.

2. Article in the Christian Index, October 7, 1893.

3. Ibid, July 21, 1900.

4. Ibid, July 25, 1903, excerpt from the article "Memphis District Conference."

5. Ibid, July 25, 1903.

6. Ibid, January 9, 1904, "He Dropped the Mask He Wore."

7. Ibid, January 16, 1904.

8. Nichols, D.D., T. H.: History of the West Tennessee Conference of the CME Church in America, Publishing House of the CME Church, 1909.

9. Article in the Christian Index, January 23, 1904.

10. Ibid, January 30, 1904.

11. Ibid, February 6, 1904, "Sanctified People Increasing and Forever Harshly Judging Others" by Rev. George W. Spearman.

12. Ibid, February 13, 1904.

13. Ibid, February 13, 1904.

14. Trenton Herald-Democrat, March 25, 1904: Trenton, Gibson County, Tennessee Public Library.

15. Article in the Christian Index, October 29, 1904.

16. Ibid, January 28, 1905.

17. Ibid, January 28, 1905.

18. Ibid, January 28, 1905.

19. Ibid, January 28, 1905.

20. Ibid, February 18, 1905.

21. Minutes of the Forty-third Session of the West Tennessee Annual Conference catalogue 1924.

CHAPTER FOUR: CHARLES HARRISON MASON AND SIBLINGS

1. 1870 United States Federal Census.

2. Clemmons, Bishop Ithiel C.: Bishop C. H. Mason and the Roots of the Church of God in Christ, Centennial Edition, Pneuma Life Publishing 1996, pp. 4.

3. Ibid, pp. 5.

4. Marriage Record of C. H. Mason and Alice Saxton, Family Search IGI Individual Record.

5. Marriage Record of Joseph Mason and Margaret White, Family Search IGI Individual Record.

6. Marriage Record of I. S. Nelson and Easter Cole, Family Search IGI Individual Record.

7. Marriage Record of Jerry Mason and Georgia Ann Kennedy, Family Search IGI Individual Record.

8. Marriage Record of Jerry Mason and Polly Kennedy, Family Search IGI Individual Record.

CHAPTER FIVE: BIRTHING PAINS OF A NEW DENOMINATION

1. Deposition of Defendant, C.H. Mason taken April 27, 1908, case number 14770, Chancery Court of Shelby County, Tennessee, Frank Avant vs. C.H. Mason, pp.99-101.

2. Ibid., pp. 102, 104.

3. Memphis, Shelby County, Tennessee Marriage Record of C.H. Mason and Lelia Washington, October 18, 1905, roll #113.

4. Memphis, Shelby County, Tennessee Property Deed, T.R. Farnsworth to Edward Loveless, et al, January 1, 1905, Shelby County Archives.

5. Pleas, Bishop Charles H.: Fifty Years of Achievements from 1906-1956: A Period in the History of COGIC reprinted by COGIC Department of Public Relations, 1991.

6. Deposition of Defendant, C.H. Mason taken April 27, 1908, case number 14770, Chancery Court of Shelby County, Tennessee, Frank Avant vs. C.H. Mason, pp.96.

7. Ibid., pp.97-98.

8. Facts in this section on the Spanish Flu, taken from articles on the Spanish Flu by Michael Finger, Memphis, the city magazine, November and December issues of 2006, published by Contemporary Media, Inc.

9. Tennessee Death Certificate of Malinda Featherston.

10. Minutes of the 1934, General Assembly of COGIC, published by the Office of the General Secretary.

11. Article in the Commercial Appeal newspaper, published in Memphis, Tennessee and part of the evidence entered in the case by the complaints, Frank Avant, etal, date unknown.

12. "Fanatical Worship of Negroes Going on at Sanctified Church" article published in the Commercial Appeal newspaper in Memphis, Tennessee, Wednesday, May 22, 1907, pp.5.

13. The Truth, religious periodical, 1906.

14. Rules of Government of the Churches of God in Christ, printed in the winter catalogue for the Winter Convention, part of the evidence entered in the case, Frank Avant vs. C.H. Mason, January 14-21, 1906.

15. Ibid, pp. 12.

16. 1910 United States Federal Census.

17. Article in the Christian Index, "A Sanctified Fight" September 14, 1907.

18. Ibid, September 28, 1907.

19. The Whole Truth, 75th Souvenir Edition, 1907-1982.

20. Jackson, Madison County, Tennessee Criminal Court document, August 15, 1906.

21. Jackson, Madison County, Tennessee Chancery Court, Minute Book #24 pp. 306, June 15, 1912.

22. 1900 United States Federal Census.

23. Tennessee Death Certificate of William M. Christian, April 11, 1928.

24. Minutes of the 1941, General Assembly of COGIC: 1934-1960 Minutes of the General Assembly, published by the Office of the General Secretary.

CHAPTER SIX: MASON'S INNER CIRCLE

1. Delaney, Rev. T.L.: The History and Life Work of C.H. Mason, chief apostle and his co-laborers from 1893 to 1924, compiled in 1924.

2. 1900 United States Federal Census.

3. The Whole Truth, Souvenir Edition, 1907-1982, pp. 8.

4. The Whole Truth, magazine of COGIC, pp. 4, July-December 2004.

5. Clemmons, Bishop Ithiel C.: Bishop C.H. Mason and the Roots of the Church of God in Christ, Centennial Edition, Pneuma Life Publishing 1996.

6. 1900 United States Federal Census.

7. Coffey, Lillian-Brooks. History and Formative Years of the Church of God in Christ with Excerpts from the Life and Works of its Founder-Bishop C.H. Mason, Reproduced by Bishop J.O. Patterson, Rev. German R. Ross, and Mrs. Julia Mason Atkins, Publishing House of COGIC 1969.

8. Memphis, Shelby County, Tennessee Death Certificate of Jerry Brooks, May 10, 1914.

9. Memphis, Shelby County, Tennessee Death Certificate of Lula Brooks, January 22, 1925.

10. Marriage Record of John Washington and Indiana Neal, Family Search IGI Individual Record.

11. The Whole Truth, vol. 4, March 1928, framed wall copies at Unity Temple COGIC, Jackson, Tennessee.

12. Marriage Record of Leonard Adams and Elizabeth Sarah Price, Family Search IGI Individual Record.

13. 1900 United States Federal Census.

CHAPTER SEVEN: EARLY LEADERS AND DEPARTMENT HEADS

1. The Journal of Negro History, Vol. 15, July, 1930, pp. 269-277.

2. Clemmons, Bishop Ithiel C.: Bishop C.H. Mason and the Roots of the Church of God in Christ, Centennial Edition, Pneuma Life Publishing, 1996.

3. Copy of the marriage license from Book A, 1873-1894, Marianna, Lee County, Arkansas.

4. Clemmons, Bishop Ithiel C.: Bishop C.H. Mason and the Roots of the Church of God in Christ, Centennial Edition, pp. 111, Pneuma Life Publishing, 1996.

5. 1880 United States Federal Census.

6. Clemmons, Bishop Ithiel C.: Bishop C.H. Mason and the Roots of the Church of God in Christ, Centennial Edition, pp. 111, Pneuma Life Publishing 1996.

7. World War 1, Draft Registration Card, 1917-18 Record.

8. Pleas, Charles H.: Fifty Years of Achievements from 1906-1956: A Period in the History of the Church of God in Christ, reprinted by the Public Relations Department of COGIC, 1991.

9. Minutes of the 12th General Assembly, December 10, 1919, Published by COGIC, Office of the General Secretary.

10. Last Will and Testament of Robert E. Hart, Will Book C pp.177, Roll #529, Jackson, Madison County, Tennessee Public Library.

CHAPTER EIGHT: FRANK AVANT VS. C. H. MASON

1. Order overruling motion to dissolve injunction, Avant vs. C.H. Mason.

2. Article in the Memphis, Commercial Appeal newspaper, "Church of God Sanctified" January 10, 1908 pp.4.

3. Taken from articles in the Memphis Appeal Avalanche, "A Bloody Riot" and "Quiet at the Curve," March 6-7, 1892.

4. Hamilton, Green P.: The Bright Side of Memphis, 1908.

5. Answer of Defendants to Petition for Rehearing, Avant vs. C.H. Mason.

6. Jackson, Madison County, Tennessee, Circuit Court, Criminal Minutes, September 15, 1908, roll #443.

7. Notice of appointment filed, May 26, 1909, by R.E. Hart, Avant vs. C.H. Mason.

8. Chancery Court papers from the case, Avant vs. C.H. Mason.

9. Final decree of the Shelby County, Tennessee, Chancery Court case, Avant vs. C.H. Mason, July 28, 1908.

10. Minutes of the Tennessee State Supreme Court case, Avant vs. C.H. Mason, May 24, 1909, Jackson, Tennessee.

CHAPTER NINE: ENEMIES OF MASON AND THE CHURCH

1. Hamilton, Green P.: The Bright Side of Memphis, 1908.

2. Deposition of Thomas J. Searcy, for the Complaints, Avant vs. Mason, April 18, 1908.

3. Ibid.

4. Deposition of William J. McMichael, for the Complaints, Avant vs. Mason, April 18, 1908.

CHAPTER TEN: FRIENDS OF MASON: MEMBERS OF COGIC AND THE COMMUNITY

1. Minutes of the 1919, General Assembly of COGIC, published by the Office of the General Secretary.

2. Memphis, Shelby County, Tennessee, Marriage license of D.J. Smith and Mary V. Britton, October 16, 1901.

3. Pleas, Charles H.: Fifty Years of Achievements from 1906-1956: A Period in the History of the COGIC.

4. Jackson, Madison County, Tennessee, Will Book C pp.177, Minute Book 33.

5. Tennessee Birth Certificate of Phillis Elizabeth Hart.

6. Social Security Death Index, of Robert Hart.

ABOUT THE AUTHOR

Deacon Calvin S. McBride is a member and secretary of the Deacon Board at Pentecostal Assembly COGIC in Jackson, Tennessee. He is a local historian/ genealogist with about fifteen years' experience. He is the archivist for the local Miles V. Lynk Medical Society, which is a member of the National Medical Association (NMA).

Deacon McBride is a U. S. Navy veteran and since 1978 had been a surgical technician and assistant. He has also worked as a licensed Tennessee State Contractor and holds a diploma in the field. He is presently working on two other books which he plans to complete in the near future.

He is the past owner of Living Waters Christian Bookstore which he operated from 1998 to 2005. Living Waters is where he displayed his collection of historical photographs of local and national African-American medical history. In 1995 his exhibit was chosen to help celebrate the Centennial Anniversary of the National Medical Association (NMA) held in Atlanta, Georgia. While in Atlanta the exhibit was featured on CNN. The exhibit was later shown at the MLK Civil Rights Museum in Memphis, Tennessee. He has been awarded numerous times in recognition of his achievements in historical research.

Deacon McBride is a member of the Board of Directors of Pacers, Inc., of Jackson, Tennessee, a community development corporation which is committed to serving the community by providing housing and education and promoting good health and nutrition for families in need.

Printed in the United States
By Bookmasters